PAUL GAUGUIN

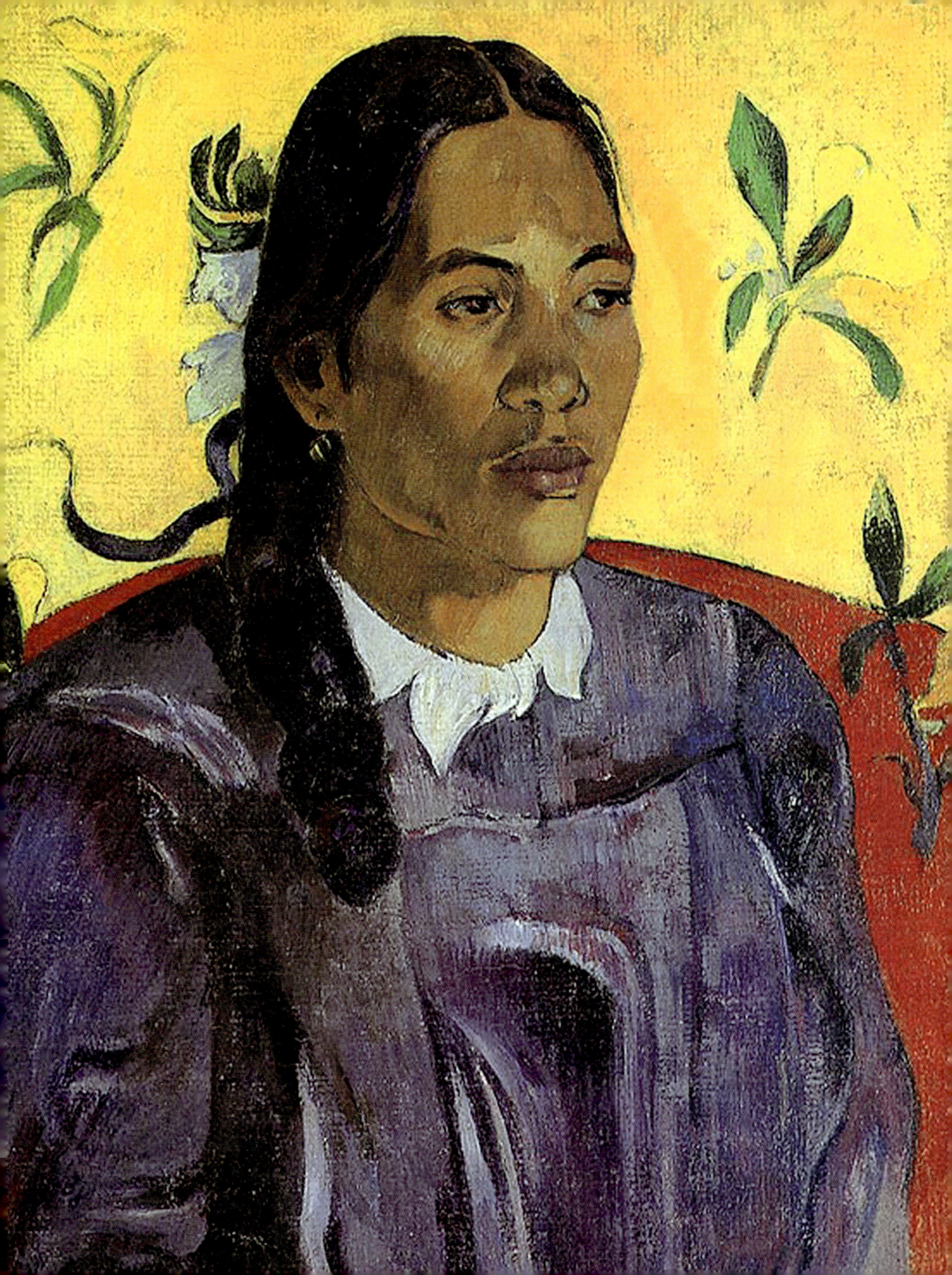

ART MASTER

PAUL GAUGUIN

CAROLINE BUGLER

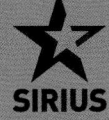

SIRIUS

SIRIUS

This edition published in 2024 by Sirius Publishing, a division of
Arcturus Publishing Limited,
26/27 Bickels Yard, 151–153 Bermondsey Street,
London SE1 3HA

Copyright © Arcturus Holdings Limited

ISBN: 978-1-3988-5098-9
AD007300UK

Printed in China

CONTENTS

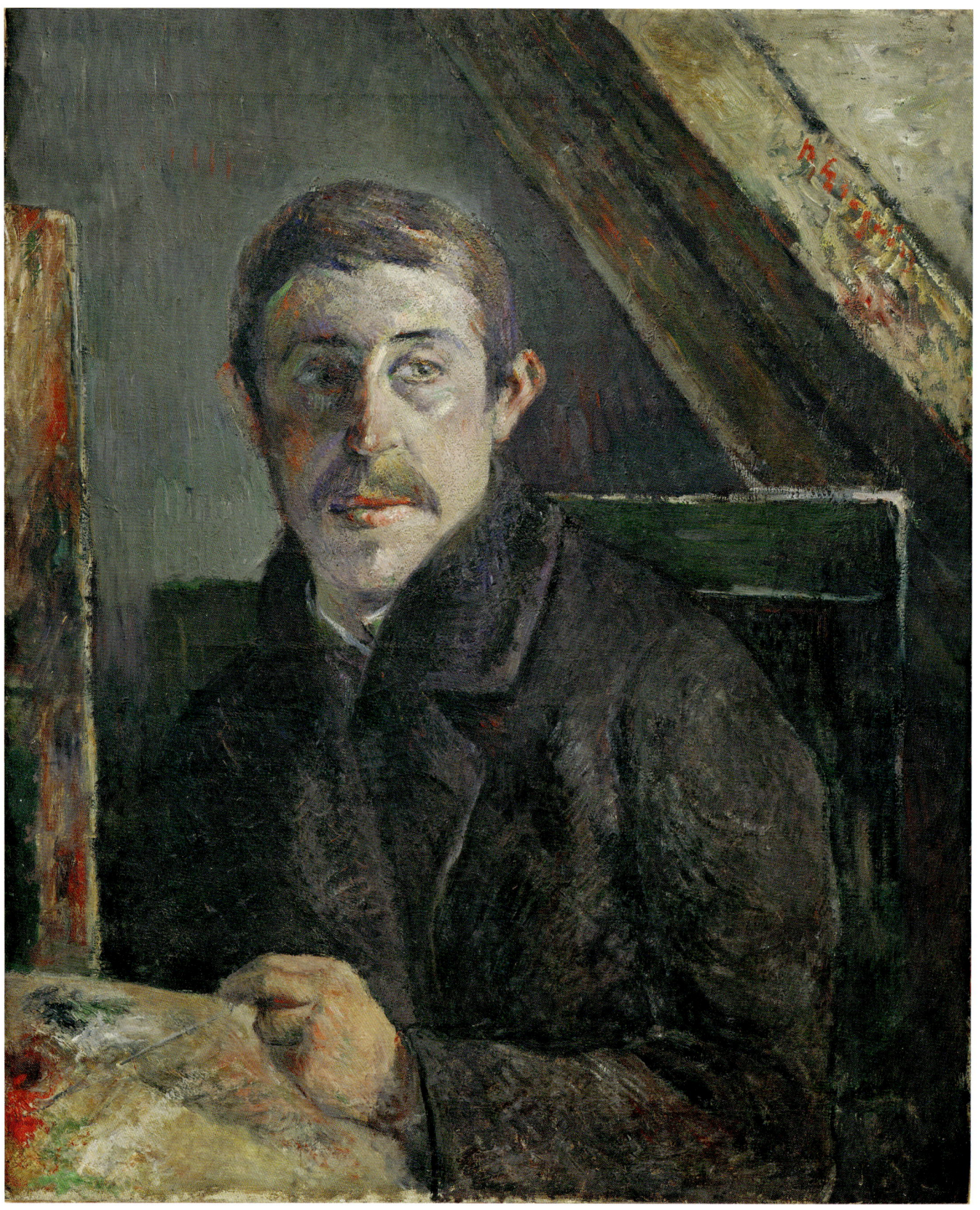

INTRODUCTION

The colourful life and equally colourful paintings of Paul Gauguin (1848–1903) have stirred the public imagination for more than a century. In many senses he appears to fulfil the modern cliché of the artist as a solitary genius who battles against the odds, is cast out from society, and sacrifices everything in order to pursue his vision with single-minded obsession. This was certainly an image that Gauguin himself was keen to promote when he wrote in 1892: 'I am a great artist and I know it. It's because I know it that I have endured such sufferings.'

Having enjoyed a successful career as a stockbroker who painted in his spare time, in his mid-thirties he relinquished the comforts of a secure job to become a professional artist with all the risks that entailed – a decision that ultimately led to estrangement from his wife and children and life in self-imposed exile in the South Seas. Gauguin was a complex, difficult and restless man who prided himself on his exotic ancestry and 'savage' nature. His early childhood in Peru left him with a taste for far-flung places, and as an adult he travelled widely in search of an elusive paradise. He sought visual and emotional inspiration in 'primitive' ways of life that would provide an antidote to what he saw as the disease of civilization, first in Brittany and then in the French overseas territories of Martinique, Tahiti and the Marquesas Islands.

Gauguin was a versatile innovator who experimented with different styles and media, trying his hand at ceramics, sculpture, woodcarvings and graphic work as well as oil painting. After initial hesitant steps as a landscapist working in the accepted style of the day, he took up with the Impressionists and adopted their bright palette and broken brushstrokes. Ultimately, though, he realized that he was more interested in the inner world of elemental myth and the imagination than in simply capturing the fleeting appearance of the natural landscape and urban scenes. His mature paintings, in which brilliant colours and strong outlines are coupled with allusive, poetic subjects, are some of the most beautiful and groundbreaking works of nineteenth-century art.

Gauguin at his Easel, *1885. This early self-portrait, painted when Gauguin was working in a cramped attic room in Copenhagen, is a defiant statement of his identity as an artist. The way the light falls through the window and the broken brushwork owe a great deal to his study of Impressionism.*

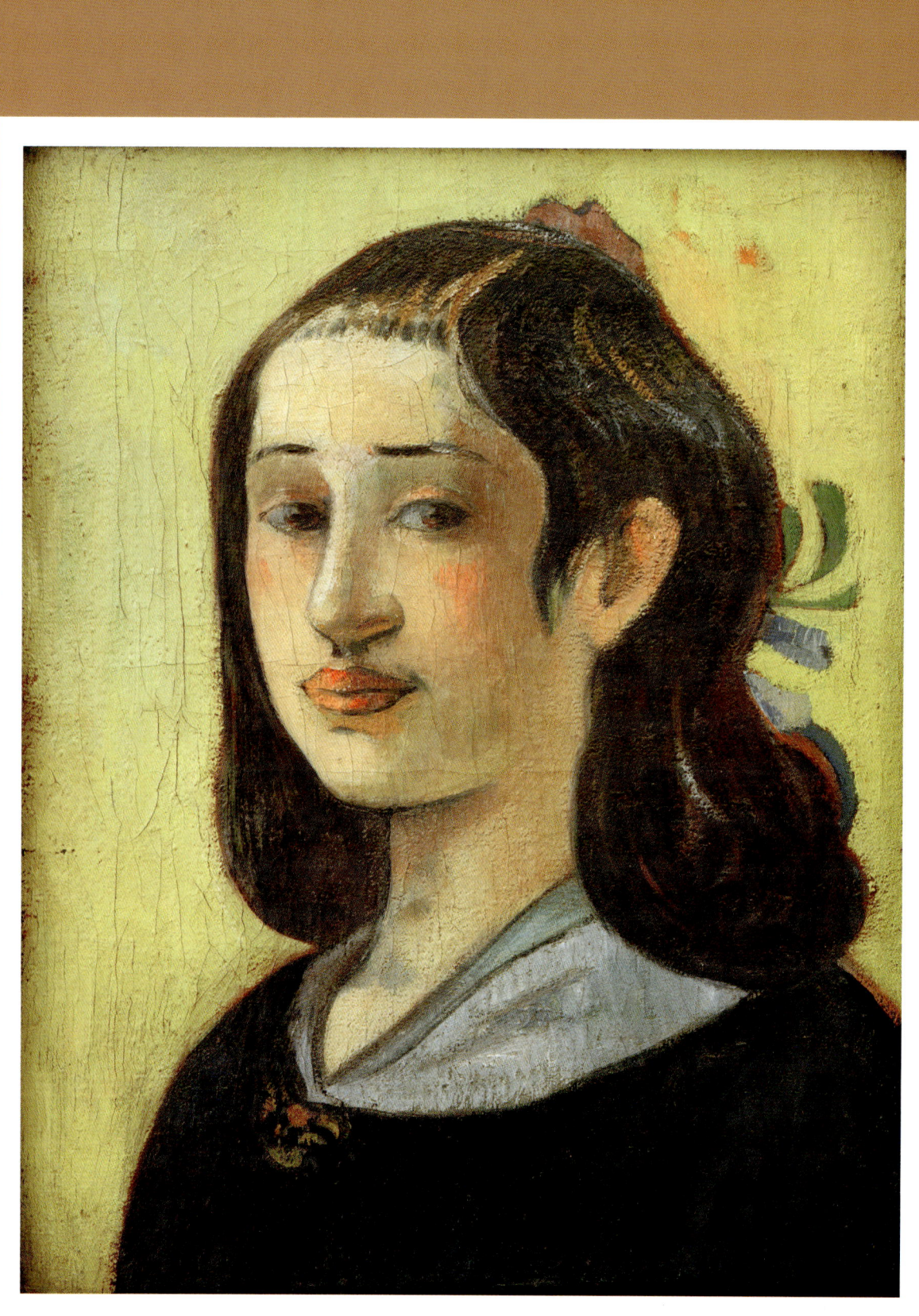

CHAPTER 1
Becoming an Artist

Paul Gauguin's unusual and exotic childhood was characterized by drama, travel and exposure to a range of visual experiences. He was born in Paris on 7 June 1848, the year that a wave of revolutions broke out throughout Europe and the French king was deposed. While he was still a baby his journalist father, Clovis, decided that the family should move from France to Peru, where he planned to set up a newspaper, and where there were family connections; Gauguin's maternal grandmother was Flora Tristan, a French-Peruvian feminist and socialist. Gauguin was clearly proud of his ancestor. He never met her, so relied on the testimony of others for information, but believed her to have been 'a pretty, noble woman' who 'used her entire fortune to further the workers' cause and travelled ceaselessly'. Abandoning her husband and three children, she had travelled to Peru in an attempt to extract a legacy from her uncle, Don Pio Tristan Moscoso, and published a memoir of her voyage. Her adventurous, unconventional life had many parallels with Gauguin's own.

Clovis Gauguin never arrived at his destination as he died at sea of a ruptured aneurysm just as the ship was rounding the Straits of Magellan. When his widow, Aline, reached Lima with her two children they were taken in by the wealthy Don Pio, who lived in some comfort in the mansion of his son-in-law, José Rufino Echenique. After Echenique became president of Peru in 1851 the family moved to the even more luxurious presidential palace. Gauguin later recalled some of the characters he encountered in his childhood, writing of 'the little Negro girl, carried to church on the little rug on which we knelt to pray. I can also see that Chinese servant of ours who was so good at ironing.' Even at this tender age Gauguin was fond of running away, and he remembered one escapade when the Chinese servant found him in a grocery shop while his weeping mother hunted high and low for him. He also had a good visual memory, so may well have remembered seeing pre-Hispanic Peruvian ceramics, Inca silver and lavish Peruvian altarpieces that would have been unknown to his European counterparts.

Those first few vivid and unconventional years of Gauguin's life in Peru provided him with raw material for the many legends he subsequently wove around himself, not least of which was his supposedly 'savage' origin. He liked to claim that he had both Spanish aristocratic and Inca heritage, later announcing that 'the Inca according to legend come straight from the sun and that's where I will return'.

Portrait of Aline Gauguin, c. 1893. *Gauguin described his mother as 'gracious and pretty' with a gentle but compelling gaze. This portrait, based on a photograph, was painted 25 years after her death and shows her as a young girl. The yellow background recalls the gold of medieval panel paintings while the flowers behind Aline's head resemble those seen as hair ornaments in Gauguin's portraits of Tahitian women.*

RETURN TO FRANCE

Aline Gauguin returned to France with her two children in 1854, when Gauguin was seven. They went to live in the Gauguin family house in Orléans, where Gauguin was enrolled in the Junior Seminary of the Saint Mesmin Chapel. He continued his studies at a pre-naval college in Paris. He was not an outstanding pupil, but received some grounding in the classics and literature. At the age of 17 he joined the Merchant Navy as a lowly sailor, later enlisting in the French Navy. He spent the next six years sailing round the world, visiting Brazil, Chile, Peru, the Mediterranean, the Arctic Circle and India. Gauguin's mother died when he was 19, and when he came back to France he was given a helping hand by the financier Gustave Arosa, a friend of his mother, who became his guardian. Based in Paris, the Arosas were a wealthy and multicultural family who spoke Spanish and French and had a network of social contacts that included artists, critics, musicians and literary figures. Gustave and his brother Auguste were also art collectors, and Gauguin saw modern French paintings hanging on their walls. Fresh out of the navy, Gauguin needed a job, and Gustave Arosa arranged for him to enter the stockbroker's office of Paul Bertin, where he was quite successful. It was not long before he met another young stockbroker, Émile Schuffenecker, who shared his interest in art and would become a lifelong friend. Schuffenecker had received some formal training as a painter, and the two aspiring artists went on painting expeditions around Paris and the suburbs.

Still Life with Oysters, 1876. *Gauguin's early mastery of realism is evident in this luxurious still life of oysters, pheasant, champagne (or sparkling cider) and a bottle of Armagnac or eau-de-vie. The thick black brushstrokes and strong tonal contrasts pay homage to the work of Manet.*

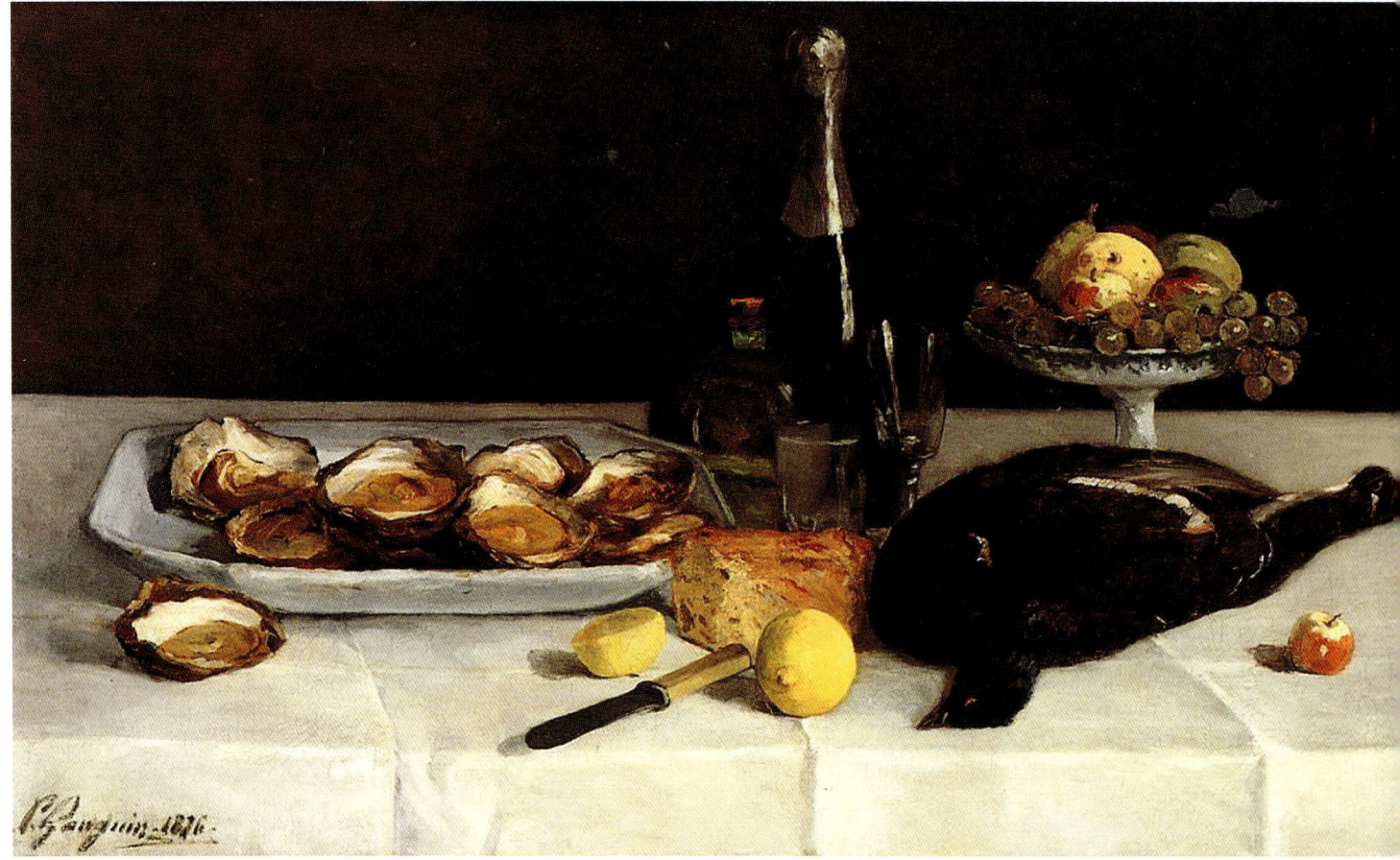

PAUL AND METTE

Things were going well for Gauguin. He was successfully establishing himself as a stockbroker and amateur artist, and he soon found love with a young Danish woman, Mette Gad, whom he probably met at the Arosas' house. Photographs show Mette to have been striking, with strong features, rather than conventionally beautiful. She was clever, independent and quick-witted and had been a governess to the children of the Danish prime minister. When Gauguin met her she was 22 and enjoying a trip abroad with her friend Marie. The two were part of a lively group of young people who enjoyed outings and fancy dress parties. In a letter home, Marie gave an account of a Christmas party in 1872 at the Arosas' house, noting that Gauguin was secretly in love with her companion. Gauguin amused himself by making portraits, sketches and caricatures of those in his circle, and creating funny outfits. In February 1873 he designed the paper outfits for a costume ball where some of those taking part were dressed as a bottle of champagne, a chandelier, a sweet, and a fan. Gauguin himself came as a soldier, while Mette was dressed as a baby.

By mid-July that year Marie was reporting that Gauguin was 'miserably in love' but was filling his spare moments with painting, adding, 'he has made great progress. Last Sunday he painted for ten hours.' As an attractive and charismatic young stockbroker with bright prospects, Gauguin must have seemed like a good catch, even if he lacked social polish. He and Mette were married in November 1873, when he was 25 and she was 23. Within a decade they had five children. Their first son, Emil, was born in 1874, followed by daughter Aline in 1877, Clovis in 1879, Jean René in 1881 and Paul in 1883. Initially Gauguin was wealthy enough to support his growing family in some comfort, but this prosperity and stability were not to last. This was partly due to circumstances beyond his control, but Gauguin's own family background hardly provided him with a model of steady family life or a permanent home. His mother had been effectively abandoned by her own mother as a child, and after she was widowed her financial position forced her to rely on the help of relatives and friends.

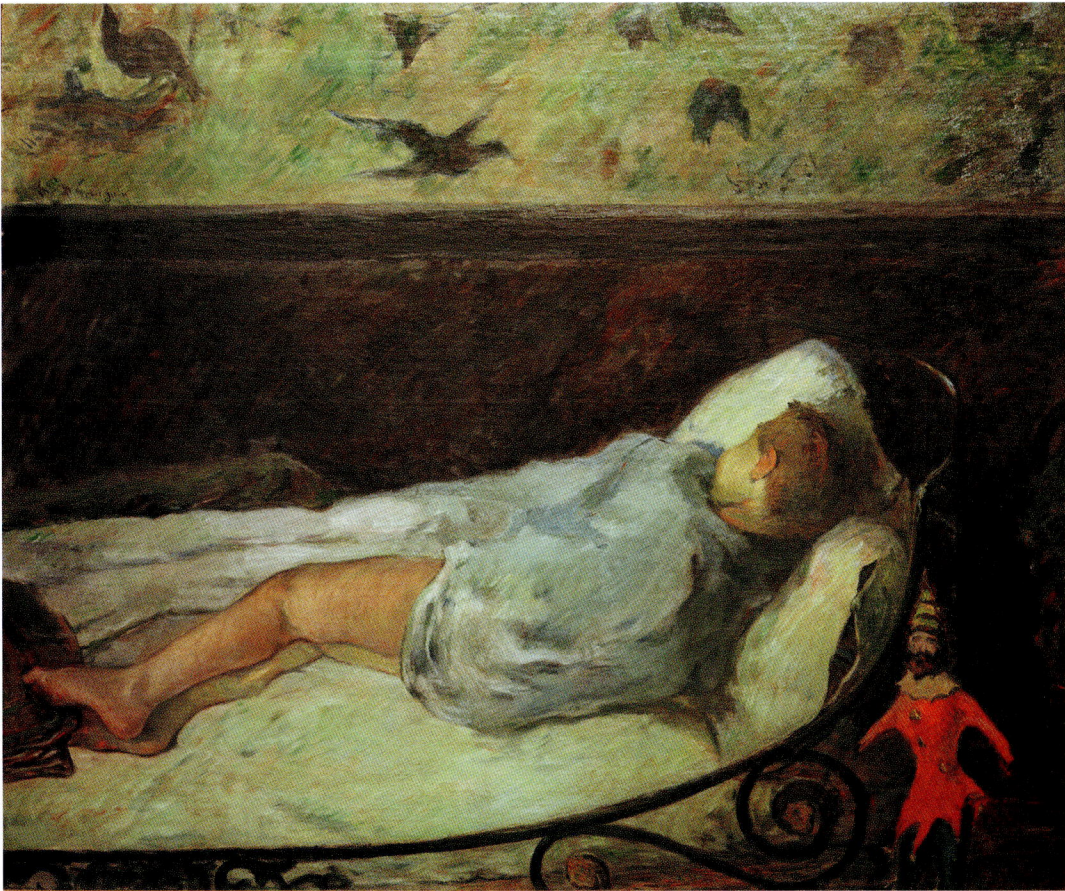

The Little Dreamer, 1881. Here Gauguin's daughter Aline lies asleep in bed. Symbolic details – birds hovering on the wallpaper above her and the slightly menacing stiff doll in a jester's costume – may provide clues to her dreams. A number of Gauguin's paintings show people sleeping, perhaps dreaming, reflecting his interest in the unconscious mind.

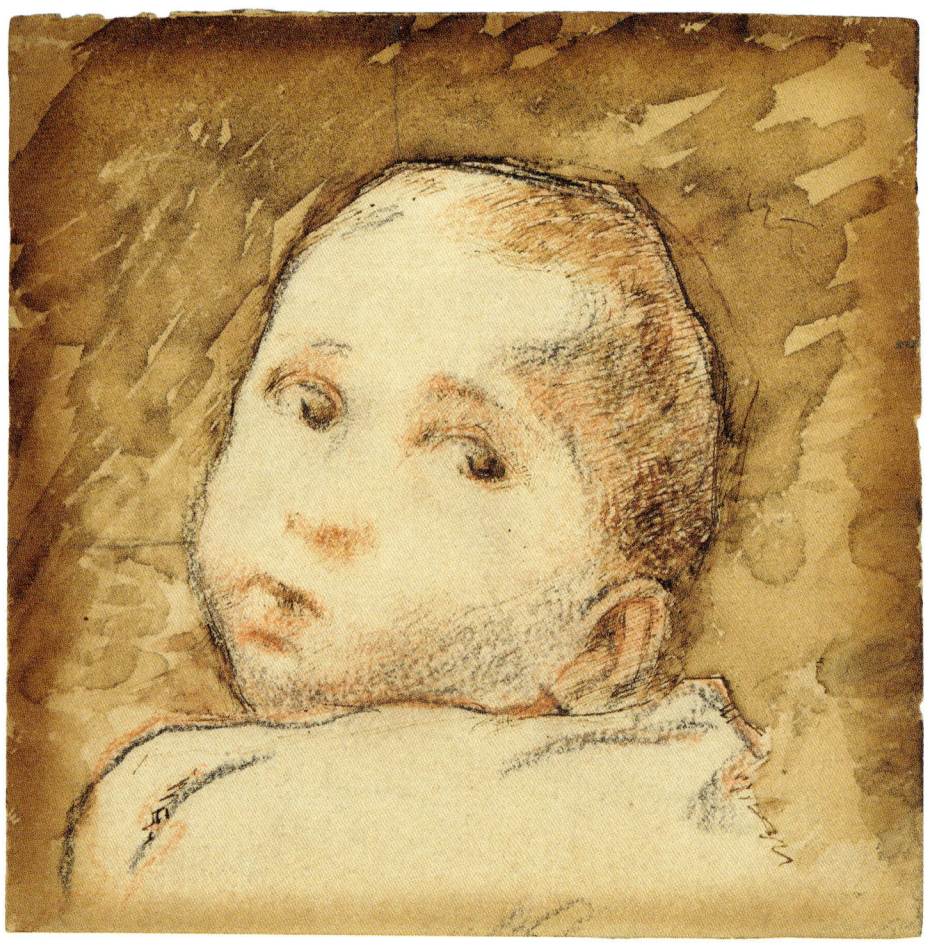

Drawing of Baby Jean René Gauguin, 1881. This intimate drawing of Gauguin's fourth child captures an apparently spontaneous moment as the baby looks over his shoulder towards his father. Gauguin may have used this drawing as a study for a wax bust of Jean René that he made the same year.

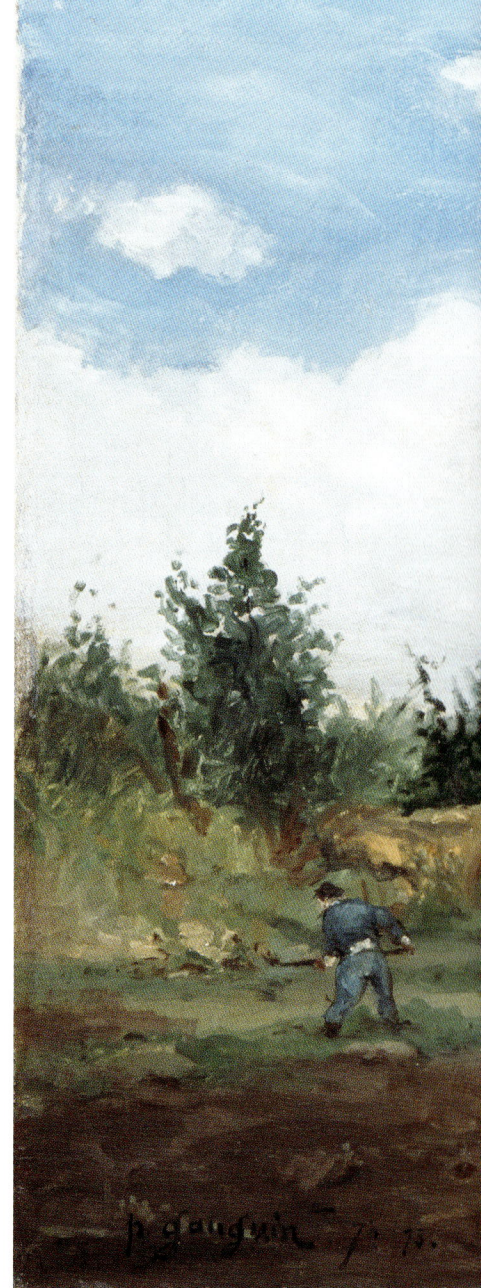

Landscape, 1873. Probably painted in one of the agricultural areas around Paris, this landscape is a remarkably skilful work for an amateur artist. The horizontal format and expanse of flat land can also be seen in the over-doors that Camille Pissarro was commissioned to paint in Gustave Arosa's apartment.

THE AMATEUR ARTIST

Gauguin attended evening art classes at the Académie Colarossi and despite his growing family responsibilities continued to spend his Sundays painting out of doors. His earliest canvases were landscapes, and he had some immediate inspiration to hand because the Arosa collection included several examples. Among them were works by the Impressionist painter Camille Pissarro – who had been commissioned to paint four pictures to go over doors in the Arosa apartment – as well as Pissarro's artistic forebears, Corot, Courbet, Boudin and Jongkind. Some of Gauguin's landscapes follow the naturalistic style of painters who worked in the forest of Fontainebleau, near the village of Barbizon, in the mid-nineteenth century, using low horizons and predominantly green tones. However, his earliest surviving picture, *Landscape*, is more adventurous and astonishingly accomplished for a Sunday painter with very little in the way of formal training.

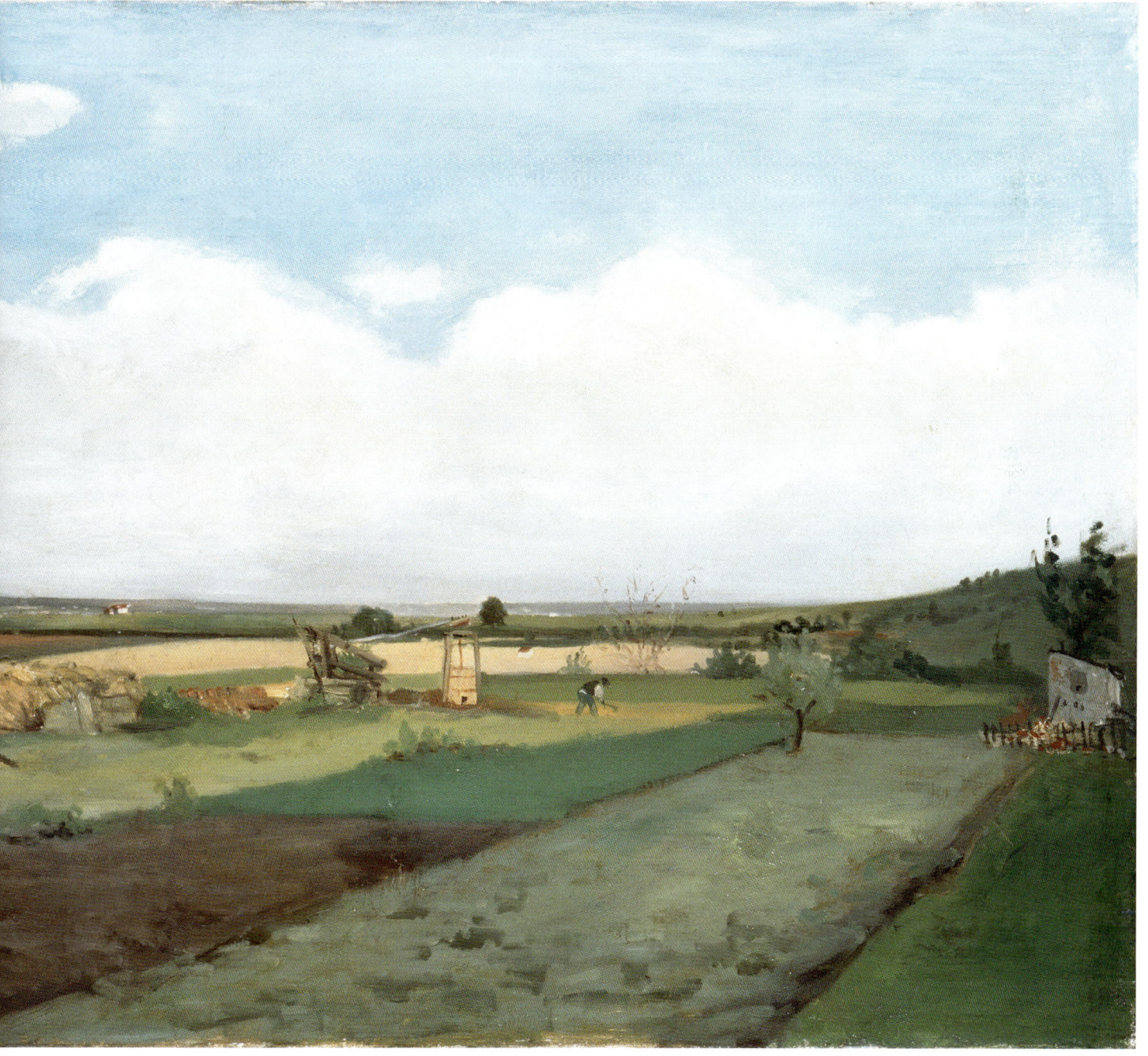

Like many artists of the time, during this early period Gauguin produced pictures in pairs – a small sketch version, perhaps painted out of doors, followed by a larger finished version. In 1876 he had a forest landscape accepted by the Paris Salon, the most prestigious annual exhibition in Paris – a great achievement for a largely self-taught artist. He was soon turning his hand to still lifes and portraits as well.

GAUGUIN THE COLLECTOR

Gauguin lost his job in 1877 and the stock market crashed in 1878. Nevertheless, he did well enough through speculation in stocks that year to start buying art, perhaps encouraged by the tidy profit that Gustave Arosa had just gained by selling his own art collection. Unlike some of the Impressionists, who acquired most of their paintings by colleagues through exchange, Gauguin bought paintings from commercial dealers and was prepared to sell them, never losing sight of the fact that art was a business. He started with works by Pissarro, buying recent ones that were relatively cheap. Gauguin was quite astute commercially, and the works he collected provided much-needed cash when he sold them later as his fortunes declined. In fact, over his lifetime he made almost as much money from selling pictures by other artists as he did from sales of his own work. Gauguin's collection was not large, but it included important works by almost all the Impressionists. He had around 50 pictures, among them six Cézannes that he was particularly attached to (and later begged Mette not to part with when she was having to sell off paintings to raise funds); Degas pastels, including a ballet dancer and a woman sewing; a painting by Boudin; a pastel by Mary Cassatt; and paintings by Guillaumin, Renoir, Sisley and Manet. Strangely, he did not buy any work by Monet, a central figure of the Impressionist movement. One of the Cézannes he owned was a large nude (now lost) and this may have been the impulse behind his decision to paint his own large nude, *Study of a Nude (Suzanne Sewing),* a subject he had never attempted before. But by 1883 Gauguin's funds were drying up, and from that point he began to sell his collection rather than add to it.

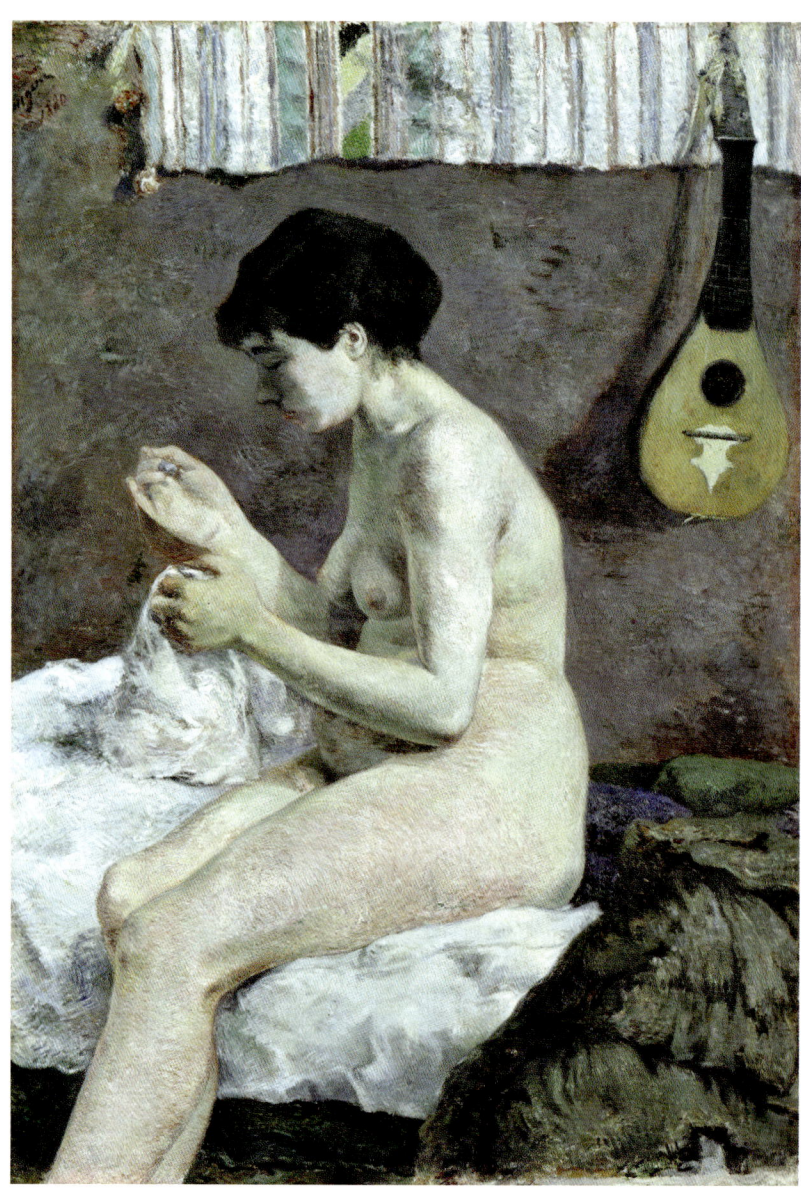

Study of a Nude (Suzanne Sewing), 1880. *This study of a young woman sitting on an unmade bed sewing does not show a classically erotic nude with obvious sensual appeal. She does not have an idealized body, nor does she look out of the canvas to engage male viewers. When the picture was shown at the Sixth Impressionist Exhibition of 1881 it caused a stir and provoked a lengthy review by the critic Joris-Karl Huysmans, who praised the realism of the picture.*

EXHIBITING WITH THE IMPRESSIONISTS

The artists who became known as the Impressionists first banded together for the purposes of exhibiting their work as a group in 1874. They were not unified by a single manifesto or style, but were broadly against academic teaching and historical subjects and committed to painting modern life in all its transience, attempting to record an impression of what the eye sees with freshness and immediacy. Gauguin would have been aware of their work from their first group show. Although his initial landscapes followed in the tradition of other mid-nineteenth-century painters such as Corot and Courbet, it was not long before he adopted the Impressionists' use of lighter tones and broken brushwork as well as their choice of subjects and predilection for views that were not picturesque in the conventional sense. A group of paintings that Gauguin made in 1875 on the banks of the Seine show his awareness of the type of urban subjects they tackled; they do not shy away from including industrial elements and reveal an interest in weather effects such as fog and snow.

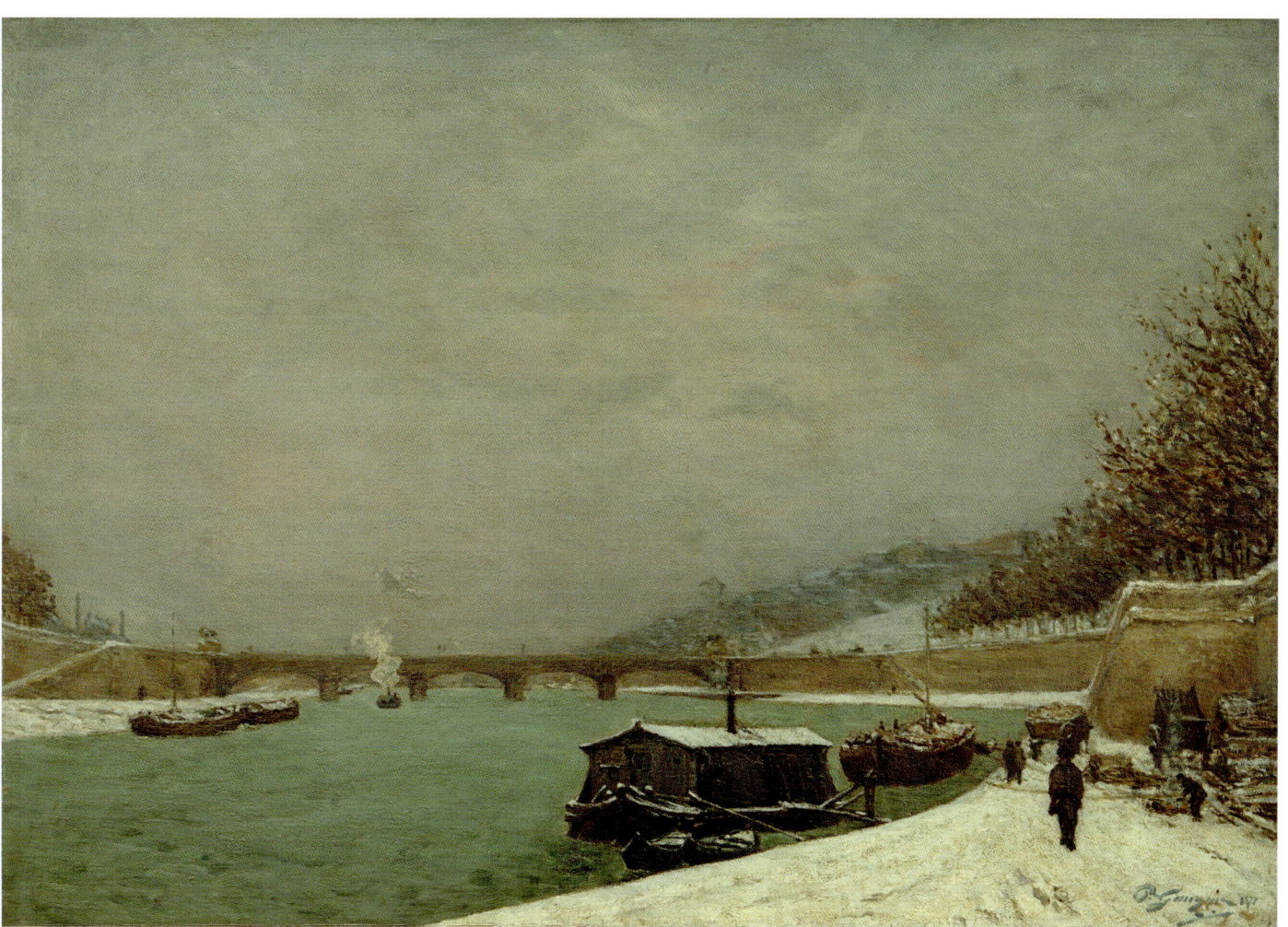

The Seine at Pont d'Iena, 1875. *Gauguin branched out from rural and suburban subjects to paint the urban scene with a series of views of the Seine that convey the unremarkable everyday activity of the river. Winter scenes were fashionable among the Impressionists, and here barges are moored alongside a snowy quay beneath a leaden sky.*

In 1879, Pissarro and Degas extended the ultimate compliment to him when they invited him to take part in the Fourth Impressionist Exhibition; he would participate in all four of the group exhibitions that followed. We cannot be sure which of his own works he submitted to the first one, apart from a sculpture of his young son Emil that was mentioned by a critic. The exhibition featured 22 works by Pissarro (two of them lent by Gauguin) and 29 by Monet. Still an amateur artist, Gauguin was in exalted company. Pissarro became a mentor and the otherwise irascible

Degas was also hugely important to Gauguin, remaining loyal to him and buying his work even when he was far away in Tahiti in later life. The admiration was mutual. Gauguin's intimate interiors, with their unusual, off-centre and apparently casual compositions, show how closely he had looked at Degas' canvases. When Gauguin painted his immediate surroundings – the garden of his home or the view from his window – he was following in Impressionist footsteps. At this time he often used his family as models, since they didn't require payment and were easily available

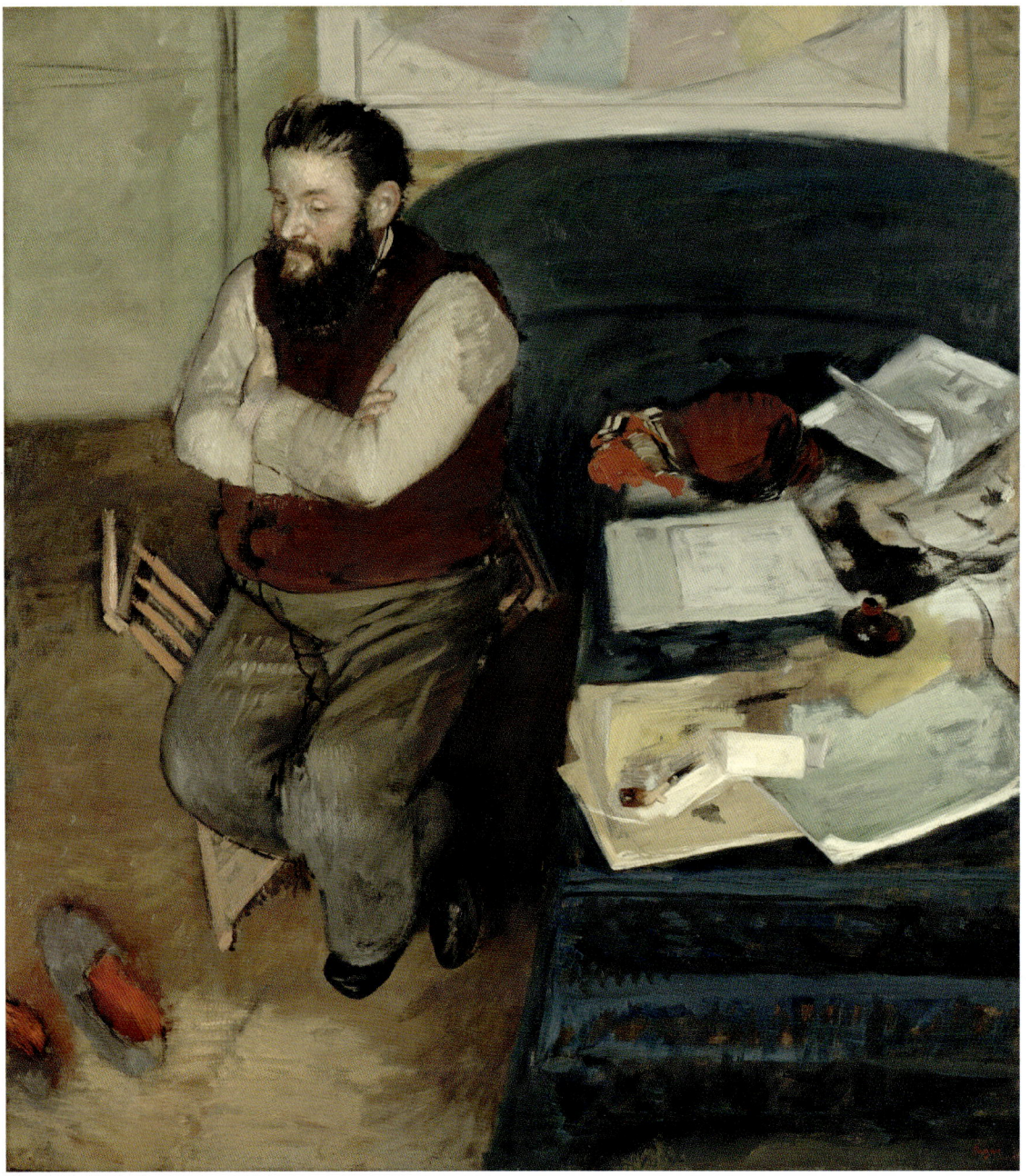

Diego Martelli, *Edgar Degas, 1879. Gauguin looked closely at Degas' innovative compositions. In this portrait of a friend, the art critic Diego Martelli, Degas chose an unusual viewpoint, showing him from above and looking away from the viewer. The picture was exhibited at the 1879 Impressionist Exhibition, in which Gauguin was invited to take part.*

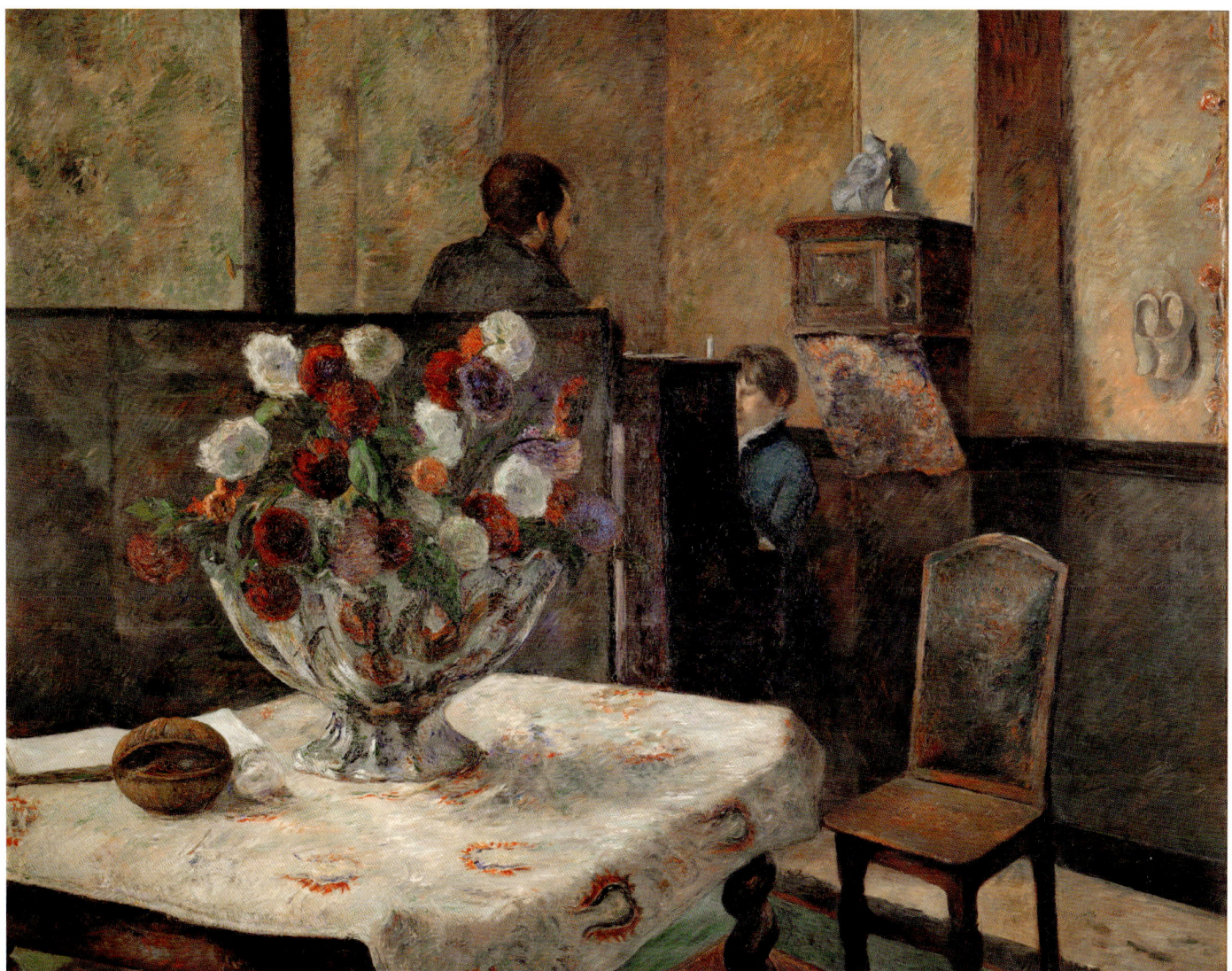

to an artist who could only paint in his spare time. His interior scenes often include ceramics or carvings he had made, pots or tankards he owned, his own paintings or those by other artists in his collection, and still life elements such as flowers.

The Impressionists disbanded as a group after their final exhibition in 1886. By this time Gauguin's work was veering off in a very different direction. He would ultimately became more interested in conveying the inner world of myths, beliefs and states of mind than the outer world of appearances.

Interior of the Artist's Home, rue Carcel, *1881. A woman (perhaps Mette) is playing the piano while a man looks on, but the human activity is relegated to the background, behind the huge vase of flowers. Incidental details – a small pair of clogs on the wall and an empty chair – hint at family life. The picture was exhibited in the Seventh Impressionist Exhibition in 1882.*

GAUGUIN AND PISSARRO

Camille Pissarro was a central figure in the Impressionist movement, a fatherly man valued for his kindness and wisdom. He was 18 years older than Gauguin, and took him under his wing, becoming a key influence on the young artist. Reflecting on his life many years later, Gauguin wrote, 'He was one of my teachers and I do not disown him.' He was familiar with Pissarro's works even before the First Impressionist Exhibition of 1874 because they were part of Gustave Arosa's collection, and he may even have met him in the Arosas' apartment. However, he got to know Pissarro really well after the Fourth Impressionist Exhibition in 1879. He also bought Pissarro's paintings, notably those from the period 1879–82, and sought out potential buyers for him among his acquaintances on the stock exchange. If the friendship was one of the reasons Gauguin collected his work, Pissarro, who was particularly short of money in

those years, must have appreciated it. Until disagreements drove them apart in the mid-1880s, the two artists regularly wrote letters to each other and sometimes exchanged work for evaluation. Pissarro was living in Pontoise outside Paris at the time, and Gauguin spent the summer of 1879 painting by his side. He continued to visit at weekends in subsequent years, on occasion working there with Cézanne as well. Pissarro was insistent on the importance of painting out of doors, and tried to banish artifice and grandeur from his depictions of nature. He chose subjects that were in themselves unremarkable – rural dwellings, villages, cottage gardens and fields, mostly painted in his immediate neighbourhood. He worked over his surfaces with small dabs of paint so that they seem to shimmer. The light, feathery touch of many of Gauguin's early works, and the interest in weather effects, owe something to Pissarro's influence.

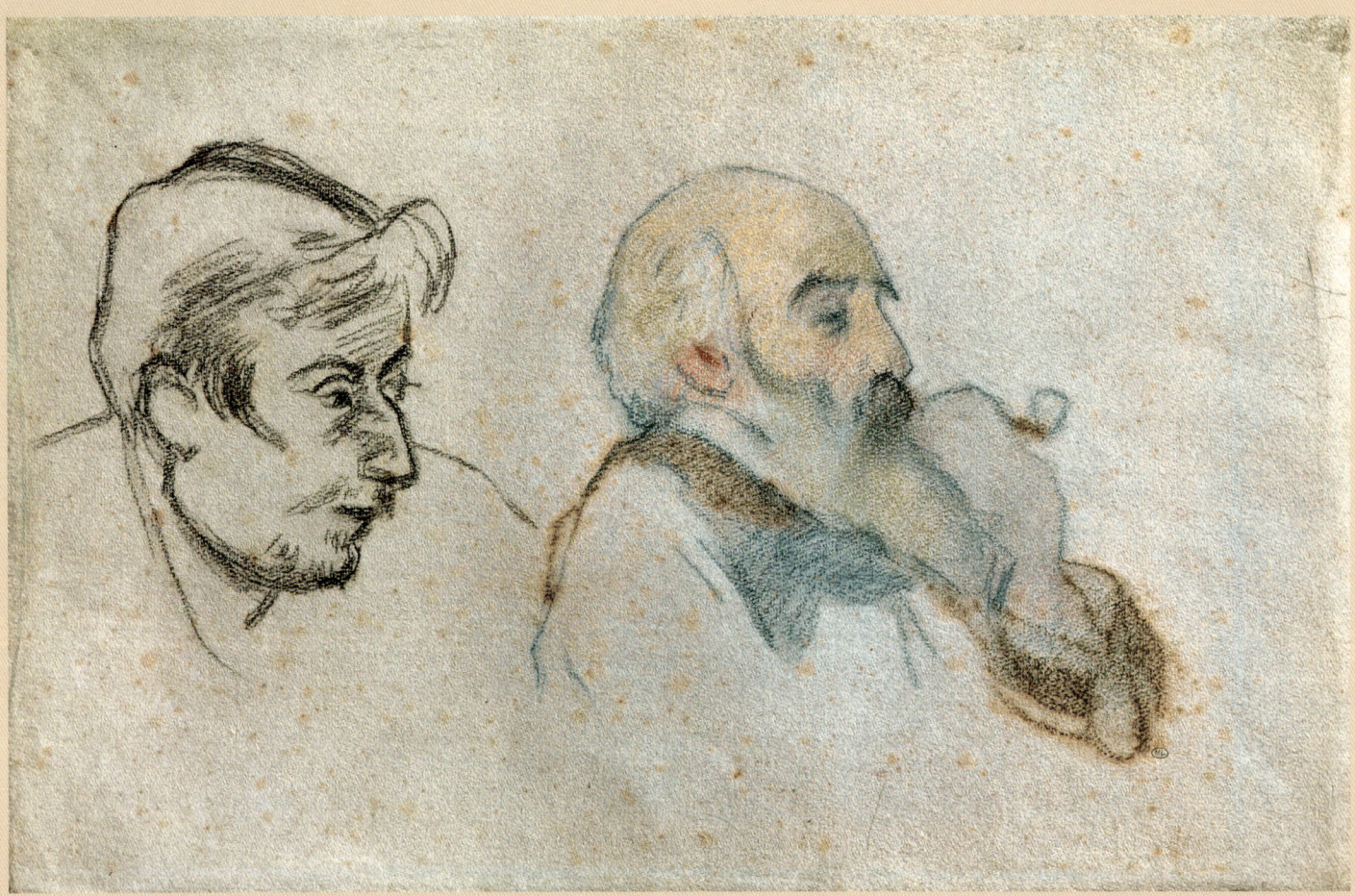

Edge of the Woods near L'Hermitage, Pontoise, *Camille Pissarro, 1879. In Pissarro's painting of woodland near his home, rustic houses are glimpsed through trees as a man slumbers in the foreground. In his early works Gauguin emulated Pissarro's technique of applying multiple small brushstrokes in a dense pattern to create an effect that Pissarro likened to knitting.*

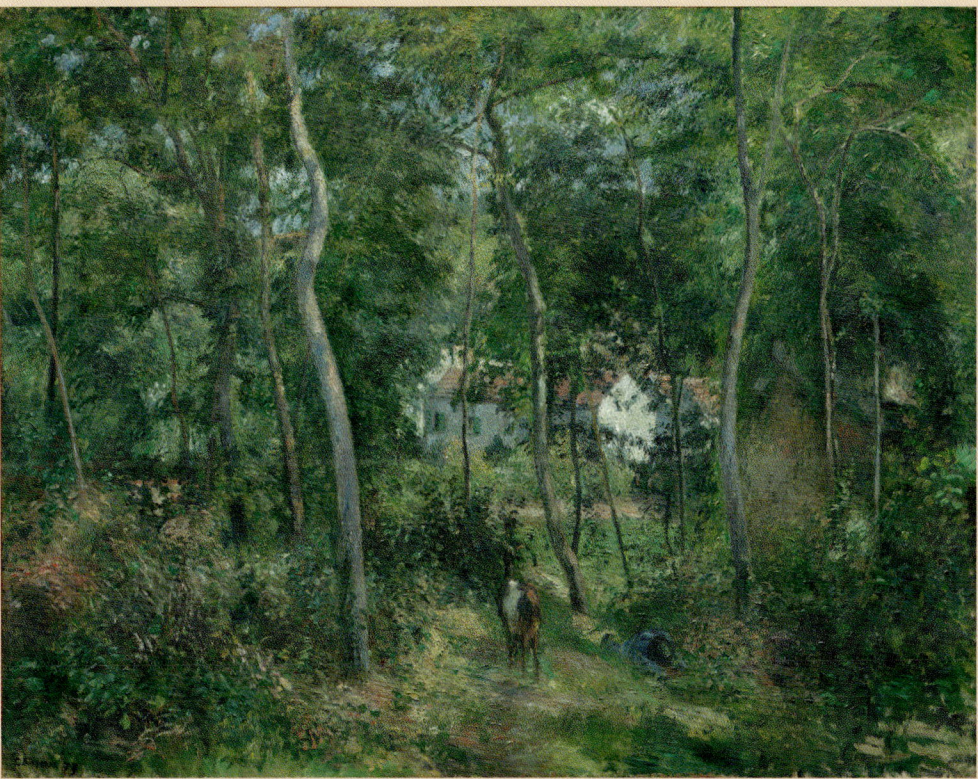

Snow at Vaugirard II, *1879. The winter of 1879–80 was particularly harsh, and several of the Impressionists recorded the snowy weather. Gauguin's rendition of a snowstorm near his home in Vaugirard reveals the influence of Pissarro, who often used a screen of trees in his work.*

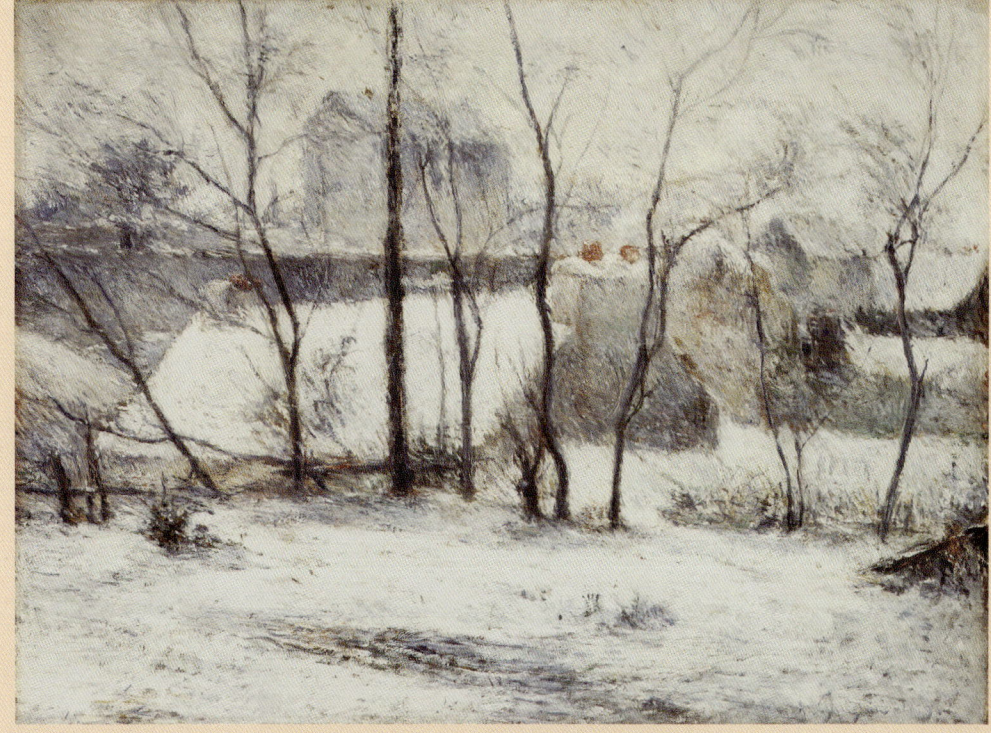

Opposite: *Double portrait drawing of Gauguin and Pissarro, 1883. Pissarro and Gauguin drew each other's portraits in pastel on the same sheet of paper. Gauguin's sketch seems almost to mimic Pissarro's style, while Pissarro's looks like a Gauguin. This may have been an act of mutual homage.*

GAUGUIN'S BEGINNINGS AS A SCULPTOR

In 1877, Gauguin moved his family from a luxurious apartment in the 8th arrondissement in Paris on the right bank of the Seine to the suburban district of Vaugirard. The change of residence marked his entry into more bohemian and less bourgeois circles. The district was home to a number of sculptors, including his new landlord, Jules-Ernest Bouillot. Another sculptor, Jean-Paul Aubé, worked in an adjoining studio. From them, Gauguin would have acquired some technical knowledge of modelling and carving. He produced two relatively conventional but accomplished works in marble, a head of Mette and a bust of his son Emil, but he generally preferred to work in wood or wax. Sculpture became very important to him, and he showed examples of his three-dimensional works in all the Impressionist exhibitions he took part in.

Carving wood also came naturally to Gauguin. He later claimed that as a young child he had worked pieces of wood with a penknife, and he may well have been attracted to the association of woodcarving with 'primitive' or folk art rather than high art as he deplored the distinction traditionally made between fine arts and decorative art, which was seen as of lower status. Wood was his preferred medium for his sculptural work throughout his life. He designed carved furniture for his own home, but realized that making such objects was hardly a commercial venture since few people would buy it.

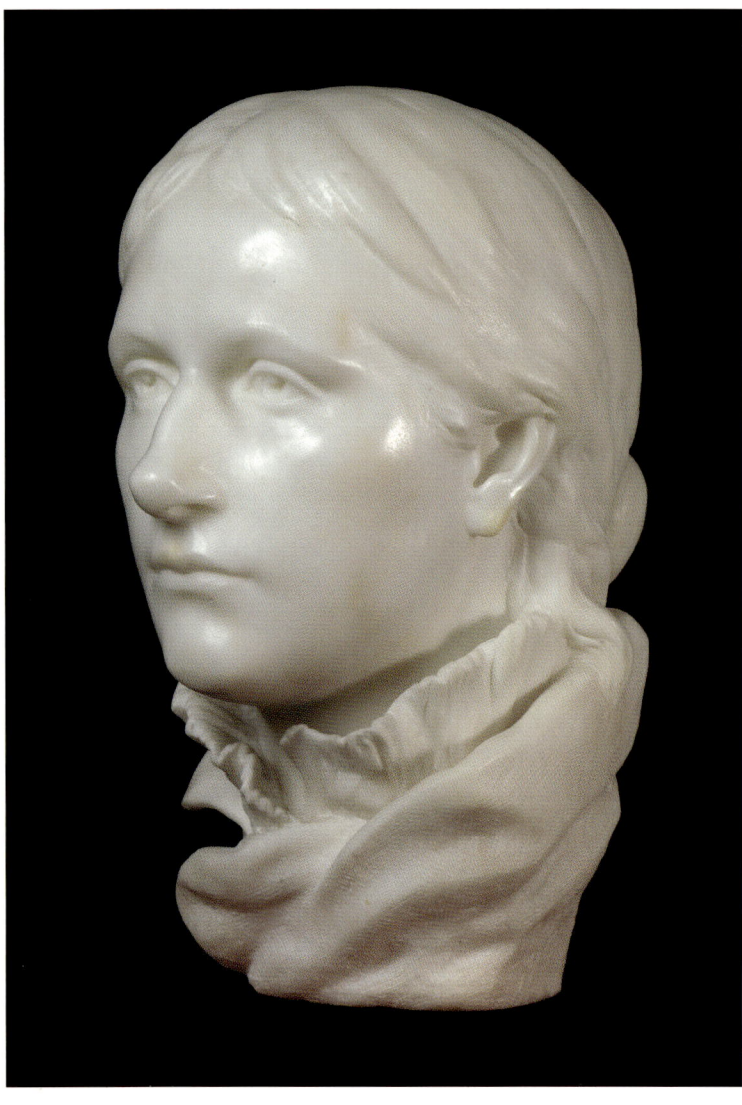

Portrait of Mette Gauguin, 1877. *Gauguin produced only two marble sculptures, this bust of his wife and one of his eldest son, Emil. As a highly finished, quite conventional work it is very unlike the deliberately rough wood carvings of his maturity, and the sculptor Bouillot, who was his landlord, may have helped him with its execution.*

Opposite: La Toilette, 1882. *Gauguin produced three-dimensional works throughout his career. He sent this wood relief of a nude girl in a landscape as a gift to Pissarro, and was delighted that it was to his mentor's taste. When the ceramicist Ernest Chaplet saw it he recognized Gauguin's talent and hired him to produce designs for his workshop.*

Gauguin's Family,
rue Carcel (Garden in
Vaugirard), *1881. The
theme of figures in a
garden was popular
with the Impressionists.
Gauguin used his family
as models for this picture.
The maid is shown with
three of the children, but
the figures are unfinished
and do not seem to relate
to each other, creating a
sense of unease.*

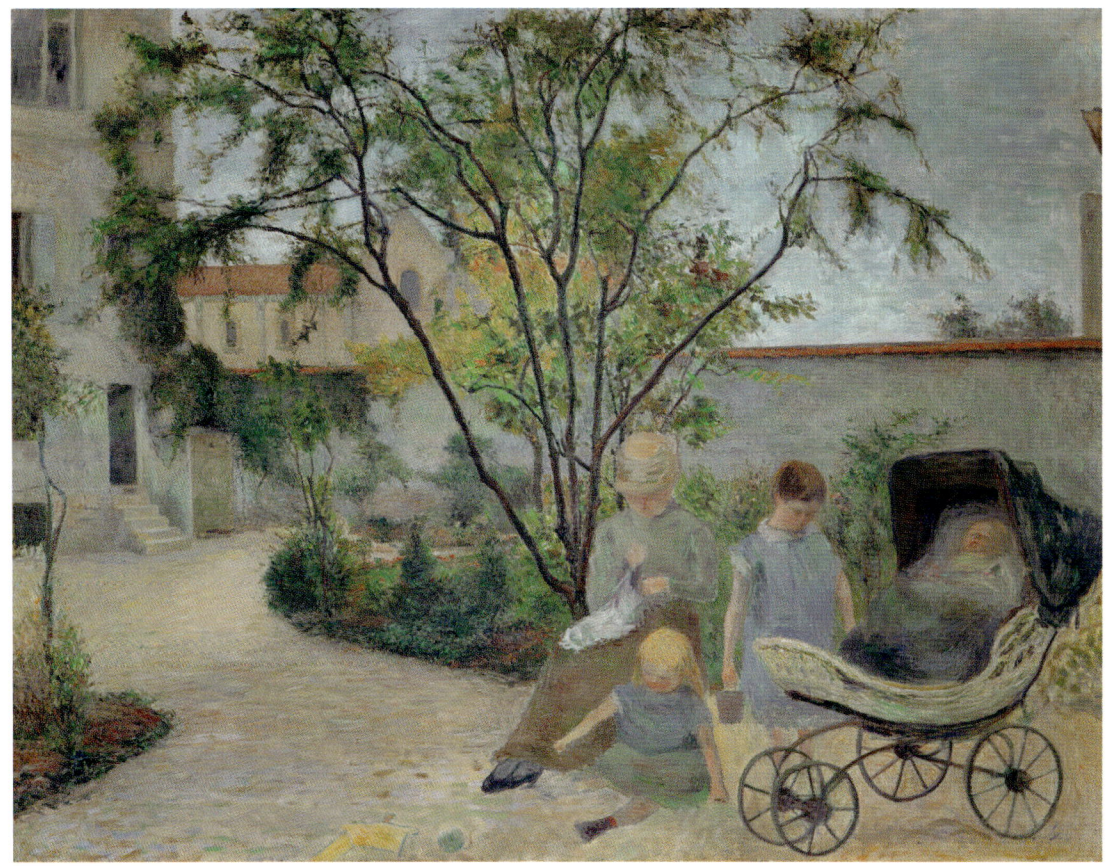

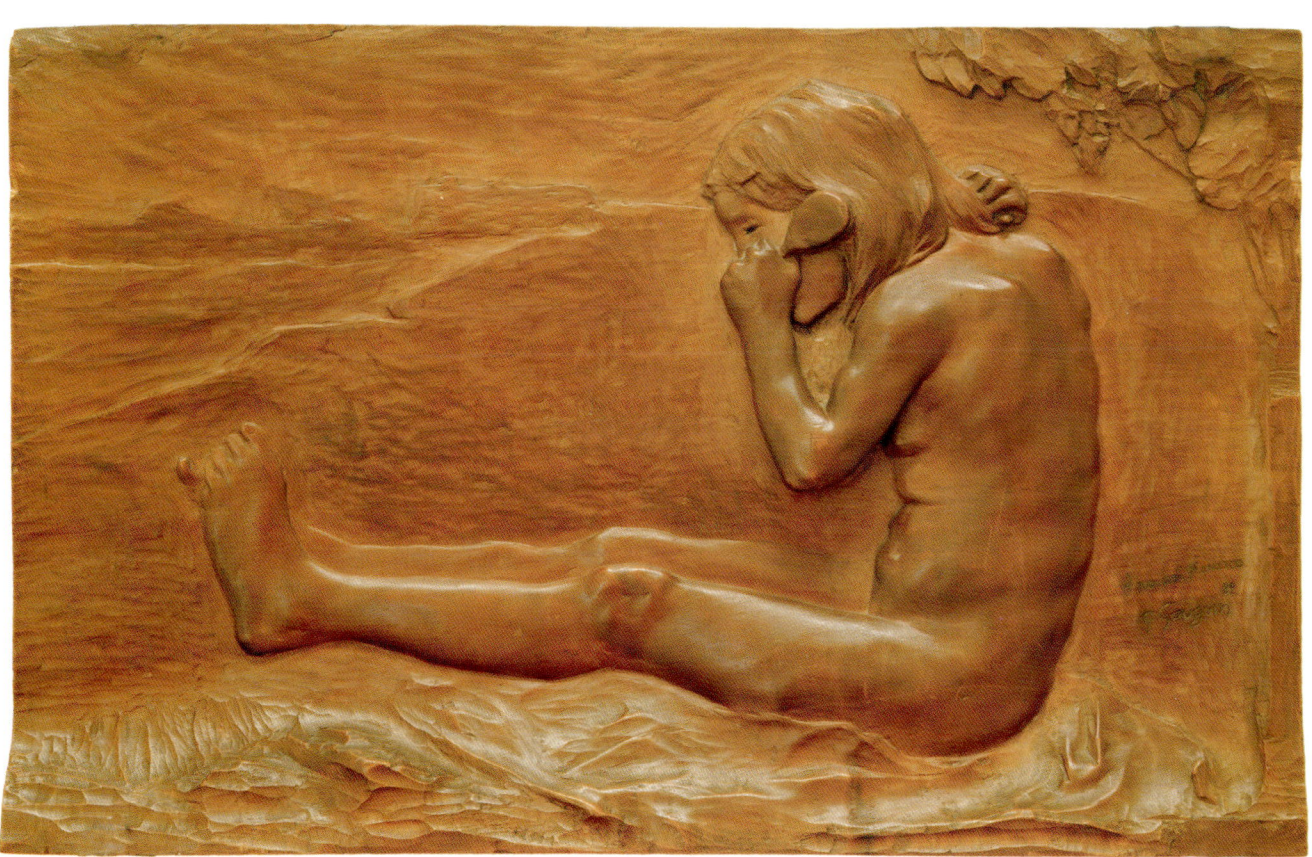

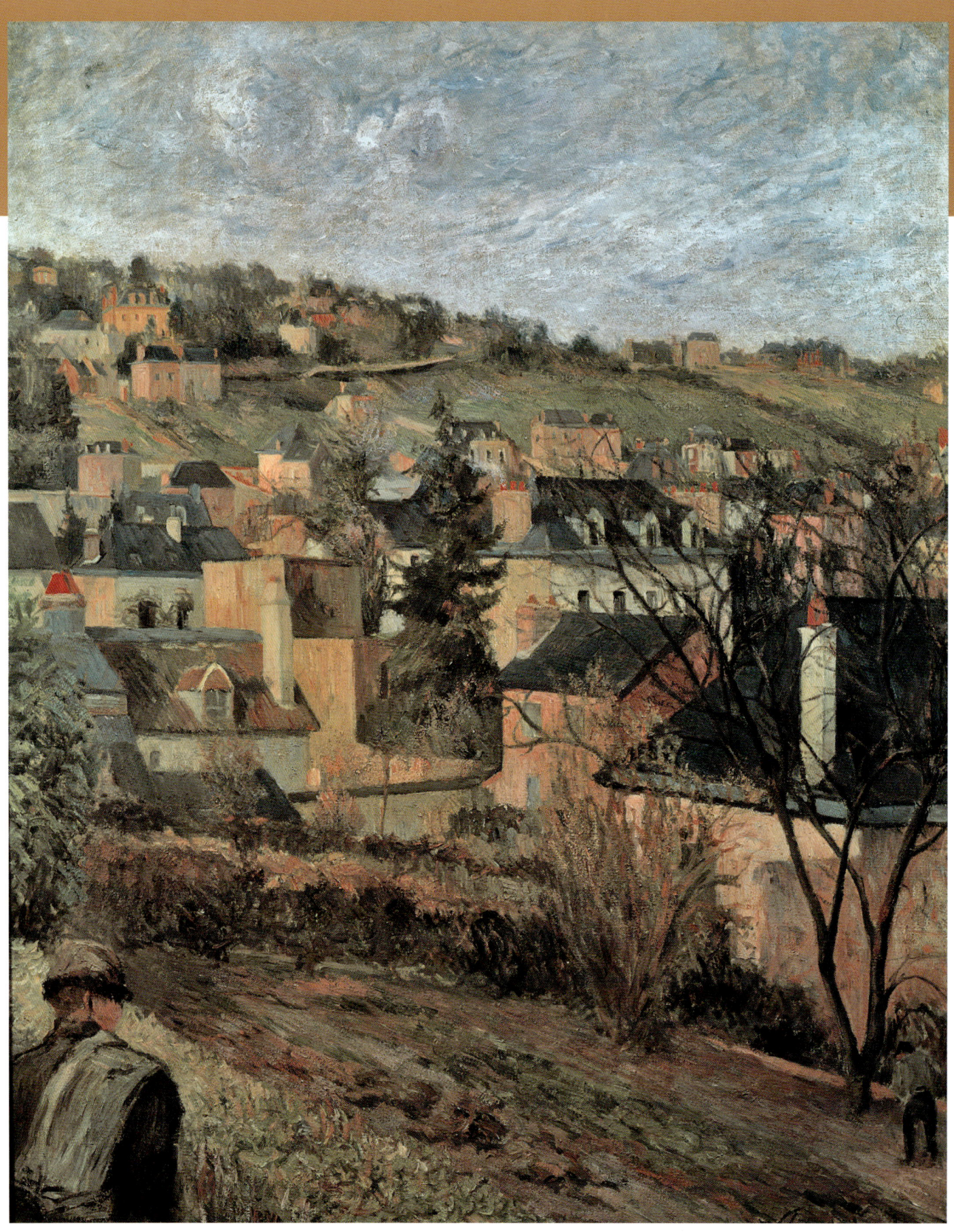

CHAPTER 2
Early Travels

Gauguin's prosperity was not to last. At the beginning of 1882 the Union Générale bank failed, the French stock market collapsed again and Gauguin's earnings went into decline. Although he complained to Pissarro that he was bored to death in an office job and did not have enough time to devote to his art, that was soon to change when he made the decision to leave the world of high finance. He was seriously beginning to think that he might be able to make a living from painting, although not everyone was as optimistic. Pissarro, who was more of a realist, was worried that Gauguin was being naïve, but he continued to support his ambition in practical ways. The two artists periodically painted together at Pontoise, near Pissarro's home, sometimes alongside Cézanne. Gauguin's wife Mette was expecting her fifth child, so was not delighted at the family's change in fortunes.

In January 1884 Gauguin, Mette and the children left Paris for Rouen, where life was cheaper and where he hoped to sell his paintings to wealthy businessmen. Rouen was a beautiful city, with a medieval centre, a great Gothic cathedral, churches, and quays bustling with activity, which had attracted many artists in the past. However, Gauguin did not choose to portray its obviously picturesque sights, concentrating instead on landscapes, gardens, portraits and still lifes.

A DANISH INTERLUDE

Gauguin's hopes for a new life in the city were soon frustrated, as he failed to find new patrons or business opportunities. Nor was his art selling in Paris, where the art market remained in a depressed state following the stock market crash; the art dealer Paul Durand-Ruel, who had promoted the work of the Impressionists, was now buying far fewer pictures. After less than a year, Mette left for Denmark with two of the children to see if the family might have a better future in her native country, where their eldest son, Emil, was already being educated. Gauguin soon followed them with the other children, and for a while endeavoured to make a living as a tarpaulin salesman. He had reasonable contacts in the Scandinavian art world through Mette's relatives and hoped this would help him market his work, but it turned out to be a miserable interlude for him. He did not speak Danish and his relationship with his in-laws was not easy. He was painting in a tiny attic room while the salon downstairs was reserved for his wife, the students to whom she gave French lessons, and other visitors. He offended several people by his behaviour and tensions with Mette were unbearable. In letters to his friends Gauguin admitted that he had contemplated hanging himself, but he had no intention of giving up his artistic ambitions. He confessed to Schuffenecker: 'Here [in Copenhagen] I am more than ever tormented by art, and

Blue Roofs, Rouen, 1884. In this meticulously painted view, Gauguin depicted all the details of the buildings on a hill in northern Rouen. He was missing close contact with Pissarro as his artistic mentor, but the relatively ordinary suburban scene was exactly the type of subject that Pissarro favoured.

although I have to worry about money, and look for business, nothing can deter me.'

A particularly cold winter meant that painting out of doors was difficult, although Gauguin did produce some wintry views and atmospheric snow scenes as well as innovative interiors. In May 1885 his brother-in-law, the artist Frits Thaulow, helped him organize an exhibition of his work, but it didn't sell. Isolated from the artistic world of Paris, Gauguin began to reflect on his work, setting down his thoughts in his 'Synthetic Notes', in which he argued that painting was 'the most beautiful of all the arts' because it unites all the senses, and that the impressions of the senses are superior to rational thought. He also maintained that certain lines and colours have intrinsic qualities: some lines would be experienced by everyone as melancholy, for example, and some colours would inevitably be associated with nobility or boldness. Gauguin further elaborated on the science of colour, saying that although the Impressionists had been criticized for putting colours side by side rather than blending them, nature did the same, and that in any case this painterly practice produced a more vibrant result. He was increasingly feeling that the foundations of his art lay in ideas, the world of thought, rather than the act of painting itself. In a long letter on the philosophy of art written to Schuffenecker, who had also abandoned the world of stockbroking to become a painter, he advised his friend not to labour over his pictures but to work 'freely and frantically', saying that 'a great feeling (sentiment) can immediately be translated – dream freely and seek the simplest form'.

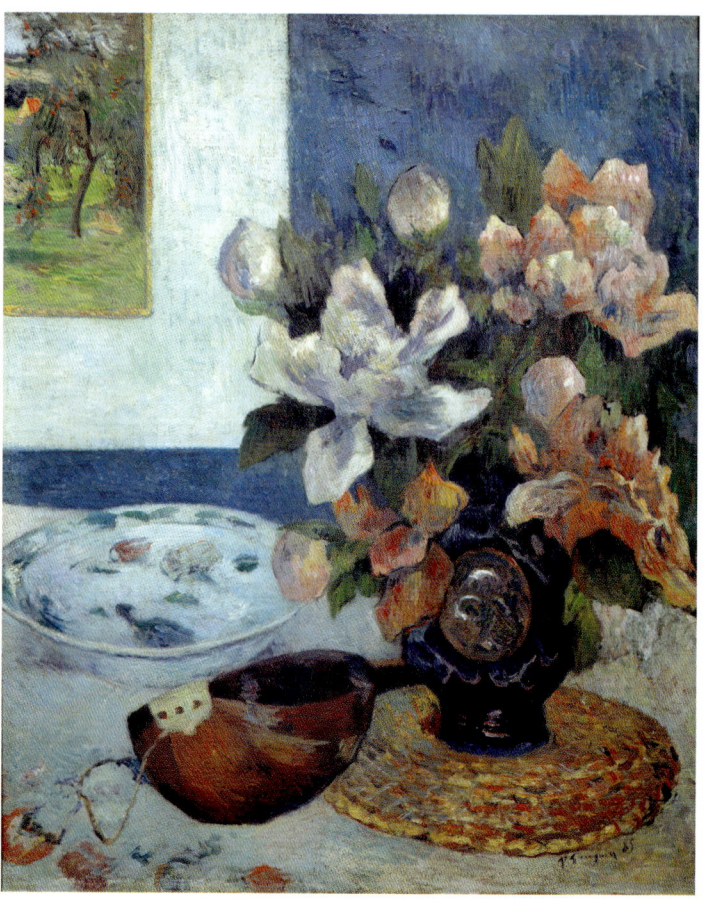

Still Life with a Mandolin, 1885. The objects in Gauguin's still lifes often have a very personal meaning. Here the mandolin echoes the instrument in a painting by Corot that belonged to his guardian Gustave Arosa, while the picture in a white frame hanging on the wall behind the vase of Chinese peonies is a painting from Gauguin's own collection by Armand Guillaumin.

A GARRET IN PARIS

By June 1885 Gauguin was back in the French capital, while Mette remained behind in Copenhagen. He was living in a cold rented garret, but appeared more cheerful. His son Clovis had come to Paris with him, although Gauguin's reduced circumstances meant he had to send him to lodge with his wealthy sister Marie, who then paid his fees at boarding school. From this time on, Gauguin and his wife led separate lives, but they remained in close contact by letter for the next decade, both continuing to hope that he would manage to make enough money as an artist to support the family. For a while he eked out a living working as a bill-poster for a French rail company. He regained contact with the Impressionists and exhibited 18 paintings, most of them landscapes, and a carved wood relief in their eighth and last group show in 1886. The work received a lukewarm reception from the critics, who seemed more interested in the paintings of Seurat, whose monumental *Sunday Afternoon at La Grande Jatte* was the talk of the show. Seurat's meticulous pointillist technique explored the optical possibilities produced by the juxtaposition of minute dots of complementary colour. Many saw this as an exciting new development – a new 'scientific' direction for Impressionism – but it was not one that Gauguin wished to follow.

PONT-AVEN

Following the disappointment of the last Impressionist exhibition, Gauguin turned his thoughts to possible voyages that might inspire his art. The previous summer he had spent a few weeks painting seascapes at Dieppe, and in the summer of 1886 he went to the coast again, but this time to Brittany. His destination was the picturesque village of Pont-Aven, where there was an established artists' colony. Although it was remote, the village had been 'discovered' by artists three decades earlier, and it was made more accessible by the opening of a new railway line in 1862. It soon became a popular destination during the summer months for painters based in Paris, in part because of the low cost of living and also because of the beauty of the Breton

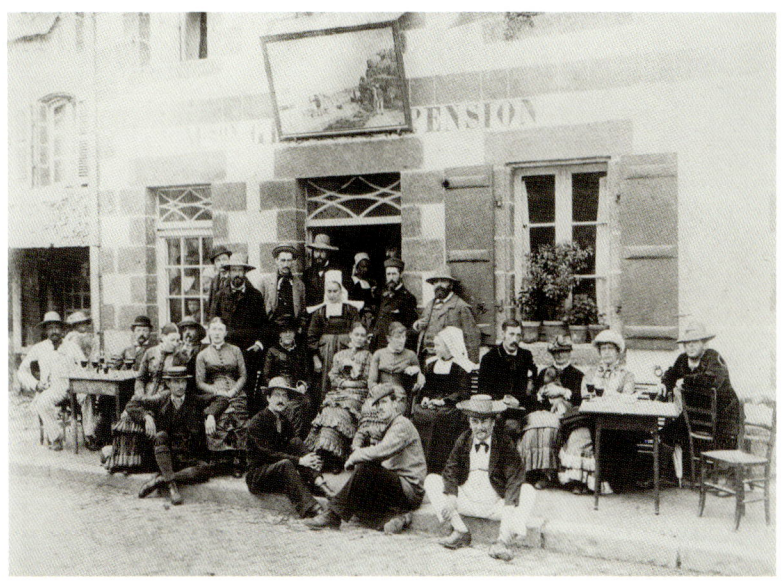

Guests and staff in front of the Pension Gloanec, 1888. Wearing a stiff white headdress, the landlady stands in the doorway of the inn, surrounded by staff and guests. Gauguin is sitting in the middle of the front row. The inn was known for its excellent food, which was served at communal tables, and the dining room was decorated with works by many of the artists who stayed or ate there.

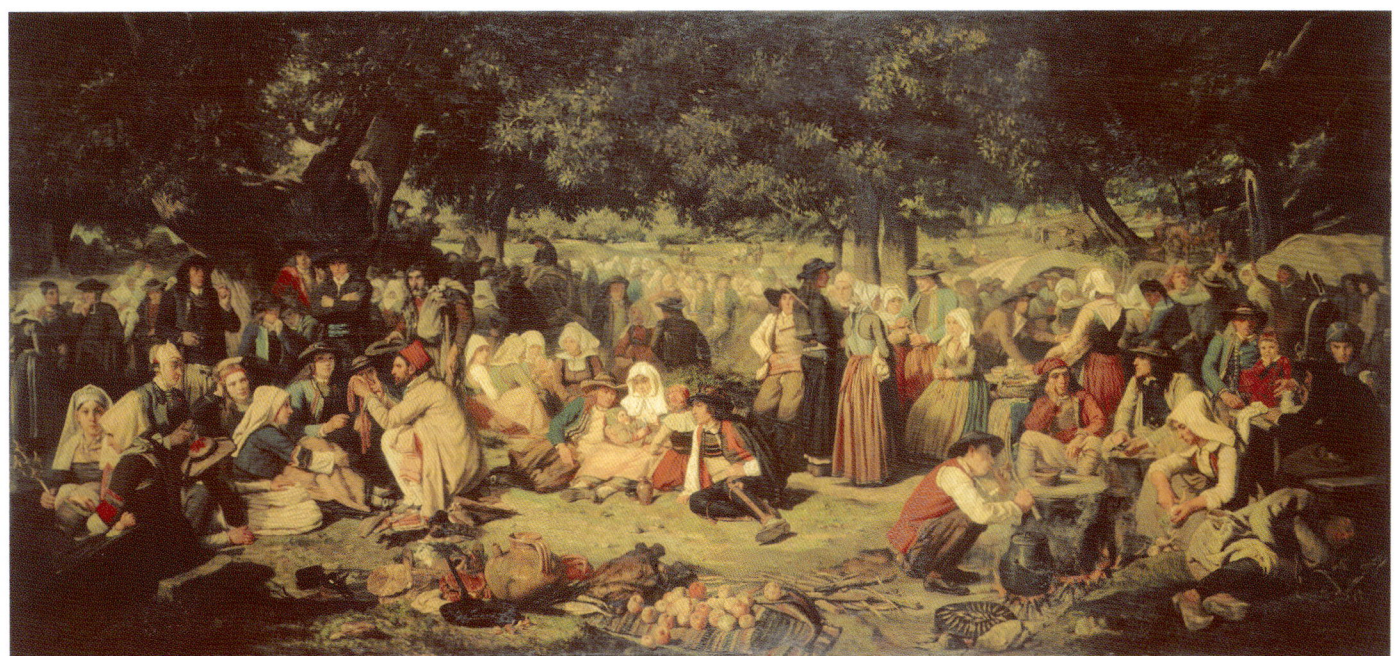

Breton Pardon (Pardon Day in Brittany), *Pierre-Charles Poussin, 1851. The ancient traditions of Brittany became popular subjects for French artists in the second half of the nineteenth century. Poussin's painting shows pilgrims who have gathered for the Pardon day at Guingamp. At Pardons the faithful would be granted absolution for their sins in return for joining a procession to worship at selected shrines.*

Women and children in traditional Breton costumes, Pont-Aven, c. 1900. Bretons asserted their unique cultural identity through traditional costume. Women generally wore a distinctive white starched headdress (the form of which varied according to region), a dress, apron and lace-trimmed embroidered shawl. Men wore baggy knee breeches, a hat, waistcoat and shirt.

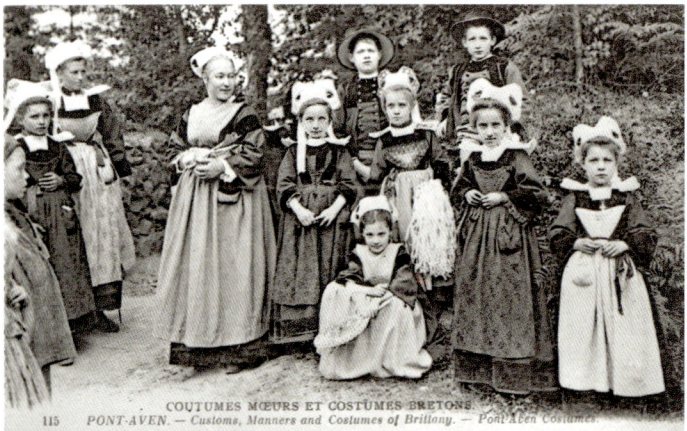

landscape and the area's colourful folklore and religious customs. Several artists had already successfully exhibited paintings with Breton subjects at the Paris Salon, notably Pierre-Charles Poussin, whose vast panoramic *Pardon Day in Brittany*, a record of a traditional religious penitential ceremony, had set the fashion for such scenes when it was exhibited there in 1852.

Gauguin booked into the Pension Gloanec, a popular inn with artists because of its good cheap food and inexpensive rooms. He stood out as an eccentric figure, adopting the traditional Breton man's embroidered vest and wooden clogs. At the age of 38 he was older than many of the artists staying in the village, with a richer and more varied experience of life and a temper that frightened off those who challenged him. He attracted a number of acolytes who listened to his pronouncements on art. 'Everyone

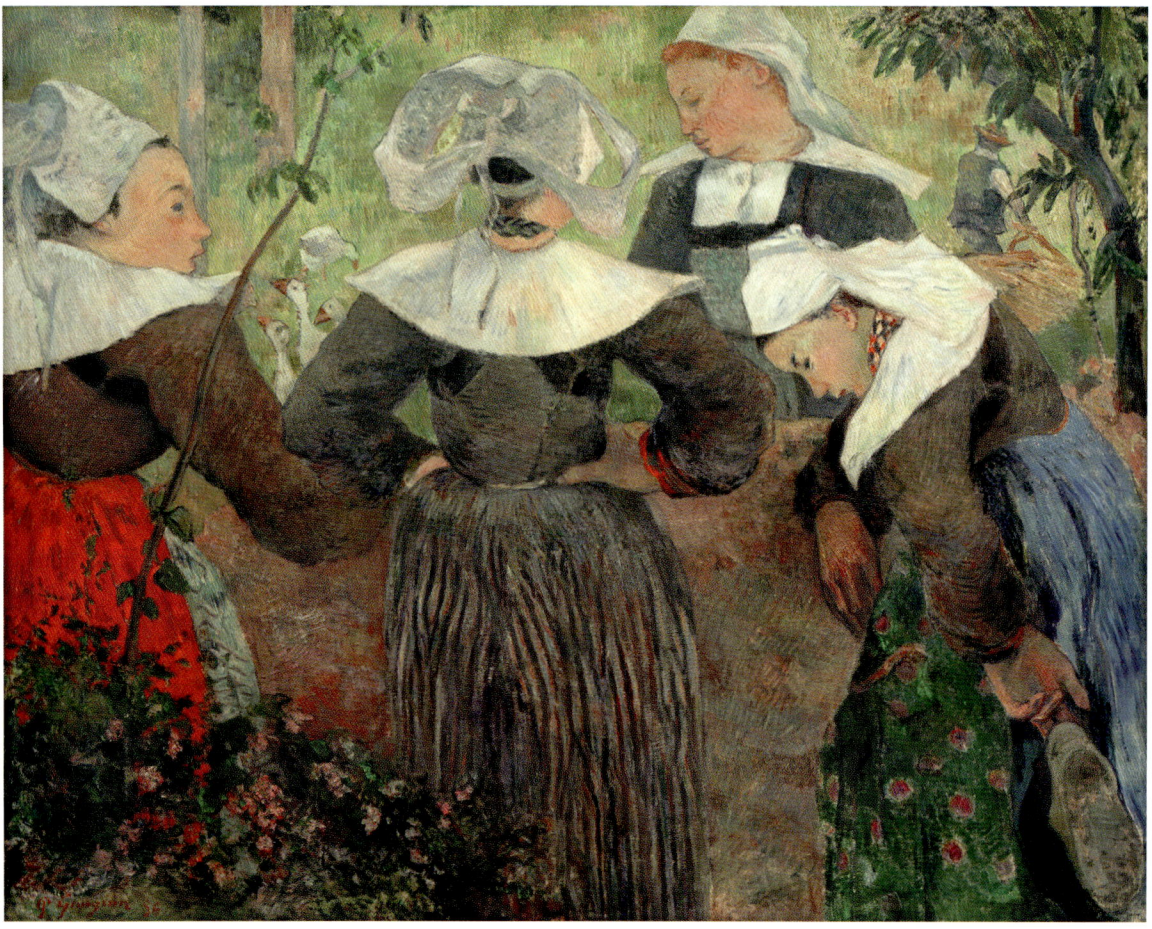

Breton Women Chatting (Four Breton Women), 1886. *Gauguin's decision to paint a group of peasant women and his light palette reveal the continuing influence of Pissarro, but the unusual, deliberately awkward poses may also owe something to his study of Degas' figure scenes. The picture was painted in the studio in Paris, based on coloured drawings made on the spot.*

considers me the best painter in Pont-Aven,' he wrote to his wife, 'and they all fight for my attention and advice.' The first of his disciples was Charles Laval, who would later join him on his voyage to Martinique. The Breton villagers were so used to being the subject of paintings that they were happy to model for painters for a fee. During this first visit Gauguin painted several pictures that marked a new development in his art. Unlike some of the Salon painters, Gauguin did not concentrate on the obvious folkloric or religious scenes, but chose to depict the daily life of the village and the everyday costumes. His drawing style was becoming simpler, and his colours brighter.

ADVENTUROUS CERAMICS

Gauguin's bold drawings of people and animals became the basis for decorations of the ceramics he was starting to make. Back in Paris that winter, he worked alongside the ceramicist Ernest Chaplet, who was collaborating with Félix Braquemond, the artistic director of Charles Haviland's ceramic workshop, on the production of artistic stoneware. This was a potentially lucrative commercial venture, and Gauguin was

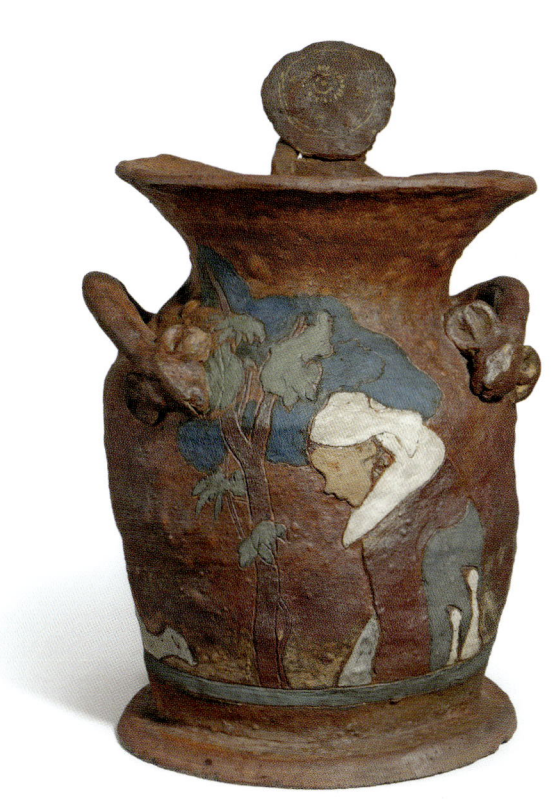

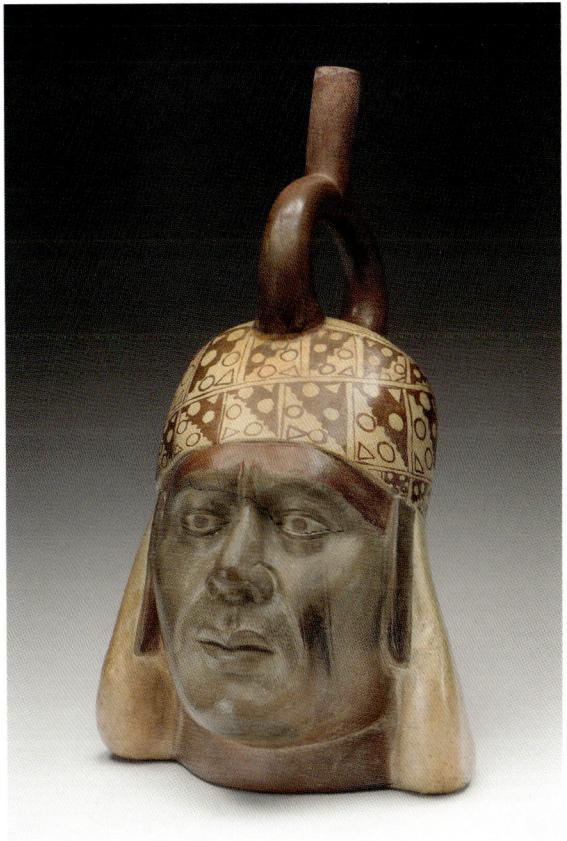

Breton Woman and a Young Breton, 1886–7. The sketches Gauguin made of Breton subjects provided motifs for paintings, ceramics and carvings. Here a Breton girl in a similar pose to one of the figures in Breton Women Chatting *appears on an unglazed stoneware vase that owes something to the example of the Moche pots he had seen as a child in Peru.*

Portrait Vessel of a Ruler, 100 BC–AD 500. Gauguin admired the extraordinary ceramic vessels produced by the Moche artists of ancient Peru. 'Making ceramics is not an idle pursuit,' he wrote. 'Ages and ages ago this art was continually in favour among the American Indians.' This finely modelled portrait of an elite member of society shows him as a man with specific individual characteristics.

clearly excited by the new challenge and the idea that he might have stumbled across a fresh source of income. The expectation was that Gauguin would decorate vases made by Chaplet, but he soon wanted to create his own pots, although he was worried that his highly unusual creations would not prove saleable. That Christmas he wrote to Mette: 'I am making ceramic sculpture. [Schuffenecker] says they are masterpieces and so does the manufacturer, although they are probably too artistic to sell.'

Gauguin's concern turned out to be well-founded. He described the 55 initial pieces he

made as 'monstrosities', and that may well be how many potential purchasers saw them. Some were relatively straightforward and functional, but others were sculptures rather than usable vessels, unlike anything seen before. Crude and lumpy, moulded by hand rather than on the potter's wheel and mostly unglazed, they had more in common with the pre-Columbian pottery he had seen as a child in Peru. One critic, Albert Aurier, described the pots as 'strange, barbaric and savage ceramics, in which the sublime potter has kneaded more soul than clay'.

MARTINIQUE

Life in the capital was proving as hard as ever for Gauguin, and he was forming a plan for a new, more ambitious journey. 'What I want most of all is to flee Paris,' he wrote to Mette. 'I am off to Panama to live like a *savage*.' With Charles Laval, he embarked on a ship bound for Panama in April 1887, intending to visit the island of Taboga in the Gulf of Panama. The two artists hoped to explore commercial possibilities connected with the Panama Canal, which was being constructed at the time, but ended up working as temporary clerks. After a bout of dysentery, they travelled in June to the more congenial environment of Martinique, a French protectorate they had admired on their journey out, where they found a hut to rent on a plantation. It seemed to be an earthly paradise, and Gauguin even suggested to Mette that she and the children might join him there one day. The countryside was beautiful, lush and tropical, with coconut, fruit and palm trees, and Gauguin particularly admired the people: 'Every day brings a ceaseless coming and going of island women in colourful faded finery, with their infinite variety of graceful movements.' He set out to record the island in a series of colourful landscapes, some of which included people, mainly women, going about their daily business, picking mangoes, carrying baskets on their heads. He seemed pleased with what he had done, confiding to Schuffenecker,

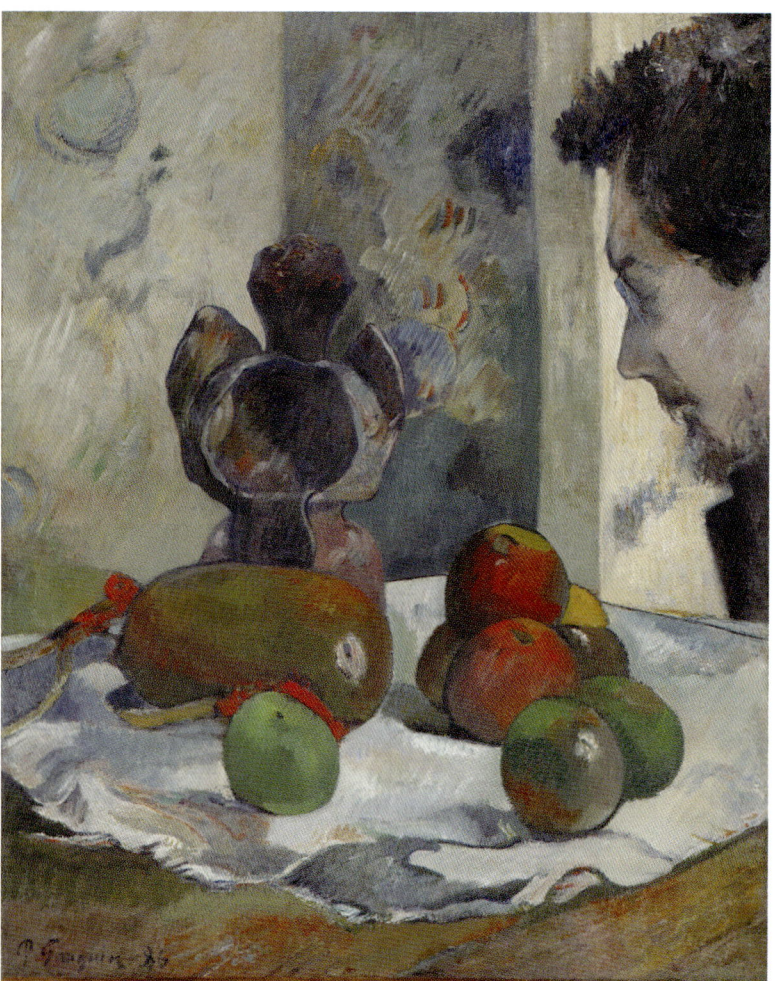

Still Life with Laval's Profile, 1886. Gauguin combined a profile portrait of his friend Charles Laval with one of his own clay pots in a highly original composition that combines a homage to Cézanne in the still life of apples and to Degas, who favoured similar off-centre arrangements in which people are abruptly truncated by the picture frame.

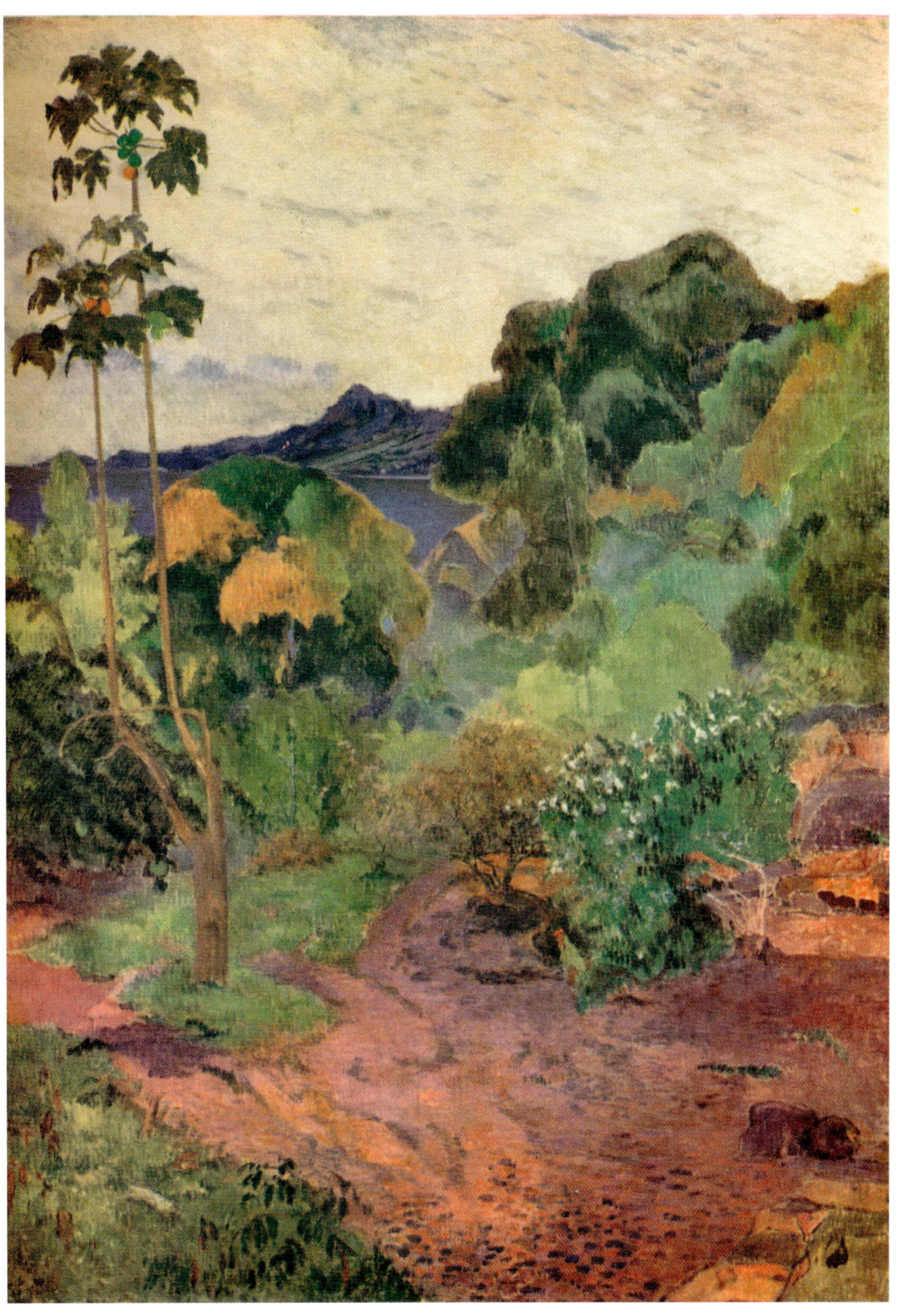

Tropical Vegetation (Martinique Landscape), 1887. *Gauguin depicted the Martinique landscape as an unsullied paradise in a dense tapestry of vibrant patches of colour created with fine brushstrokes. The deep hues feel quite different from the lighter Impressionistic palette of his Brittany pictures painted the previous year.*

'I shall bring back a dozen canvases, four of which have figures far superior to those of my Pont-Aven period … despite my physical weakness, my painting has never been so light, so lucid (with plenty of imagination thrown in).' But the dysentery that Gauguin had contracted in Panama caught up with him, and in November he returned to France in a much weakened state.

Back in Paris, the new paintings earned Gauguin two new admirers: Vincent Van Gogh and his brother Theo, who was working for the picture dealer Boussod, Valadon & Cie, where he was keen to promote avant-garde art. Theo bought some of Gauguin's pottery and paintings, including *Picking Mangoes*, and put the work on show in his gallery. With money in his pocket, Gauguin could now afford to travel back to Brittany, where he intended to focus with increased intensity on his painting, away from the distractions of the capital. He wrote to Mette that he was going to work for seven or eight months solidly in order to immerse himself in the character of the people and the place where they lived.

Picking Mangoes, Martinique, 1887. *The powerful physiques and graceful movements of the women at work in the Martinique countryside impressed Gauguin. He wrote to Schuffenecker: 'They chat incessantly while carrying heavy loads on their heads. Their gestures are quite extraordinary; their hands play an important role, in harmony with the swaying of their hips.'*

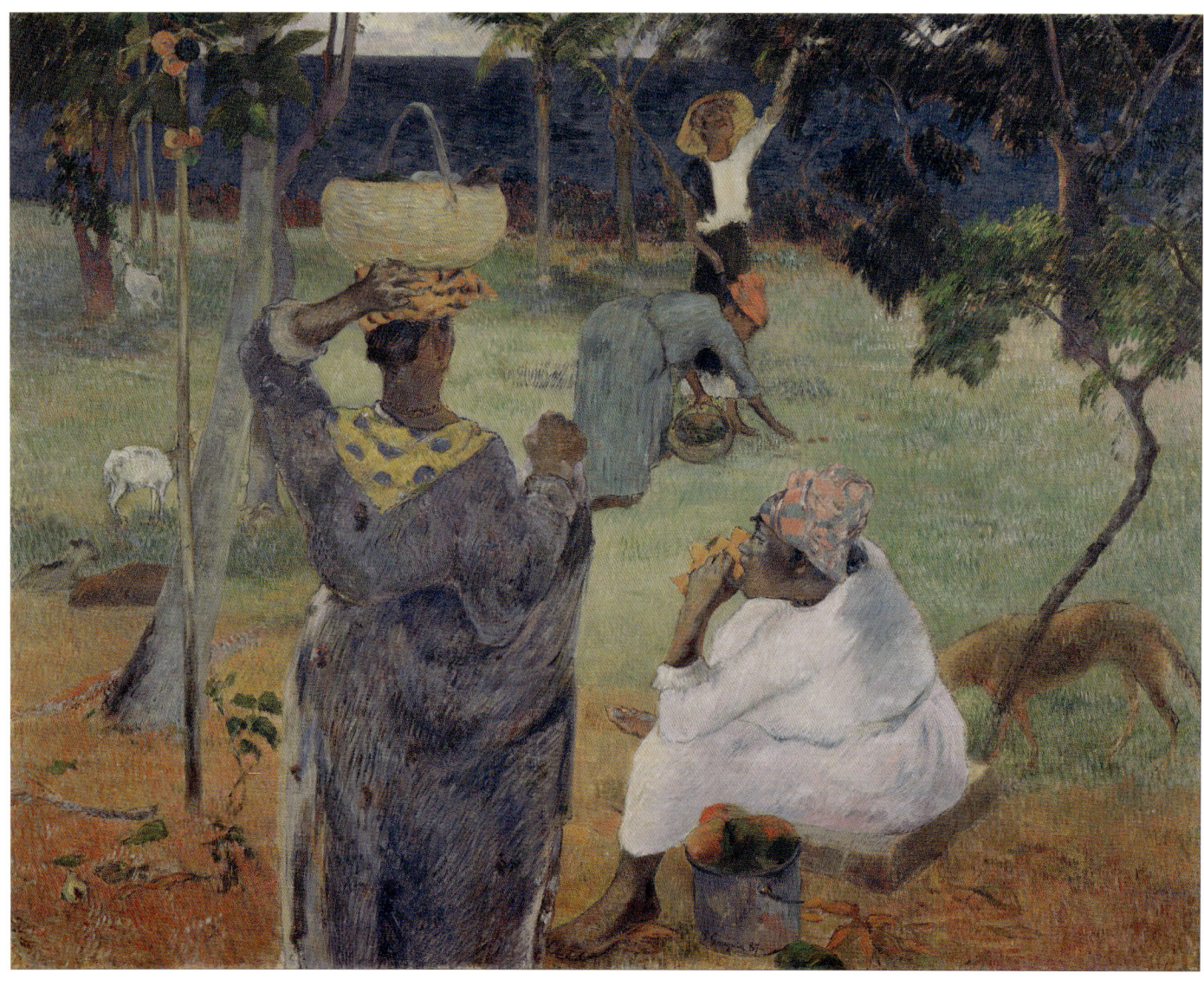

A NEW APPROACH

Gauguin's extended second stay in Brittany, from late January to October 1888, was to prove highly important as it marked an important transition in his art – a break with Impressionism and a move towards dramatically simplified shapes, larger areas of matt colour and an unnaturalistic representation of space. Like many other painters who visited the region, he admired what he saw as the pagan Celtic character of the people and their customs, the fact that they were resistant to modern ideas and seemed remote from the Graeco-Roman tradition on which so much French academic art was founded. 'I love Brittany,' he wrote to Schuffenecker. 'I find the wild and the primitive here. When my clogs resonate on this granite ground I hear the muffled and powerful thud that I'm looking for.' Gauguin had a productive time, completing almost 60 known pictures during his stay. He painted the countryside, the appearance of the first flowers of spring, young boys bathing and wrestling, and dancing at harvest time.

The Swineherd, 1888. Just as he had observed rural life in Martinique so Gauguin set about recording agricultural labour in Brittany, conveying the characteristic gestures of the people in the landscape. He began to simplify forms, using larger blocks of colour bounded by strong contours.

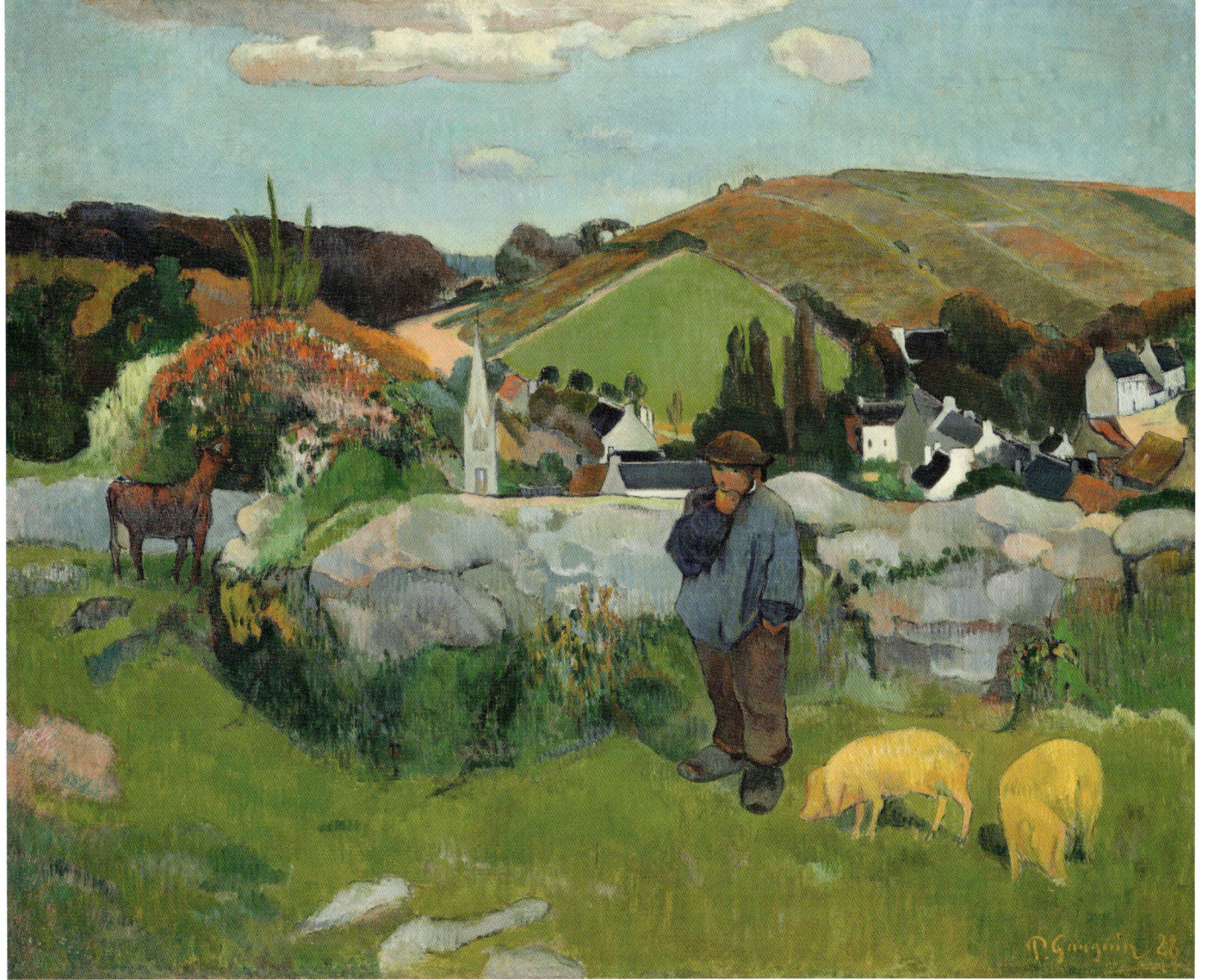

While many artists found Gauguin eccentric and unapproachable, he once again attracted a band of artistic disciples. During that summer, the young Émile Bernard, who had studied alongside Vincent Van Gogh at Fernand Cormon's studio in Paris, travelled to Pont-Aven specifically to seek him out. Although Bernard was younger than Gauguin, and in some senses deferred to him, Gauguin was impressed by his work, particularly its simplified forms and bold dark outlines inspired by stained glass enamels and popular prints. This new style of painting, with its heavy outlines, had been dubbed 'cloisonnism' by one art critic because it was reminiscent of the enamelling technique in which metal partitions or *cloisons* are used to divide one area of bright colour from another. Bernard was later to complain bitterly that Gauguin had stolen the credit for the invention of this new way of painting, but it is difficult to disentangle the sequence of events in its development.

Certainly *The Pardon (Breton Women in the Meadow)*, which Bernard painted that autumn, was a prime example of this new style and Gauguin's *Vision of the Sermon*,

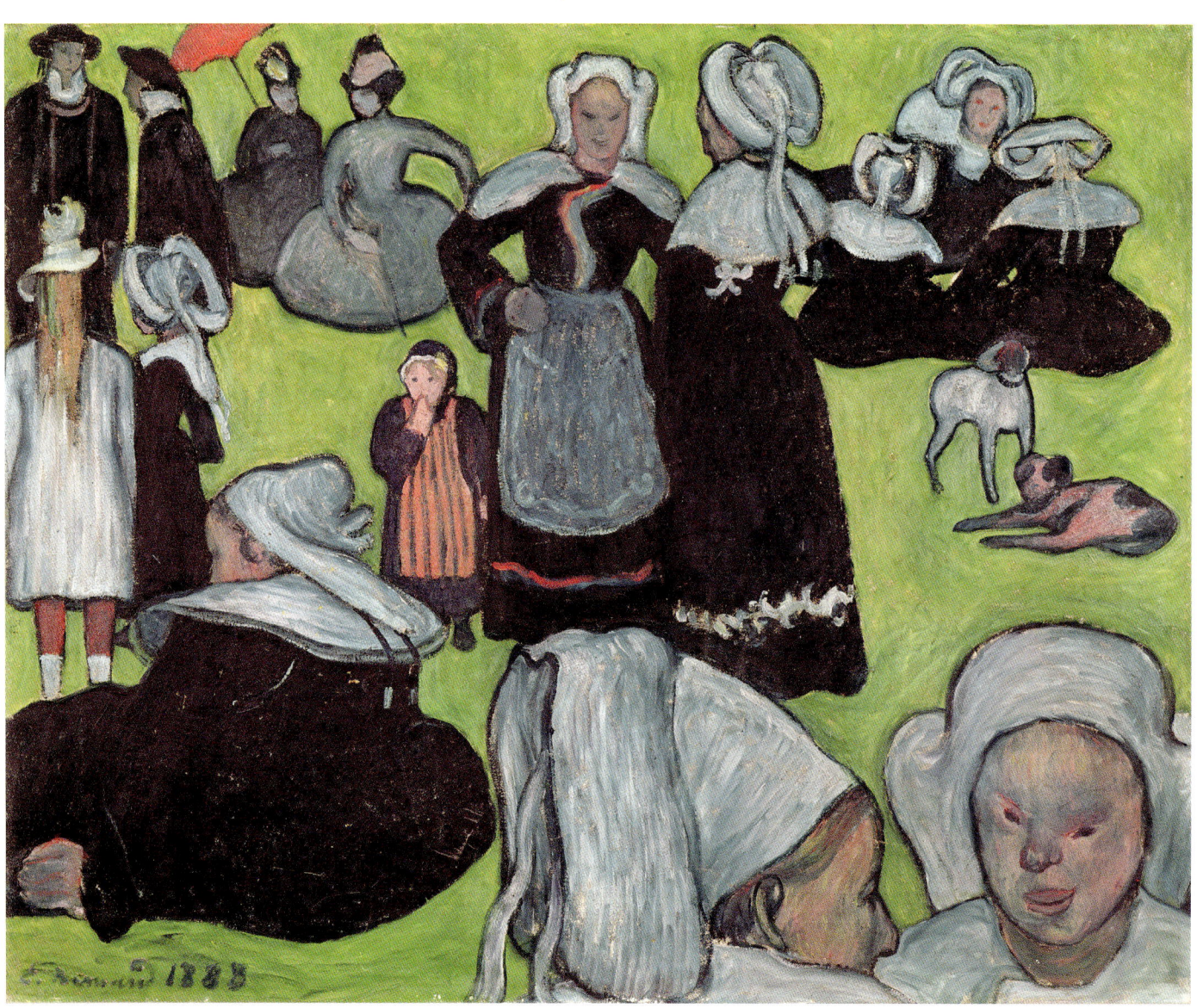

The Pardon (Breton Women in the Meadow), *Émile Bernard, 1888. The talented 20-year-old artist painted this picture after seeing the religious procession in Pont-Aven. With its bold areas of colour contained within strong outlines, absence of horizon or colour modulation to distinguish between foreground and background, it was startlingly innovative.*

which may have been begun slightly before or after it, treats a similar religious subject in a not dissimilar manner. Both paintings were inspired by a visit the two artists made to the Pont-Aven Pardon that took place every autumn. Bernard was a Christian, and his sister Madeleine, to whom Gauguin was attracted, was devout. Their presence in Brittany seems to have awakened in Gauguin a fresh interest in religious customs, although he was generally critical of the established Church. Sadly for Gauguin, Madeleine was in love with Laval. And sadly for all of them, both Madeleine and Laval were to die in their mid-twenties of tuberculosis. Two more of Gauguin's young disciples that summer in Pont-Aven were Maurice Denis and Paul Sérusier. When Sérusier showed Gauguin a painting for his advice, Gauguin responded by accompanying him to the Bois d'Amour, a wood on the edge of Pont-Aven, to give him a lesson on painting with pure colour straight from the tube without attempting to create a literal record of what was in front of him. The result was *The Talisman* (1888), a tiny picture on the back of a cigar lid. When Sérusier took it back to Paris he told his friends that it was 'based on the concept, still unknown to us, of the painting as a flat surface covered in colours assembled in a certain order'. Posterity has come to see it as an important step forward in the development of abstract painting.

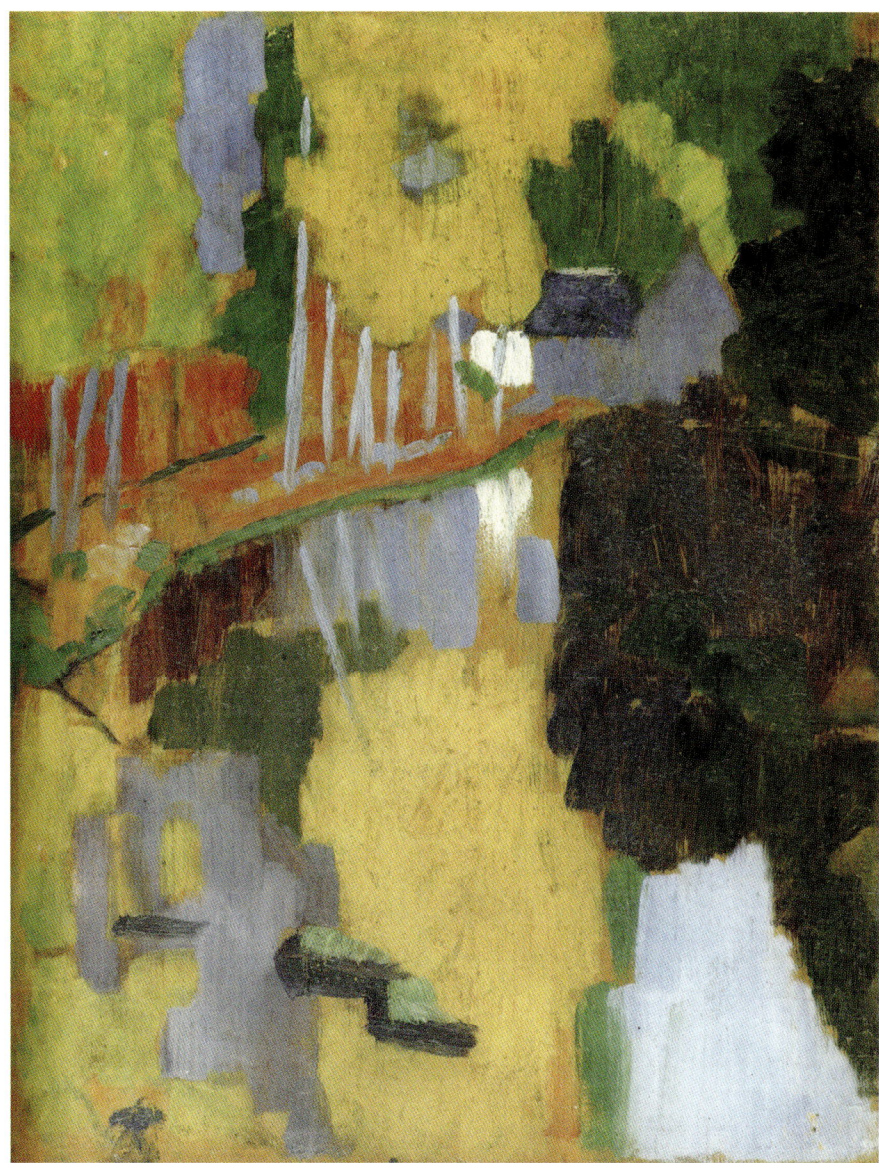

The Talisman, *Paul Sérusier, 1888. Although one can make out features such as the wood, the path and the beech trees on the river bank, they are all represented as blocks of unnaturalistic colour. Gauguin had told Sérusier: 'How do you see these trees? They are yellow. So, put in yellow; this shadow, rather blue, paint it with pure ultramarine; these red leaves? Put in vermilion.'*

THE VISION OF THE SERMON
(JACOB WRESTLING WITH THE ANGEL)

Dating from 1888, this work amounted to a manifesto of a new style of painting which Gauguin developed with his young friends in Pont-Aven.

The Old Testament book of Genesis (32:22–32) relates the story of Jacob who, after fording the river Jabbok with his family, spent a whole night wrestling with a mysterious angel. Gauguin took his inspiration from the story to show the religious experience of a group of traditionally dressed Breton women and a tonsured cleric who have just listened to a sermon based on it. As with many of his paintings, their features are slightly caricatured. He intended to convey the sense of their private experience, as he explained in a letter to Van Gogh: 'For me the landscape and the fight only exist in the imagination of the people praying after the sermon.' Gauguin offered it to the church at Pont-Aven, but it was turned down.

In order to convey the idea that this is a painting about the power of imagination, Gauguin flattened space so that the spectator cannot situate the composition in the real world. The figures are set against a violent red background with no shadows to indicate their position in space. The people in the foreground have their eyes closed or turned downwards; they are not looking at a scene played out before them but imagining it. The giant tree trunk bisecting the composition separates them from the scene they are visualizing. The motif of the two wrestling figures reflects Gauguin's interest in the martial arts, and echoes the pictures he had painted that summer of wrestling boys.

The whole composition, with its broad areas of vivid colour, strong outlines and lack of traditional perspective owes a great deal to the Japanese prints that were much admired by both Gauguin and Van Gogh.

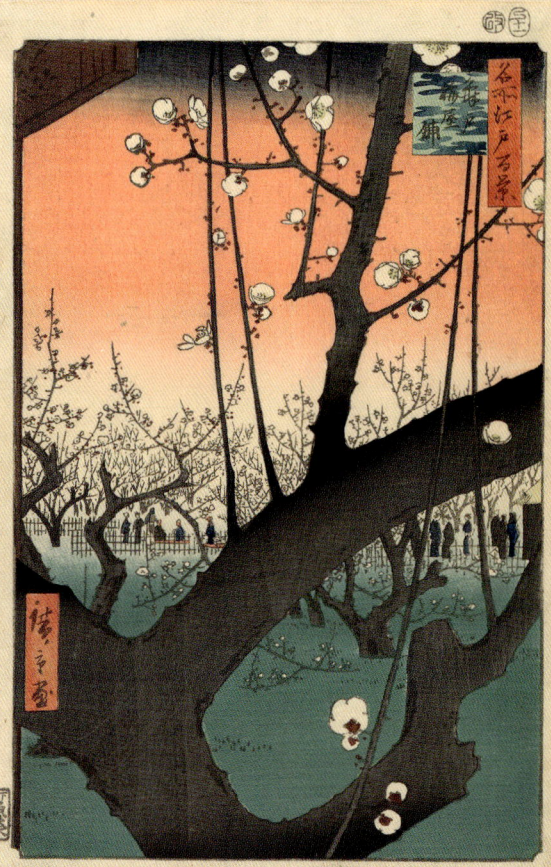

Plum Garden at Kameido, *Utagawa Hiroshige, 1857.*
Gauguin and Van Gogh shared an admiration for Japanese prints. In Hiroshige's print, one of his One Hundred Famous Views of Edo, *diagonal tree branches slice across the foreground, creating a compositional precedent for Gauguin's use of a branch to bisect the composition in* The Vision of the Sermon. *Van Gogh owned a copy of this print and copied it in oils.*

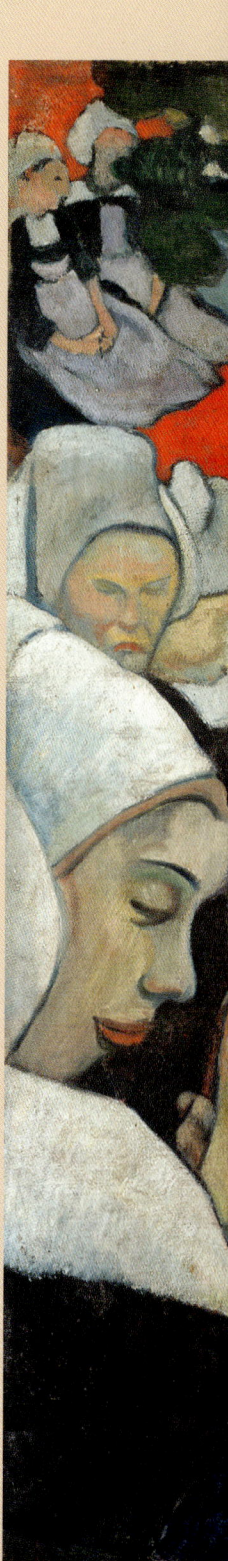

The Vision of the Sermon (Jacob Wrestling with the Angel), *1888. Gauguin described this painting to Van Gogh: 'A group of Breton women are praying, their costumes very intense black. The coifs very luminous yellowy-white. The two coifs to the right are like monstrous helmets.' It has been suggested that he gave his own features to the monk in the right-hand corner, making himself a participant in the vision.*

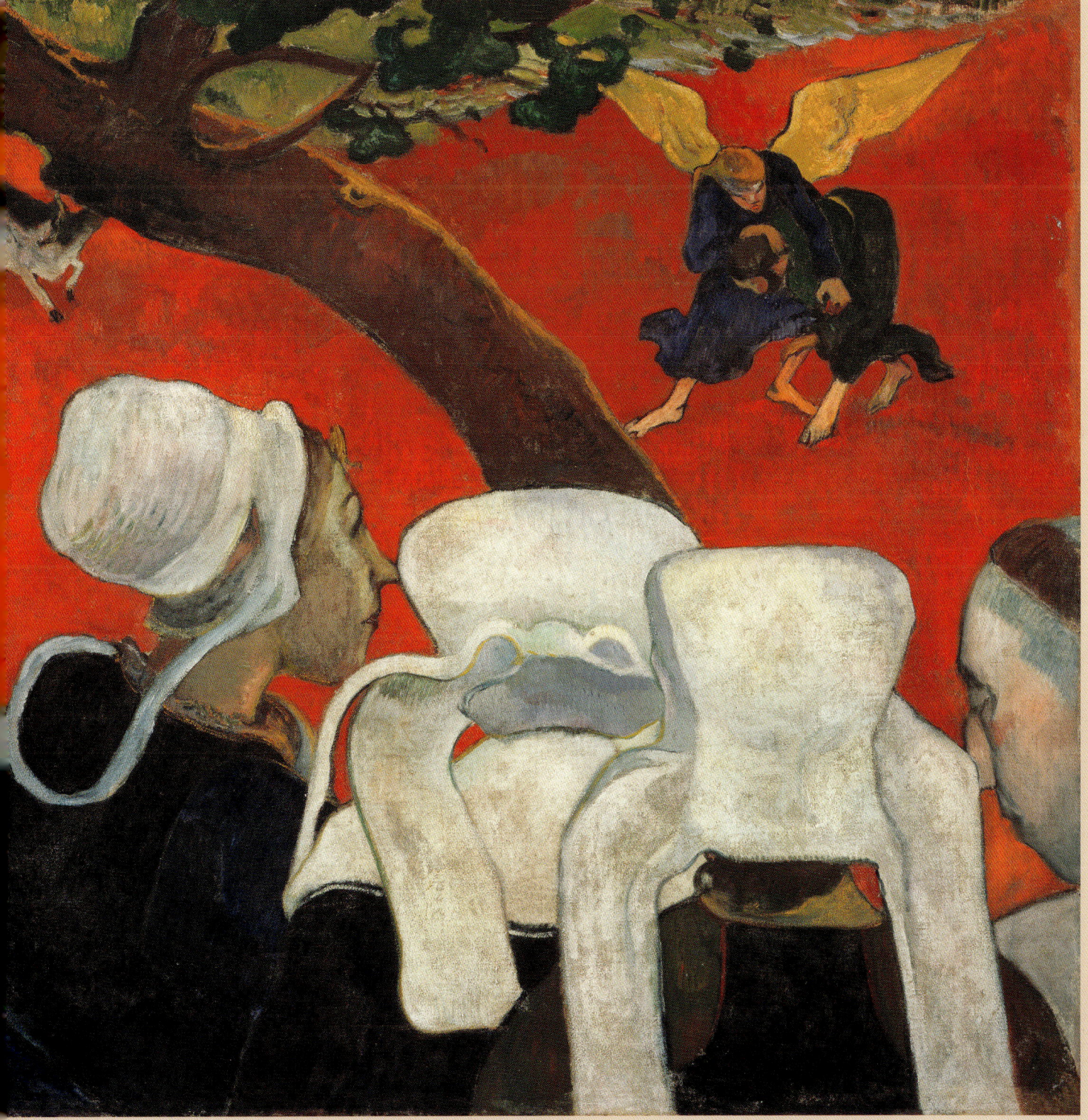

A STUDIO OF THE SOUTH

Vincent Van Gogh had not been invited to join the little colony of artists in Pont-Aven, but he kept in contact with Gauguin and Émile Bernard by letter. He had moved to Arles in the south of France, and was nurturing hopes that Gauguin would join him in the house he had just rented. He wrote to Gauguin and asked whether he and Bernard might paint each other's portraits in exchange for two of his own. Bernard was reluctant to paint Gauguin, saying he was too afraid of him, and in the end the two artists painted their own likenesses but included a small portrait of each other in the background. Gauguin showed himself as Jean Valjean, the hero of Victor Hugo's novel *Les Miserables* (1862), who lived his life as an honourable outcast shunned by society. He exaggerated his hooked nose and gave himself red-rimmed eyes, 'to suggest the red-hot lava that set our painter's soul ablaze'. The profile portrait beside him is that of Émile Bernard. Van Gogh remarked that the picture contained 'not a hint of cheerfulness'.

In return, Van Gogh sent Gauguin a portrait of himself with a shaven head in the

Self-Portrait with Portrait of Émile Bernard (Les Miserables), 1888. Gauguin saw his self-portrait as the solitary outsider, Jean Valjean, as 'a portrait of us all as poor victims of society, taking revenge on it by doing good'. He told Van Gogh that he intended the yellow floral background 'like the wallpaper in a young girl's bedroom' to represent his artistic purity.

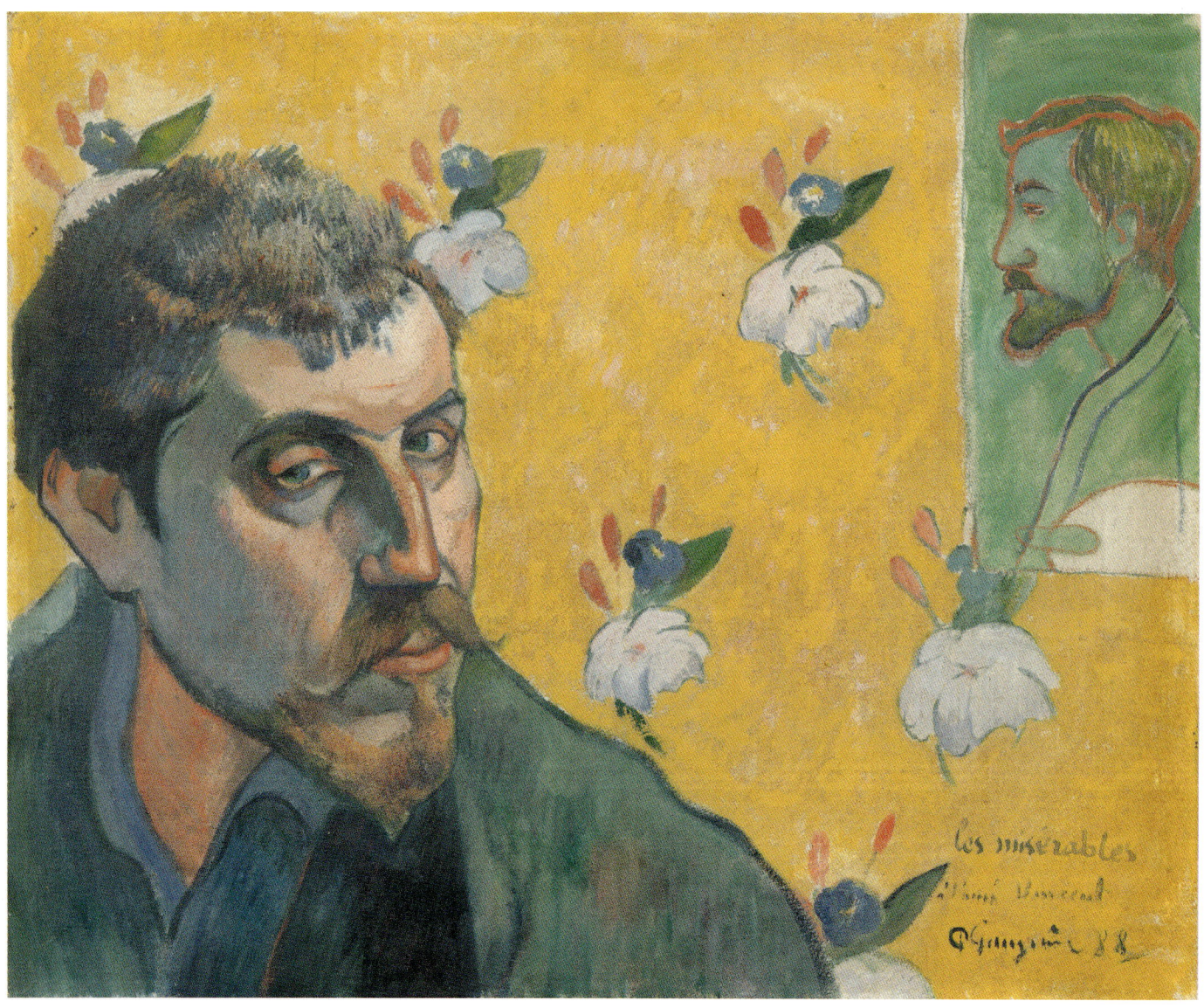

guise of a *bonze*, a Japanese monk or priest. This reflected his hope that Gauguin would help him fulfil his dream of founding a community of artists who would live together in a simple brotherhood, rather like Japanese monks. There was some talk of Laval and Bernard joining them as well. Gauguin did not want to alienate Theo Van Gogh, who offered to buy his paintings, support the household financially and pay his travel expenses, so after much prevarication he accepted Vincent's invitation and boarded the train for Arles, arriving on 23 October 1888. Van Gogh had worked himself into a fever of excitement anticipating Gauguin's arrival, and had hung some of his paintings of sunflowers in Gauguin's bedroom. For his part, Gauguin busied himself organizing the domestic details, devising a budget (which included a sum allocated for visits to the local brothel) and settling down to paint. Van Gogh found Gauguin remarkable and fascinating, 'an unspoiled creature with the instincts of a wild beast'. For a short while the future looked rosy. The two artists worked together and Van Gogh wrote to Theo: 'The house is going very, very well and is becoming not only comfortable, but an artists' house.' Unlike Van Gogh, who was profoundly moved by the nature he saw around him, the changing weather and autumnal colours, Gauguin found the rather flat landscape around Arles less attractive than the rugged Brittany countryside, and was disappointed in the appearance of the town. He turned his attention to its inhabitants, particularly the women. One of them was Madame Ginoux, who ran the Café de la Gare, where the two artists often ate and drank. Gauguin painted her at a table in the café with her absinthe and soda siphon and a slightly world-weary air, a streak of smoke running across the background. Van Gogh, who had also painted the café in a different composition devoid of figures, evidently liked the picture more than its maker did, as Gauguin described it in a letter to Émile Bernard as 'not my kind of subject'.

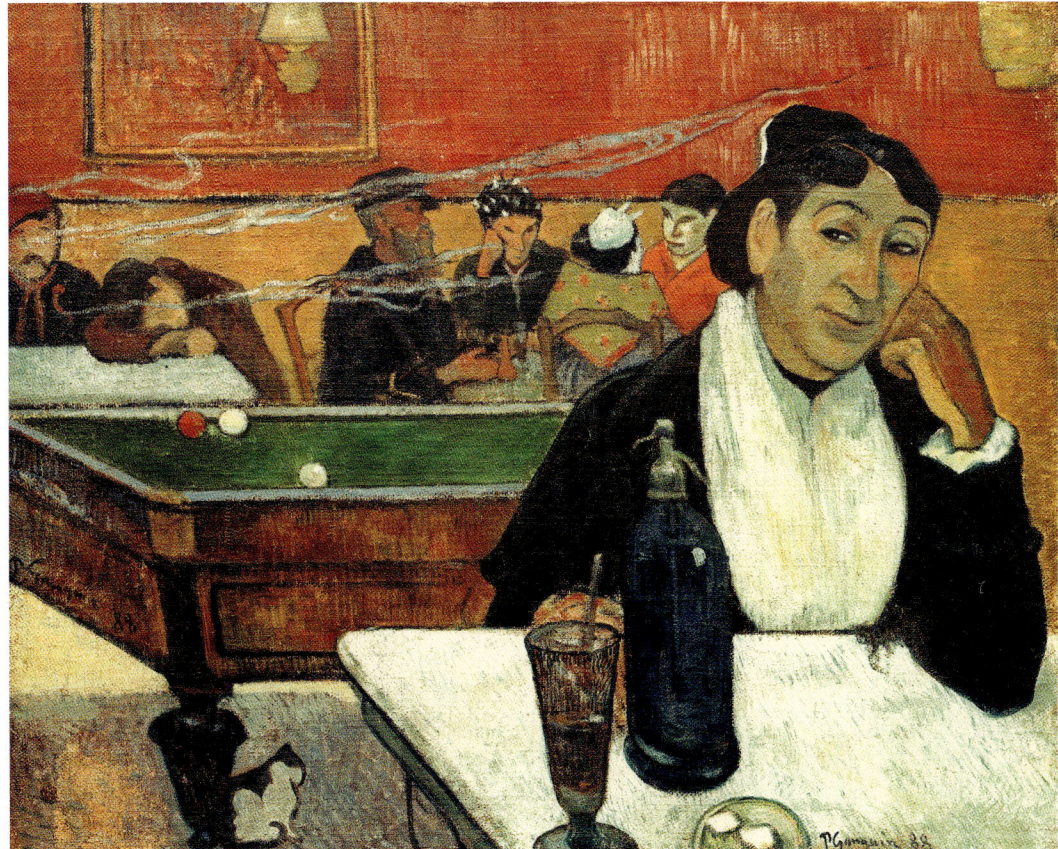

Café at Arles, 1888. *The Café de la Gare is given a slightly louche air. In the background one man is slumped over a table and three prostitutes, one of whom has her hair in curlers, sit together. The man conversing with them is the postmaster Joseph Roulin, whose portrait was painted by Van Gogh.*

The Grape Harvest (Human Misery), 1888. Gauguin worked from memory to produce this extraordinary mix of Breton motifs and southern French setting. The foreground figure, which he reused in many works, conveys a mood of utter dejection, although the cause of her misery is not immediately obvious. The woman watching over her wears the traditional Le Pouldu black hood of mourning.

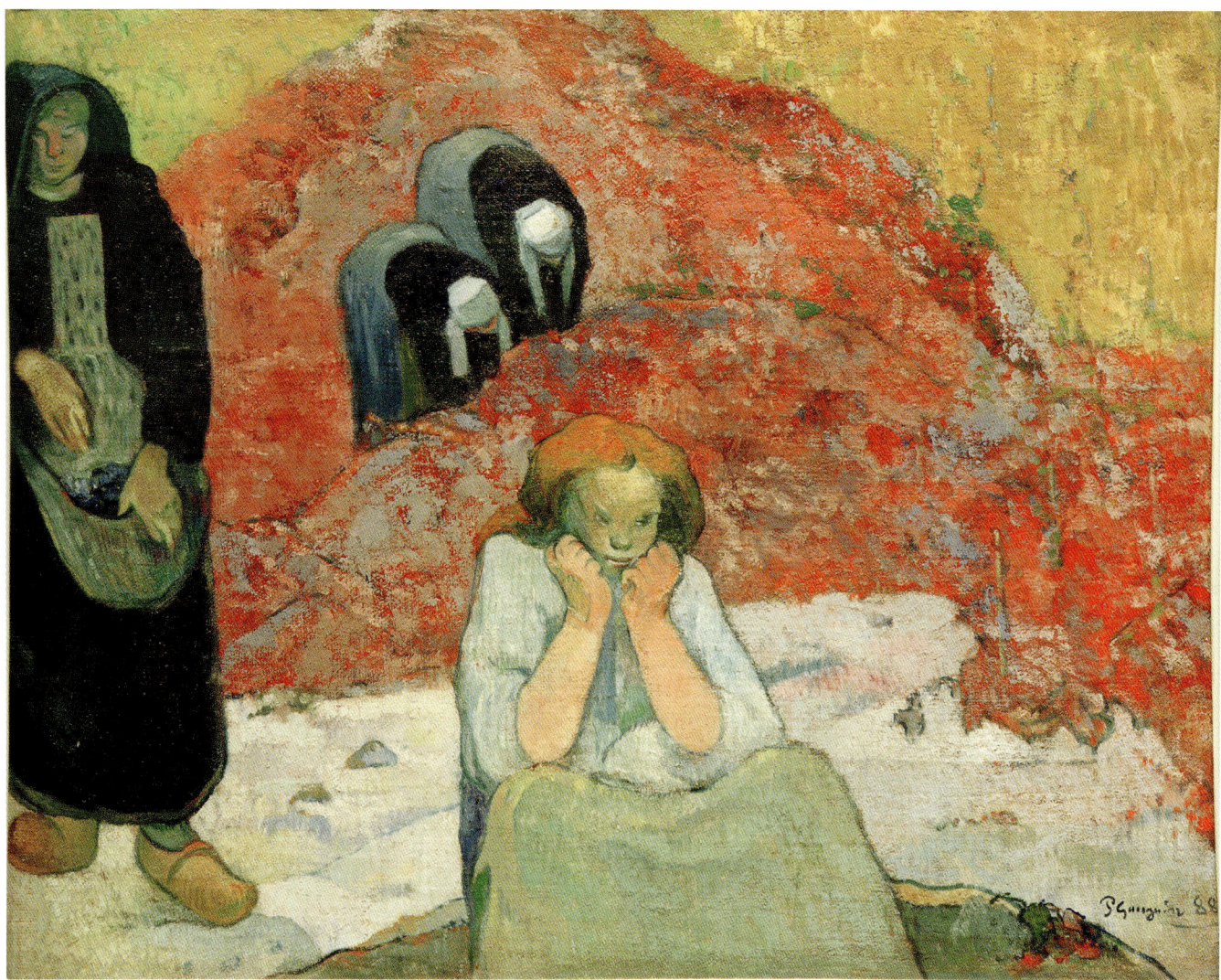

He was much happier with the strange composite picture *The Grape Harvest* or *Human Misery*. Although it was based on a scene of southern France it includes two women in Breton costume in the background, an odd foreground figure whose pose is reminiscent of a Peruvian mummy he had seen in the Ethnographic Museum in Paris (see page 63), and a Breton woman in clogs on the far left. Van Gogh described the painting as 'very fine and very strange' when he saw it in progress. Gauguin also made a portrait of Van Gogh at his easel painting sunflowers, which Van Gogh described as 'me gone mad'.

The two months Gauguin spent in Arles were productive ones for his art, but tensions soon manifested themselves and Vincent's hopes for a permanent brotherhood of artists were dashed. It was not long before the two artists were having 'electric' arguments as the differences in their personalities and opinions asserted themselves. Gauguin favoured an art based on imagination and memory, but Van Gogh's work was founded on his close observation of the real world. Although Gauguin encouraged him to experiment with working from memory, Van Gogh soon realized that it did not suit him. By mid-December Van Gogh was reporting

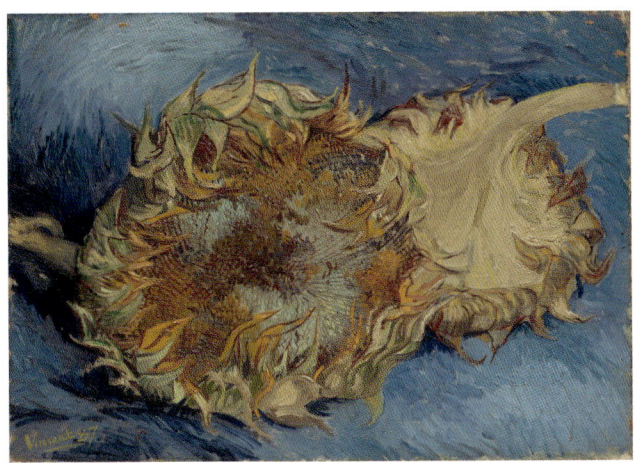

Sunflowers, Vincent Van Gogh, 1887. Even before he arrived in Arles Gauguin was familiar with Van Gogh's sunflower paintings because he had acquired two of the canvases, both showing a pair of flower heads. This is one of them. Van Gogh hung further sunflower paintings in Gauguin's bedroom to welcome him to the Yellow House.

that Gauguin had become disheartened by life in Arles, and a visit they made in December to the Musée Fabre in Montpellier seemed to confirm their divergent tastes as they were unable to agree on which artists they most admired.

Something about their relationship is expressed in a pair of canvases that Van Gogh painted of two chairs. They are symbolic portraits, one representing himself and the other Gauguin. Van Gogh's crudely made chair, seen in bright daylight, is a vision of rustic simplicity. His pipe rests on its wicker seat and there is a box of what look like onions in the background. Gauguin's, a more exotic carved armchair with two novels and a candle resting on the seat, is seen at night. Perhaps Van Gogh was saying something fundamental about Gauguin's approach to art, based on ideas and symbols, and his own work, which was closer to observable reality.

It is also notable that both chairs are empty. Van Gogh was haunted by the idea of loneliness, and dreaded the idea of Gauguin leaving. But after the notorious incident in which, according to Gauguin, Van Gogh threatened him with a razor before slicing off his own ear, Gauguin beat a hasty retreat to Paris. However, in spite of the traumatic episode, the two artists exchanged letters until Van Gogh's death two years later.

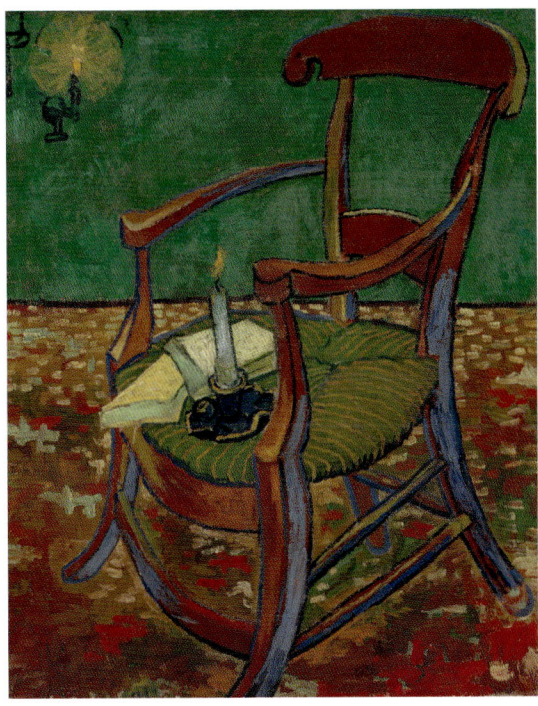

Gauguin's Chair, Vincent Van Gogh, 1888. This empty chair with a candle and two novels on its seat is Van Gogh's symbolic portrait of his friend. Years later, in Polynesia, Gauguin would paint two still lifes showing baskets of sunflowers on a chair that recall this picture and also function as a surrogate portrait of Van Gogh.

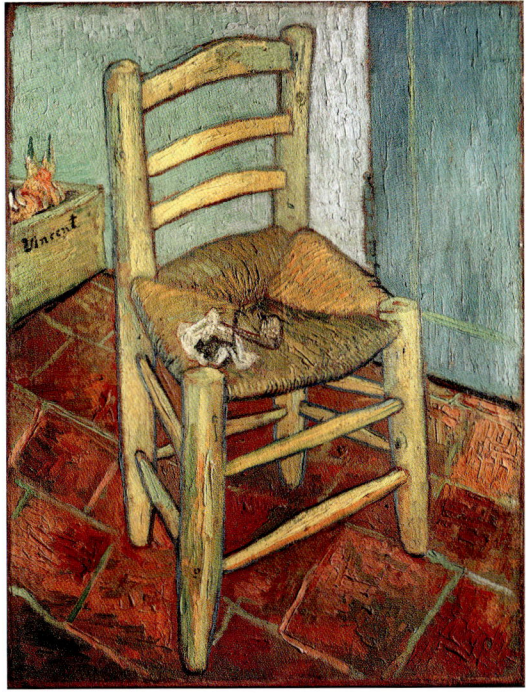

Vincent's Chair, Vincent Van Gogh, 1888. Every element in this picture conveys something of how Van Gogh saw himself, from the humble simplicity of the rush-bottomed chair to the box of bulbs that relate to his fondness for nature. The pipe may represent homely comforts, but Van Gogh was also aware that smoking had long been associated with transience in Dutch art.

THE UNIVERSAL EXHIBITION

When Gauguin returned to Paris, the Schuffenecker family provided him with board and lodging as he worked hard to re-establish himself in the art world. He was also invited to exhibit with the avant-garde group Les Vingt in Brussels. The month of May saw the opening of the Universal Exhibition in Paris, held in the Champ de Mars below the newly built Eiffel Tower. Marking the centenary of the French Revolution, it was intended to celebrate the nation's achievements in science, technology and culture. Some artists, mainly the academic painters whose work was officially sanctioned by the Salon, were invited to participate. Gauguin was not among them, but he found another way of bringing his work to public attention. He and a group of friends – Schuffenecker, Bernard and Laval included – mounted their own Impressionist and Synthetist exhibition in one of the exhibition cafés, the Café des Arts, run by M. Volpini. The reception was mixed, but it was obvious to more than one critic that Gauguin had definitively parted company from the Impressionists. His 17 paintings were admired by a younger

Schuffenecker's Studio, 1889. The artist Émile Schuffenecker was a loyal and supportive friend and Gauguin stayed in his home in 1889 when he returned from Arles. However, his portrait of the Schuffenecker family is hardly flattering, as the painter appears to cringe in the background behind his wife and daughters.

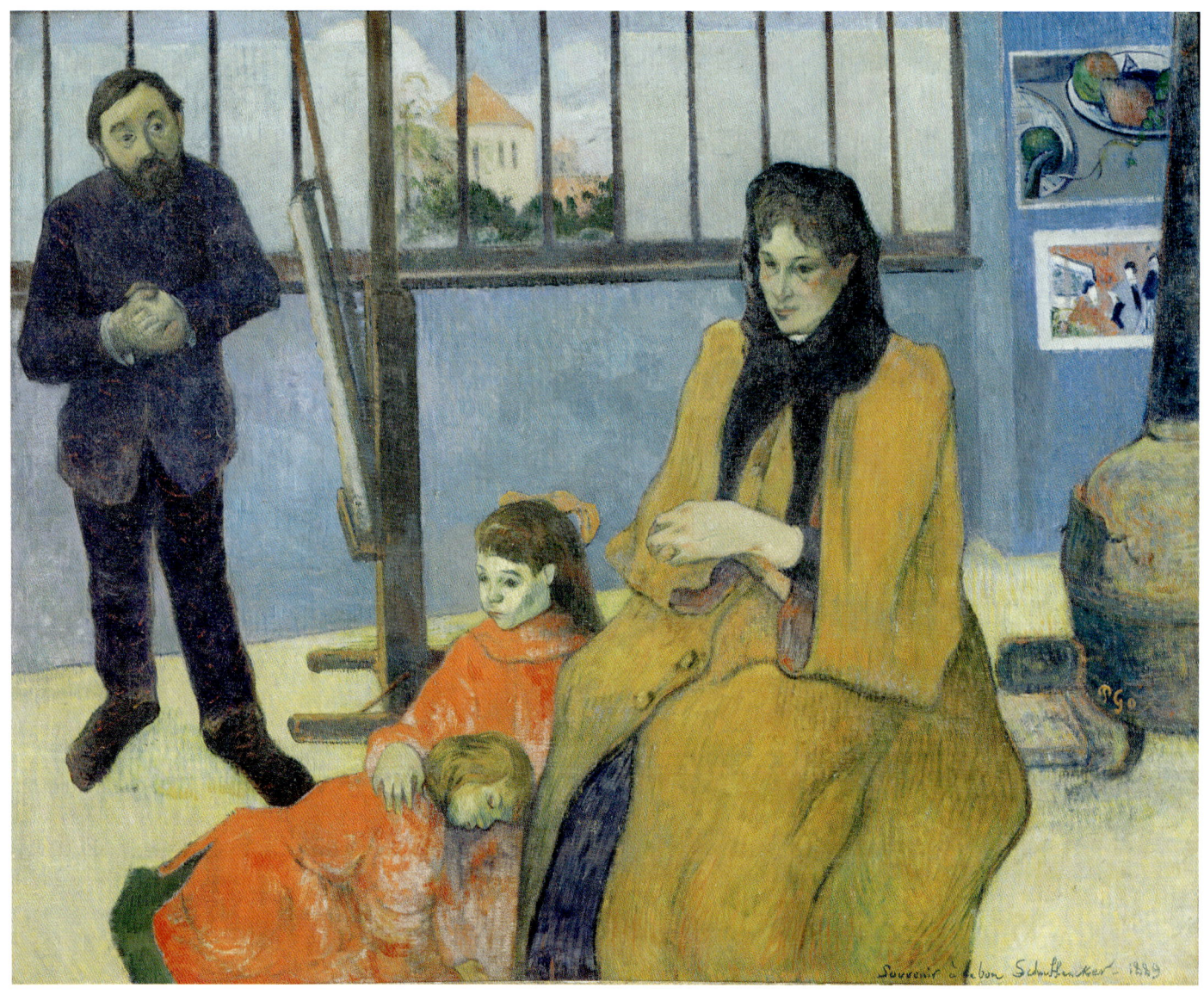

generation of artists, including Maurice Denis, Pierre Bonnard and Edouard Vuillard, who had already seen Sérusier's *The Talisman*, painted under Gauguin's tutelage. They had formed a secret society called 'Les Nabis', the Hebrew word for prophets. Motivated by a desire to revolutionize painting, they believed that art should not aim to reproduce the details of nature but prioritize an expressive use of colour and symbols.

Gauguin was also drawn to the colonial pavilions at the Universal Exhibition that were devoted to the French overseas territories of Madagascar, Martinique, Tahiti and Tonkin (northern Vietnam). He was fascinated by the displays that featured people from these countries as living exhibits, the Javanese dancers and the reproductions of carvings of temples from Angkor Wat and Borobudur. He began to dream of returning to the tropics, perhaps to Madagascar or Tonkin, to found a studio of the tropics, which he had started to think about while he was staying in Arles. His next trip, though, was a return visit to Brittany in June.

PONT-AVEN AND LE POULDU

This time Gauguin found Pont-Aven too full of tourists, so he spent some time further west, in the more remote village of Le Pouldu, where, as he wrote to Van Gogh, 'the peasants have a medieval air and do not have the sense that Paris exists or that we are in 1889'. By this stage he was carefully stage-managing his image as a 'savage', and imagining that this was how others saw him too. As he wrote to Mette: 'I live here like a peasant. They call me the Savage.' Various artists joined him there, including Sérusier and the Dutch artist Meijer de Haan, whom Gauguin described as his pupil and who gave him financial support. Marie Henry, who ran the inn at Le Pouldu, was happy to let her guests decorate the walls and doors of the dining room. Marie-Angélique Satre, the keeper of a hotel in Pont-Aven, also obliged him by posing for her portrait. In this highly unusual work the rather bovine-looking sitter is shown in Breton costume and contained in a circle in the way that popular actors were often shown in Japanese prints as well as early Christian images of saints or the

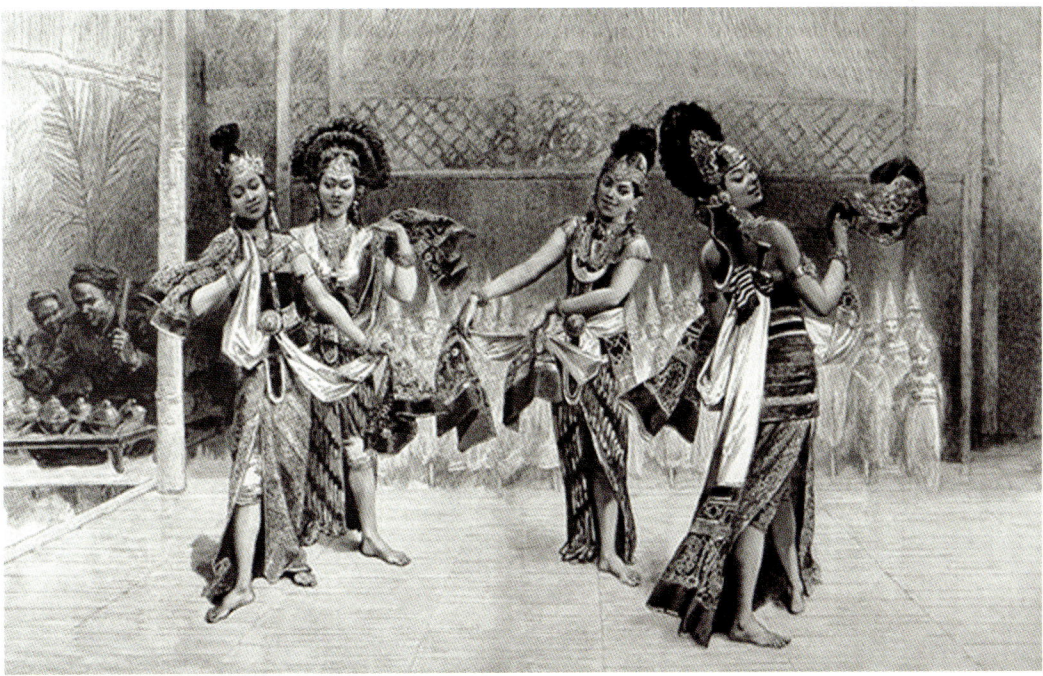

Dancers in the Javanese village at the Universal Exhibition, 1889. The Universal Exhibition in Paris featured people from around the world. Gauguin saw the Javanese dancers, the 'Negro village' and Buffalo Bill's Wild West show, as well as reproductions of impressive monuments of Southeast Asia.

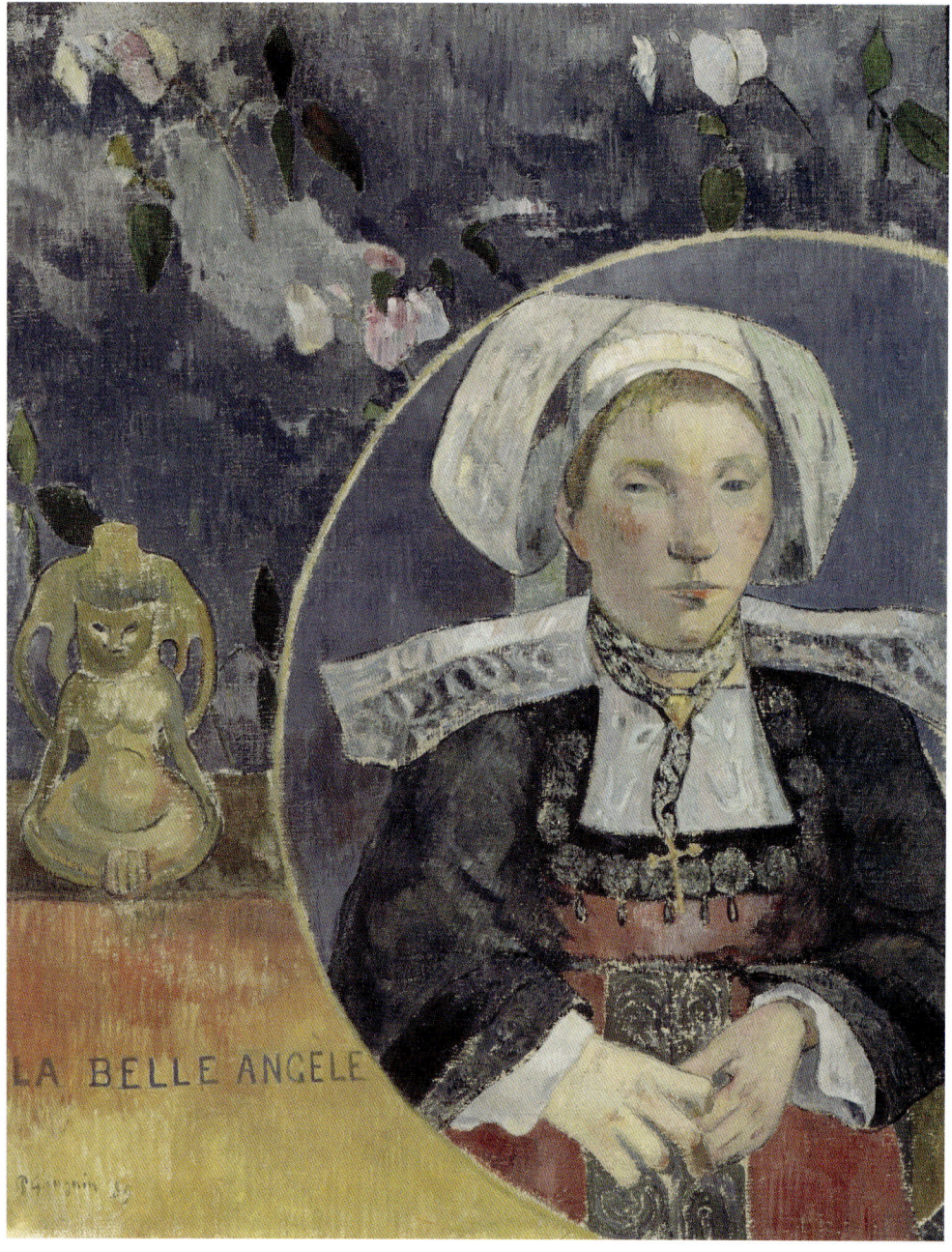

La Belle Angèle (Portrait of Mme Satre), 1889. *In Gauguin's highly unusual portrait the pious Marie-Angélique Satre is contained within a circle, isolated from the flowery wallpaper in the background and the ceramic sculpture – perhaps one of Gauguin's own or a Peruvian piece – showing what appears to be a pagan idol.*

deceased. Madame Satre refused the picture when Gauguin offered it to her as she had found out that his fellow artists had made fun of it. Two years later, Degas bought it.

Gauguin also turned his attention to the Brittany countryside and the hard lives of the peasants who lived there, tending their animals, harvesting and gathering seaweed. He produced another religious work, *The Yellow Christ*, which was based on a wooden crucifix he had sketched in the old chapel at Trémalo near Pont-Aven. Instead of showing it in its original chapel setting he placed it outside against the dunes of Le Pouldu, turning it into the kind of sculpted calvary that was a feature of the Breton countryside, exaggerating its size and adding three praying women at its base – perhaps the three Marys traditionally shown at the Crucifixion transformed into Bretons. One critic,

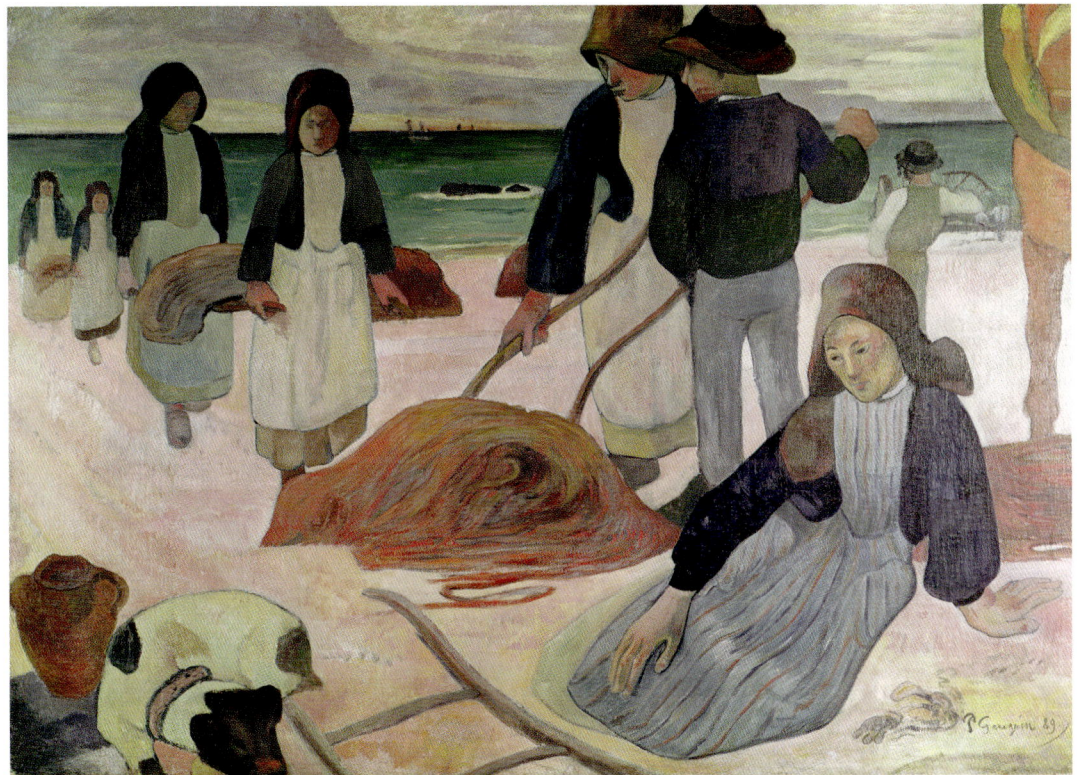

The Kelp Gatherers II, *1889.*
Seaweed was harvested in
Brittany for use as fertilizer
and as a source of iodine.
Gauguin's scene of people
gathering it on the beach
is subdued in mood and
has a simplified linear style
that reflects the influence of
folk art and children's book
illustrations.

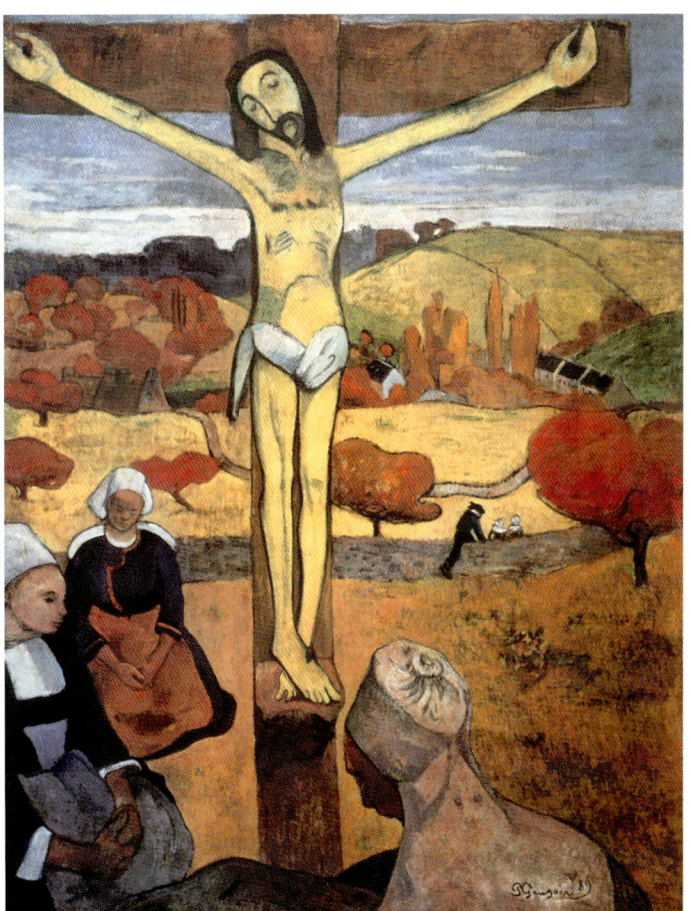

The Yellow Christ, 1889. *Gauguin was*
fascinated by what he saw as the 'primitive'
character of Breton religious observance. The
matt yellow colour of Christ, which may reflect
the discoloured wood of the crucifix on which
the image was based, stands out against the
autumnal hues of the landscape.

Octave Mirbeau, pointed out the many sources that had fed into the image when he wrote of Gauguin's 'unsettling, savoury mingling of barbaric splendour, Hindu reverie, Gothic imagery, and subtle obscure symbolism'. Gauguin followed this picture with a green version of the calvary, showing Christ being lifted down from the Cross.

Taking inspiration from Breton carved furniture, he turned his hand once again to woodcarving, making a polychrome cabinet and carving a panel entitled *Soyez amoureuses, vous serez heureuses (Be in Love and You Will Be Happy)*. Both this carving and *Loss of Virginity*, a painting of a naked young girl lying in the Breton landscape, reveal Gauguin's growing interest in Symbolism, an artistic and literary movement which favoured dreams, visions, mysticism and often obscure imagery rather than naturalism and realism. The young artists surrounding Gauguin in Brittany were closely allied to Symbolist ideas, and Gauguin was also aware that by attaching himself to the new movement he would endear himself to the Parisian avant-garde. He needed good publicity as he was thinking of selling his works to fund the tropical adventure he was planning. Having abandoned an earlier idea of going to Madagascar, which he now felt was 'too close to the civilized world', he set his sights on Tahiti in the hope that he would renew himself 'in unspoiled nature, to see nothing but savages, to live as they do'.

Gauguin auctioned 30 paintings at the Hotel Drouot, Paris's major auction house, which netted him 10,000 francs. With enough money to make his dream a reality, he organized a farewell banquet for himself at the Café Voltaire in Paris and paid what would turn out to be his final visit to his wife and children in Copenhagen. No doubt he hoped to convince them that his growing artistic reputation would help to make his trip a success and enable him to support his family on his return.

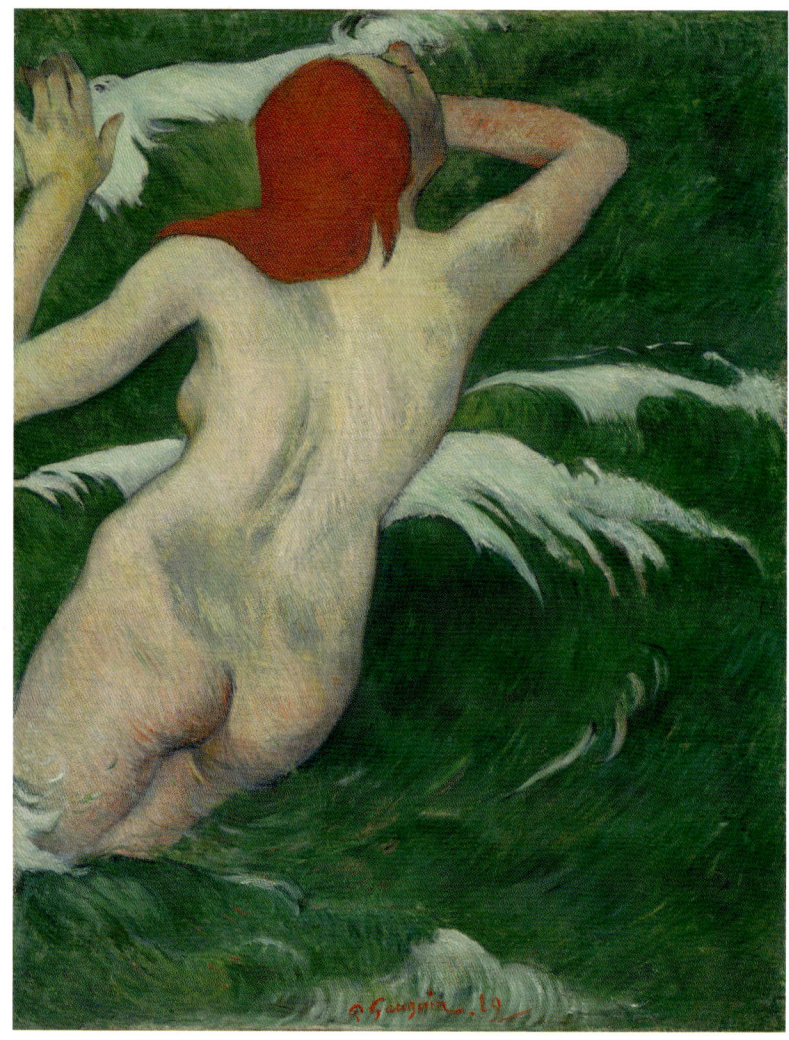

In the Waves, 1889. *The back view of a female figure leaning forward is a motif that recurs in Gauguin's art. Here the woman is throwing herself into waves that resemble those seen in the Japanese prints he so admired. He subtitled the work 'Ondine' after the Germanic fairytale of a water nymph who sacrifices her soul to marry a man, with tragic consequences.*

The Loss of Virginity, *1890–1. A pale naked girl lies on the ground, holding a plucked flower symbolizing her lost innocence, as a fox – a symbol of perversity or threat – places its paw on her heart. In the background a party of peasants, perhaps on their way to a wedding, wend their way along a path. The model was Juliette Huet, who was temporarily Gauguin's mistress in Paris and gave birth to his daughter.*

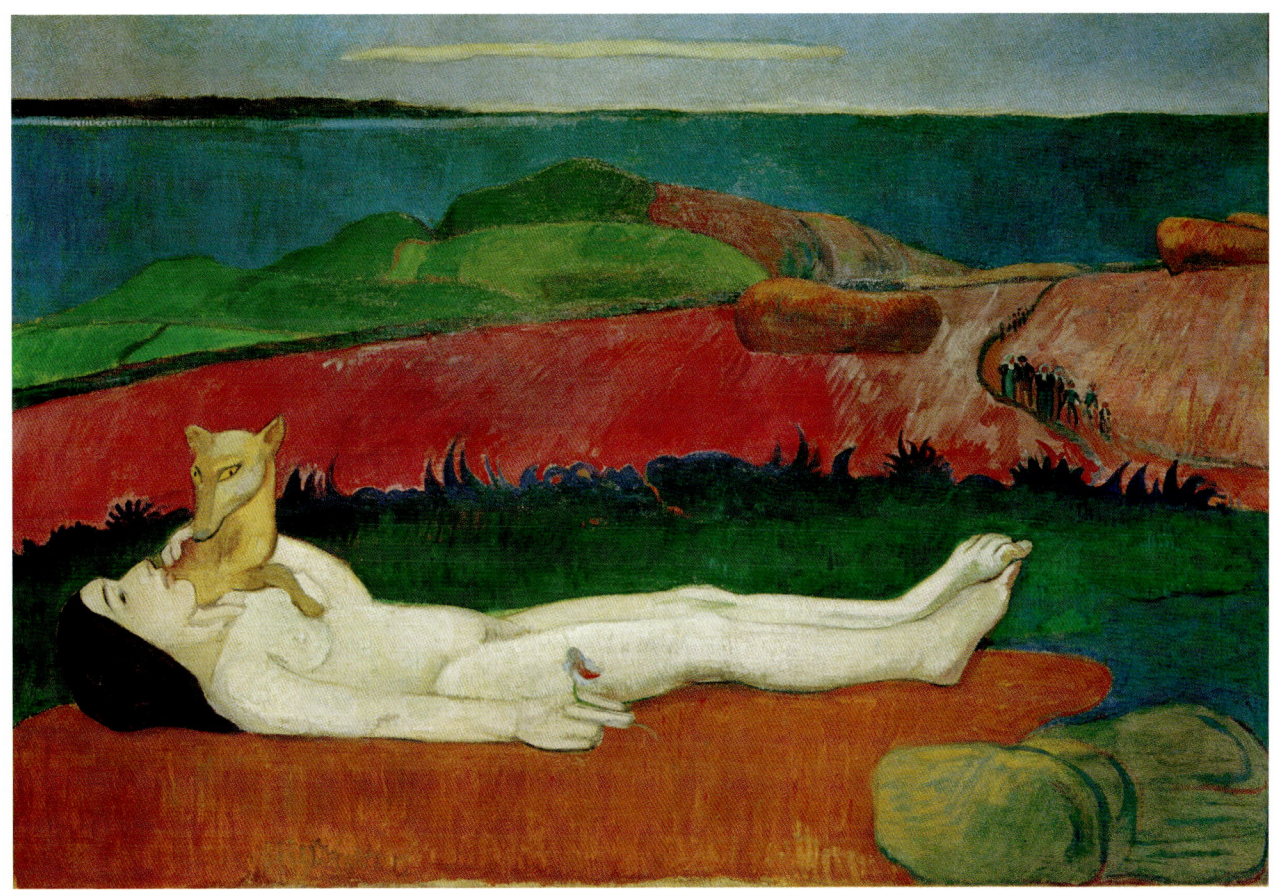

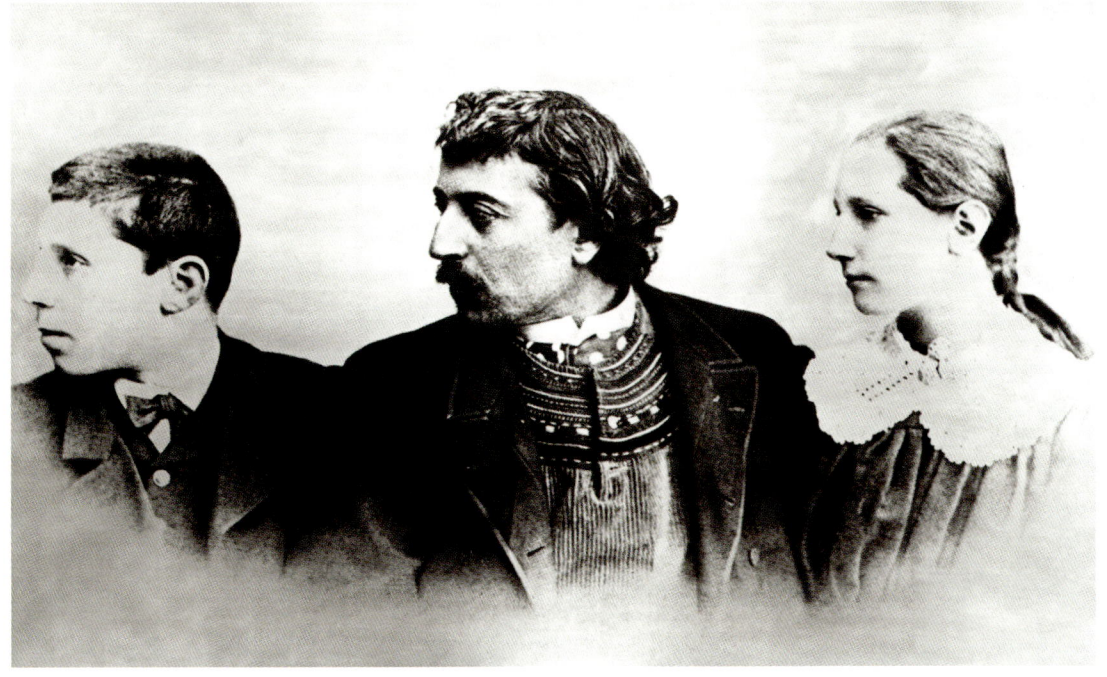

Gauguin was photographed with his two eldest children, Emil and Aline, during the week he spent with his family in Copenhagen in 1891. Their identical profile poses were no doubt intended to show their family resemblance. Gauguin is wearing his embroidered Breton shirt.

GAUGUIN'S SELF-PORTRAITS

The many self-portraits that Gauguin painted throughout his career reflect his changing self-image. He decorated the dining room of the inn at Le Pouldu with two pictures of himself, *Bonjour Monsieur Gauguin* and *Self-Portrait* (see right). The former alludes to Gustave Courbet's famous *Bonjour Monsieur Courbet*, which he had seen the previous year in the Musée Fabre at Montpellier. Courbet shows himself greeting his patron Alfred Bruyas and Bruyas' servant on a road in southern France, but whereas Courbet presents himself in arrogant mode, chin jutting out, Gauguin looks slightly lost, hunched in a greatcoat as he meets a Breton woman in a winter landscape. This is not an image of an artist who looks content with his place in the world and assured of the support of a patron, but that of an outsider who is more at ease in the company of peasants.

A more flagrant self-identification with suffering can be seen in Gauguin's *Self-Portrait*, in which his features are simplified and almost caricatural and the head disembodied. The apples, the halo and the snake entwined between the fingers must be intended to evoke the biblical Fall of Man, but the precise meaning remains opaque – perhaps intentionally so, as Gauguin enjoyed investing his works with layers of mystery.

His Jesus in *Christ in the Garden of Olives* is also a self-portrait, as the saviour who is facing his certain death has his own features, although his hair is red. The picture underlines Gauguin's own sense of martyrdom, just as he had earlier presented himself as a persecuted outsider in his self-portrait as Jean Valjean. As he wrote to Van Gogh: 'There is a road to Calvary that all we artists must tread.'

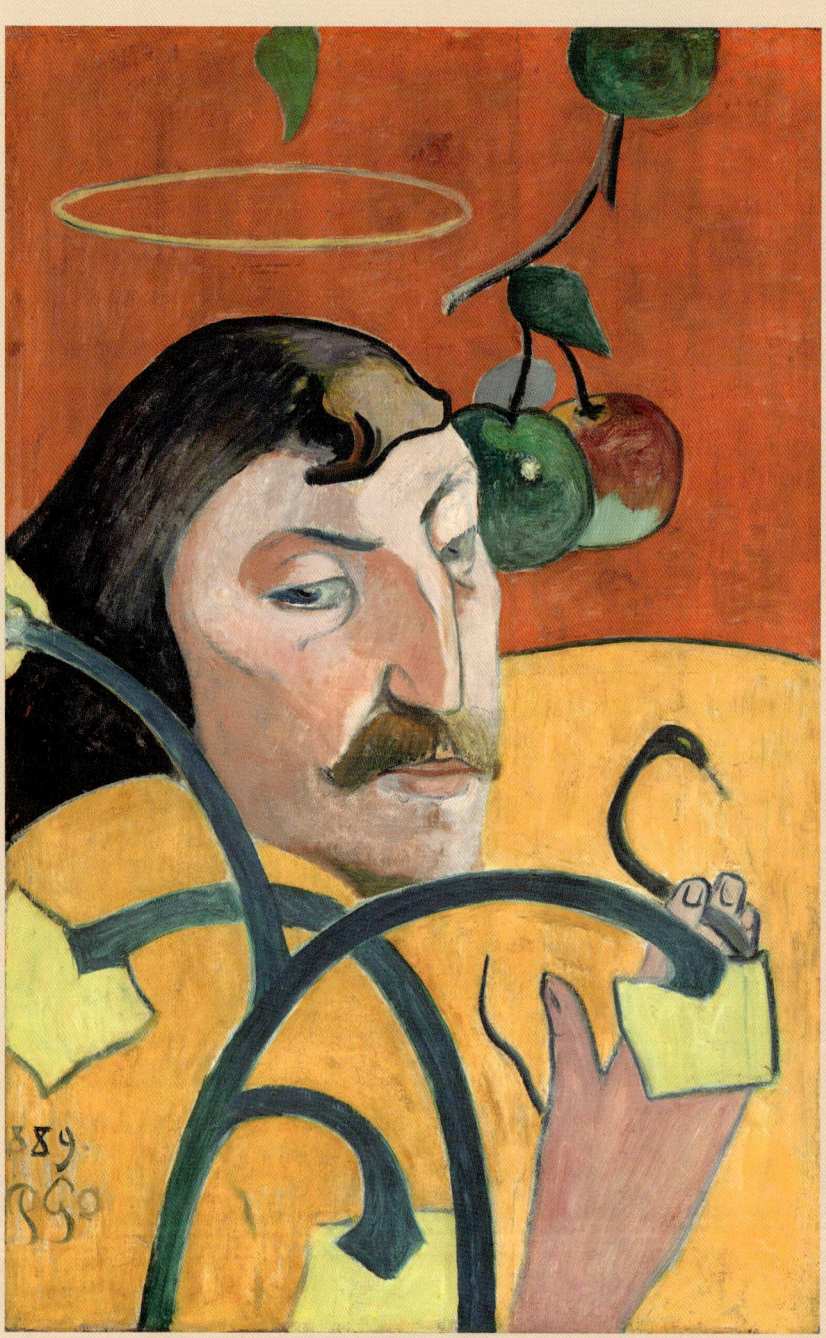

Self-Portrait, 1889. Originally painted on a cupboard door in the dining room of the inn at Le Pouldu, this portrait is astonishing for its bold modernity. Gauguin places his disembodied head and hand against two abstract areas of red and yellow. If he is an angel, as his halo indicates, he is perhaps a fallen one associated with the temptation in the Garden of Eden, as indicated by the apples and the snake.

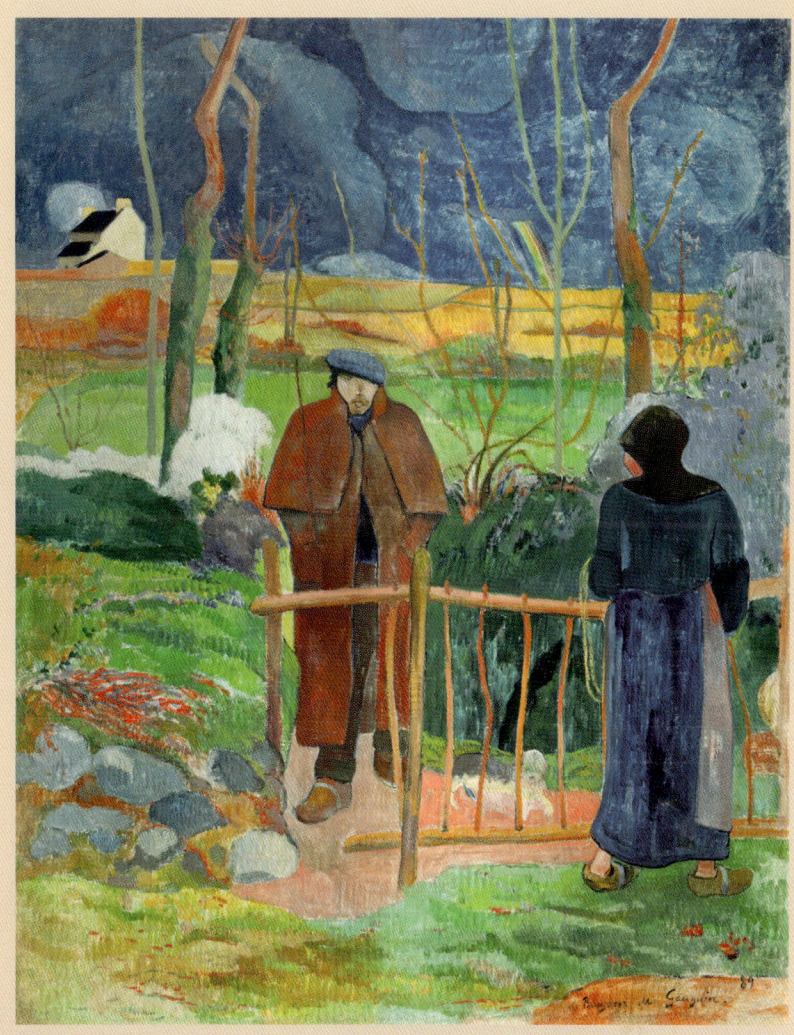

Bonjour Monsieur Gauguin, *1889.*
This portrait, which hung on one of
the dining-room doors at the inn in Le
Pouldu, shows the artist surrounded
by nature in a silent encounter with
a Breton woman. She stands on the
other side of a fence, perhaps even
turning away from him, reinforcing
the sense that he is an outsider.

Christ in the Garden of
Olives, *1889. Gauguin*
represents himself as
the despairing Christ on
the eve of his betrayal.
Shadowy figures in the dark
landscape come to lead
him away, adding a sense
of foreboding. Christ's
disciples let him down
by falling asleep instead
of keeping watch, and
Gauguin would have sensed
that his own Pont-Aven
disciples were beginning to
desert him.

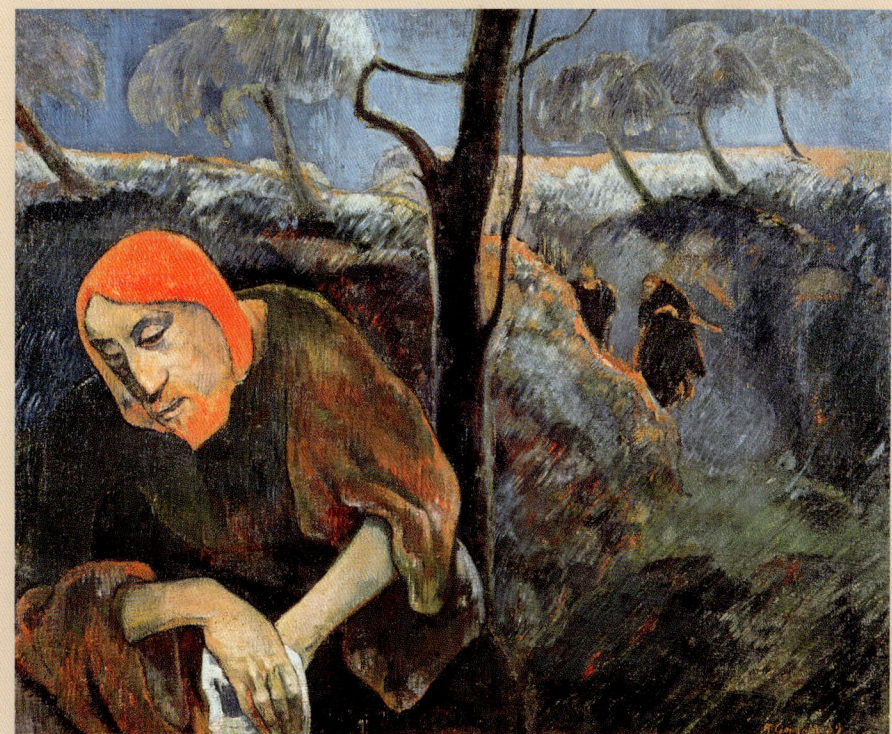

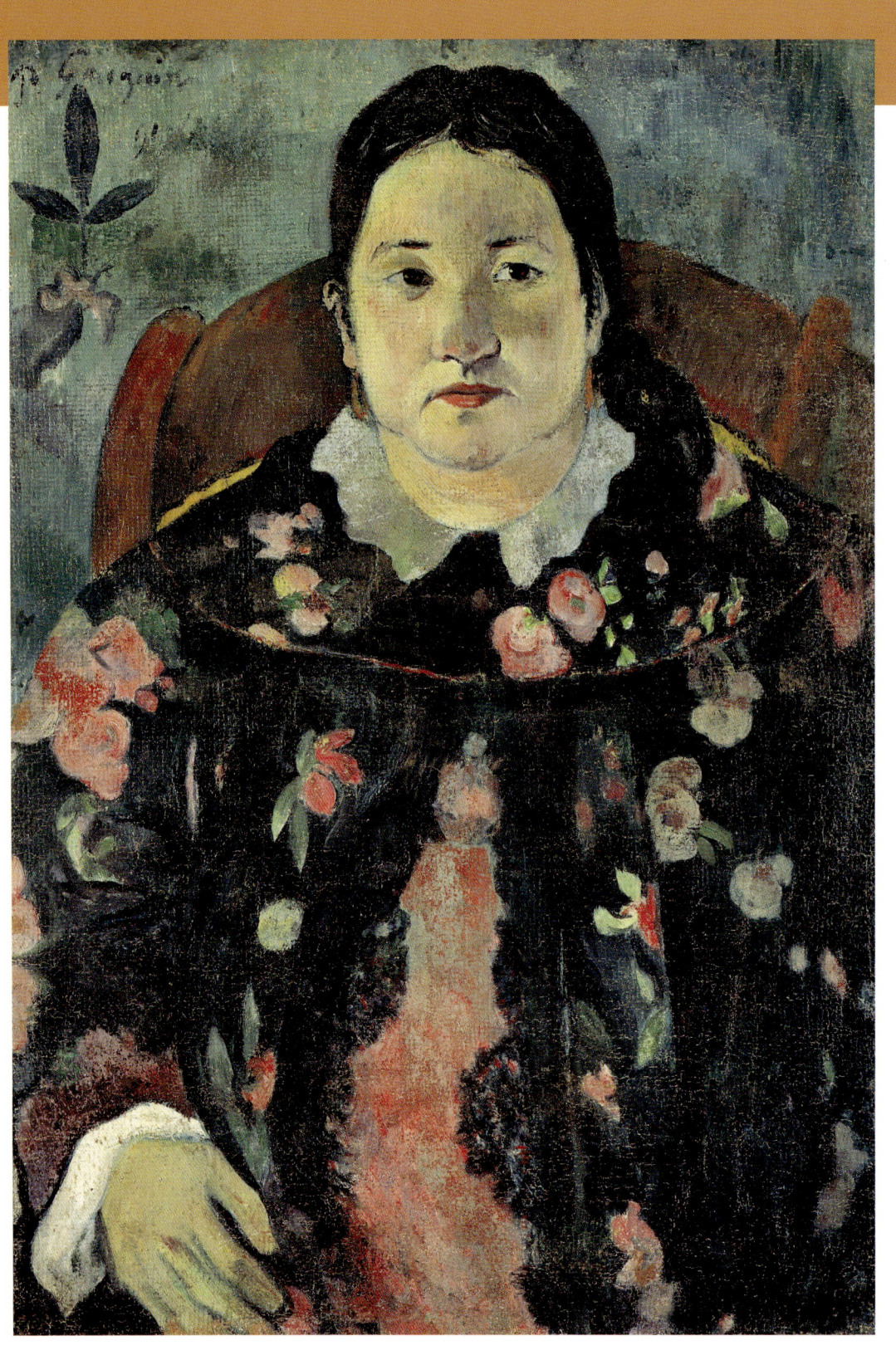

Portrait of Suzanne Bambridge, 1891. *Soon after he arrived in Papeete, Gauguin wrote to Mette: 'I think I shall soon have some well-paid commissions for portraits. I am bombarded with requests to do them.' Suzanne Bambridge was related to Tahitian royalty and would have been well placed to help Gauguin, but she so disliked her portrait that she hid it away.*

CHAPTER 3
First Stay in Tahiti

When Gauguin disembarked in the Tahitian port of Papeete on 9 June 1891 he was not stepping into unknown territory. Tahiti was a French colony, and as a French citizen he had obtained a subsidy for his passage. He also had an official mission from the French government 'to study and then paint the customs and landscapes of Tahiti' on the understanding that a painting would be bought by the Ministry of Public Instruction on his return. Furthermore, the image of the island as an exotic paradise had entered the French public imagination through a highly popular autobiographical novel, *Le Mariage de Loti (The Marriage of Loti)* published in 1880. Based on the experiences of a French naval officer, Julien Viaud (known as Pierre Loti), who had been stationed in Papeete, the narrative tells the story of a Frenchman who adopts local dress and customs and has a romantic liaison with a Tahitian girl named Rarahu.

The residents of Papeete did not know what to make of Gauguin. He was a strange figure with a disdainful air, shoulder-length hair (which earned him the nickname 'man-woman') and a cowboy hat. For his part, Gauguin was disappointed with the place, which in some respects resembled a French town and was far from the unspoilt utopia he was expecting. Tahiti may have been a tropical island, but European trade and missionaries had diluted indigenous culture and introduced Western ways of life and dress. Tahitian women had been persuaded to replace their figure-revealing garments with voluminous full-length 'Mother Hubbard' dresses. Gauguin had hoped for an encounter with innocent 'savages' but he found instead that 'it was Europe – the Europe which I had thought to shake off – and under the aggravating circumstances of colonial snobbism, and the imitation, grotesque, even to the point of absurdity, of our customs, fashions, vices, and absurdities of civilization'. Nonetheless, he hoped to turn this to his advantage by making portraits of the French governing classes, and he cut his hair and donned a linen suit in order to make himself more acceptable in polite society. He painted a few portraits, including one of an Anglo-Tahitian woman called Suzanne Bambridge, but she did not like the result and other commissions did not follow. Meanwhile, his money worries continued to fester, and he became increasingly concerned about whether or not his pictures were selling in France.

IN SEARCH OF VANISHING TRADITIONS

Soon after Gauguin's arrival, Pomare V, the last Tahitian king, died. Gauguin witnessed the events that attended his funeral, following the cortege to the royal mausoleum. The draped coffin was decorated with flowers and topped with the crown of the monarch, which seemed more European than Tahitian. The sight inspired the idea of his *Arii matamoe (The Royal End)*, which shows the decapitated head of a dead Tahitian chief resting on a pillow on the chief's seat. This was not part of the ceremony that he saw, but an entirely invented scene that also reflects the fact that a few months earlier Gauguin had attended a public execution by guillotine in Paris. He had also seen a wood carving of a head that he said supplied the idea. This conflation of myth and observed reality would come to characterize his work in Tahiti.

For Gauguin, the death of Pomare represented the passing of the last traditions. 'Shall I manage to recover any trace of that past, so remote and mysterious?' he wrote. 'To get back to the ancient hearth, revive the fire in the midst of all these ashes?' A local chief whom he met in Papeete suggested that he might find a more authentic way of life in Mataiea, some 45 km (28 miles) outside the capital. Life was less expensive there, which was an added attraction. In September Gauguin made the five-hour journey to the new area accompanied by a young woman of mixed heritage called Titi, who had previously been the companion of officials in Papeete. The landscape of Mataiea was beautiful, and Gauguin rented a bamboo hut in the compound of

Arii matamoe (The Royal End), 1892. Gauguin's picture combines many different elements. The palace and the mourning women are entirely fictional; the carpet is Persian; the carving Polynesian; and the crouching figure based on a Peruvian mummy he had seen in Paris. Tahitians did not routinely display trophy heads, but Gauguin might have got the idea from photographs of a New Zealand Maori practice.

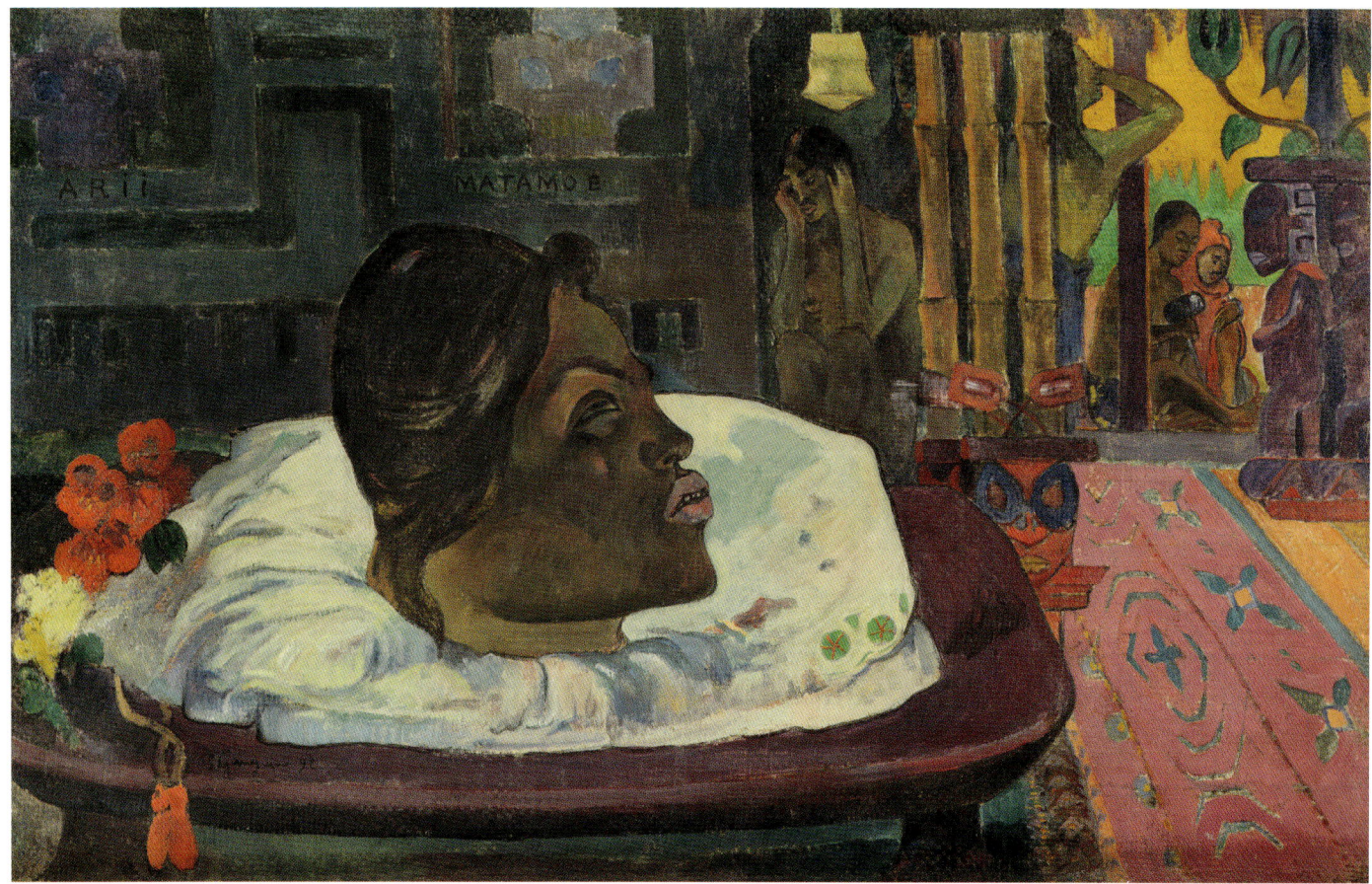

the local ruling family. He began work, starting cautiously with sketches of figures and the countryside in pencil, ink, watercolour and gouache before he attempted full-size paintings. His neighbours were friendly and hospitable, and he began to adopt their dress. Observing them as they went about their daily lives, he admired their gracefulness, their slightly androgynous appearance and their uninhibited sexuality. He noticed a man wielding an axe; a woman stowing nets on a pirogue; trees laden with fruit; people swimming in the sea and singing. He saw women carrying fruit under pandanus trees, playing a Polynesian instrument like a flute and dancing at night. While he hoped to immerse himself in the culture, he acknowledged in a moment of insight that, 'As each one was a savage to me, so was I a savage to each one of them.'

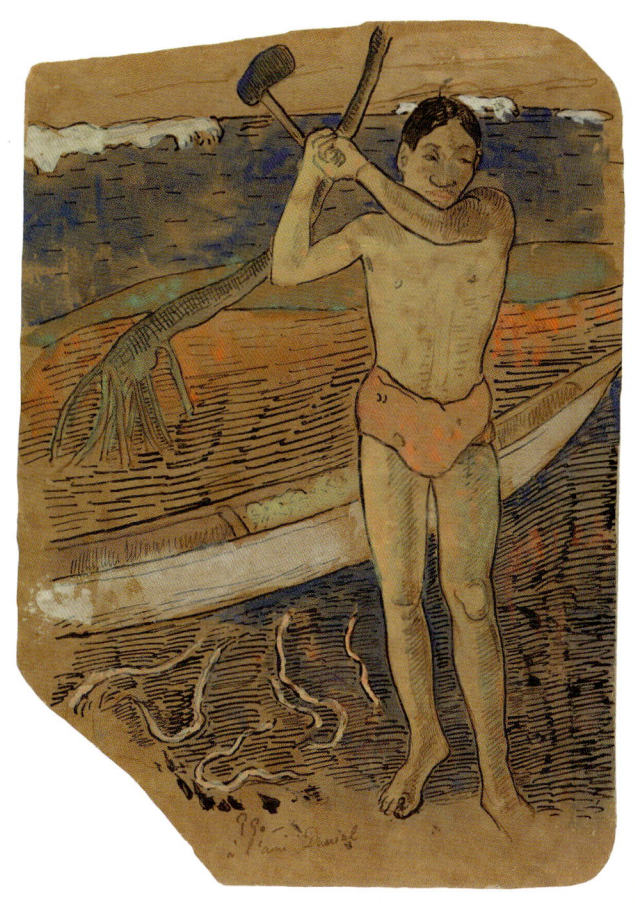

Man with an Axe, *1891–3. In* Noa Noa *Gauguin describes meeting a handsome Tahitian: 'The nearly naked man was wielding with both hands a heavy axe that left, at the top of the stroke, its blue imprint on the silvery sky.' When he noticed Gauguin, the man saw that he was hungry and arranged for a child to bring him food.*

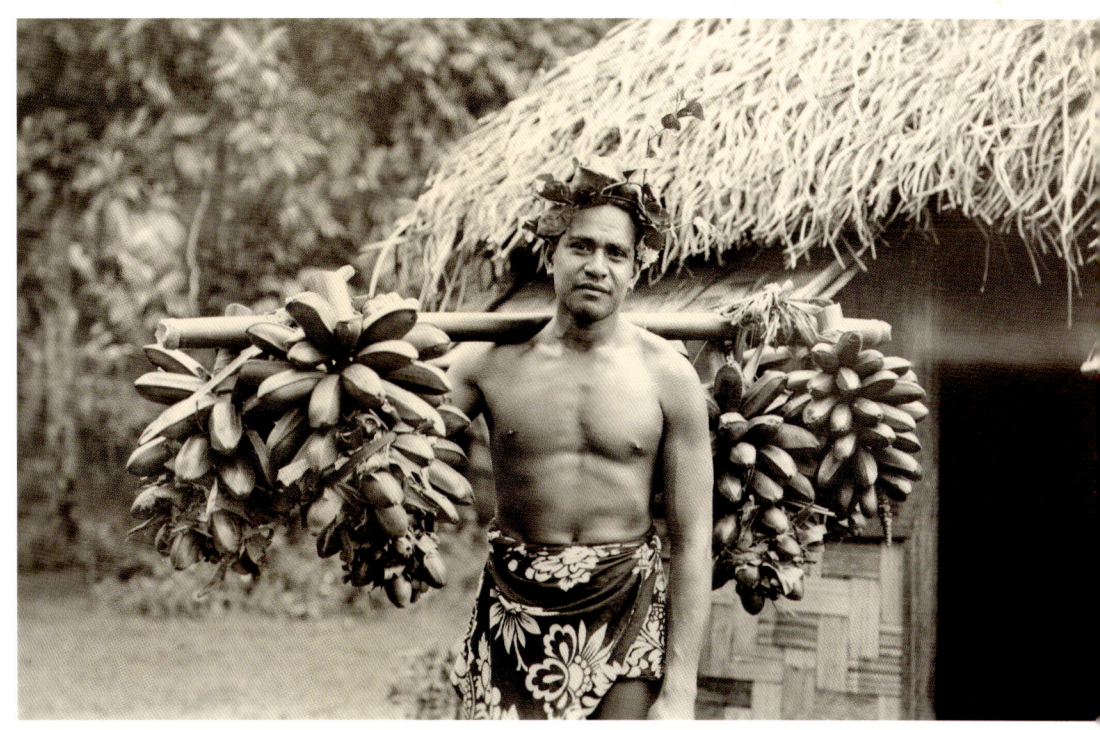

A Tahitian man carrying bananas, photographed c. 1920. *Photographers as well as artists recorded Tahitian customs and daily life, deliberately arranging their subjects in poses with appropriate props to cater for the public appetite for ethnographic information.*

Gauguin's palette increasingly reflected the brilliant tropical colours he saw around him, which he often juxtaposed in surprising combinations, but his paintings contain visual ideas he had first explored in Europe. *The Meal*, painted during his first few months on the island, is an entirely invented scene, a strange combination of still life and figures showing three children ranged behind a dining table covered with a white tablecloth staring at a giant bowl of coconut milk, oversize bananas, guavas, a calabash, oranges and a European blue faience bowl. Tahitians did not normally eat at table, and the scene is more than slightly reminiscent of the still lifes by Cézanne that Gauguin so admired. *Fatata te miti (By the Sea)* also reused one of his favourite motifs of a woman bather seen from behind, first seen in his Brittany works.

The most complex composition Gauguin made during his first year in Tahiti was *Ia orana Maria (Hail Mary)*. This was entirely based on his imagination, and had strongly Symbolist overtones, harking back to the religious subjects he had painted in Brittany. Christ sits on his mother's shoulder and both have halos. In his later Tahitian works he would engage

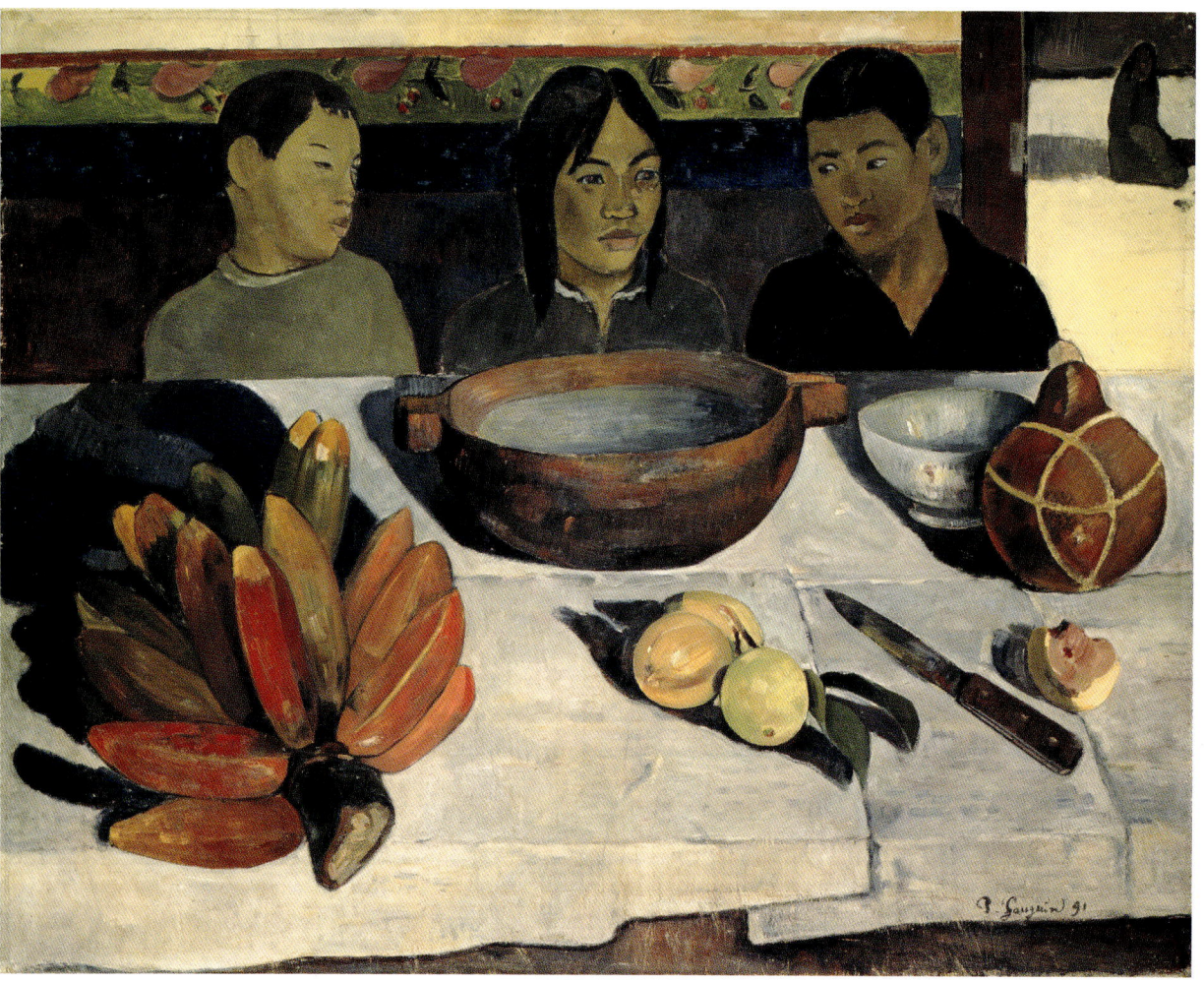

The Meal, 1891. *The outsize still life on the table includes a type of bowl generally used for serving rice or mashed taro root. Gauguin owned a similar bowl, which he decorated with his own carvings. The children seem oddly disengaged with the food in front of them and the figure glimpsed in the background adds a sense of mystery.*

Fatata te M

with Maori beliefs, but this picture is firmly rooted in the European Christian tradition, albeit transposed into a Tahitian setting. The fruit laid out in front of Mary is arranged on the type of platform that Tahitians used to make offerings to their gods. The longer Gauguin stayed in Tahiti, the more critical he became of the missionaries who were converting the population to Christianity. He started to make conscious efforts to document Polynesian mythology, which was fast disappearing, in his work.

Fatata te miti (By the Sea), 1892. The theme of the bathing woman seen from behind was a constant in Gauguin's art. Here he captures the sheer delight of two Tahitians as they plunge into the waves, the sea and sand suggested by broad sweeps of decorative colour.

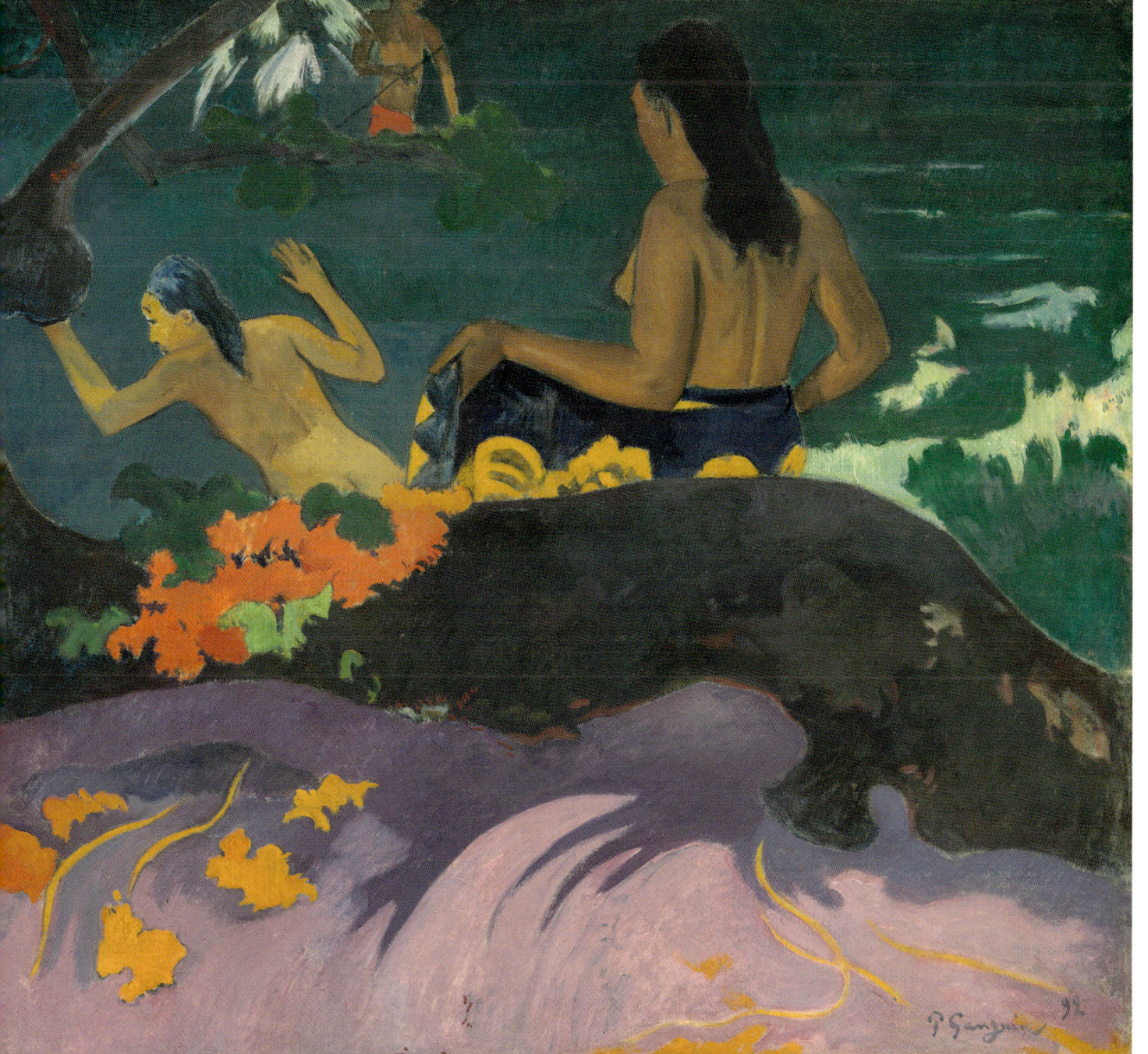

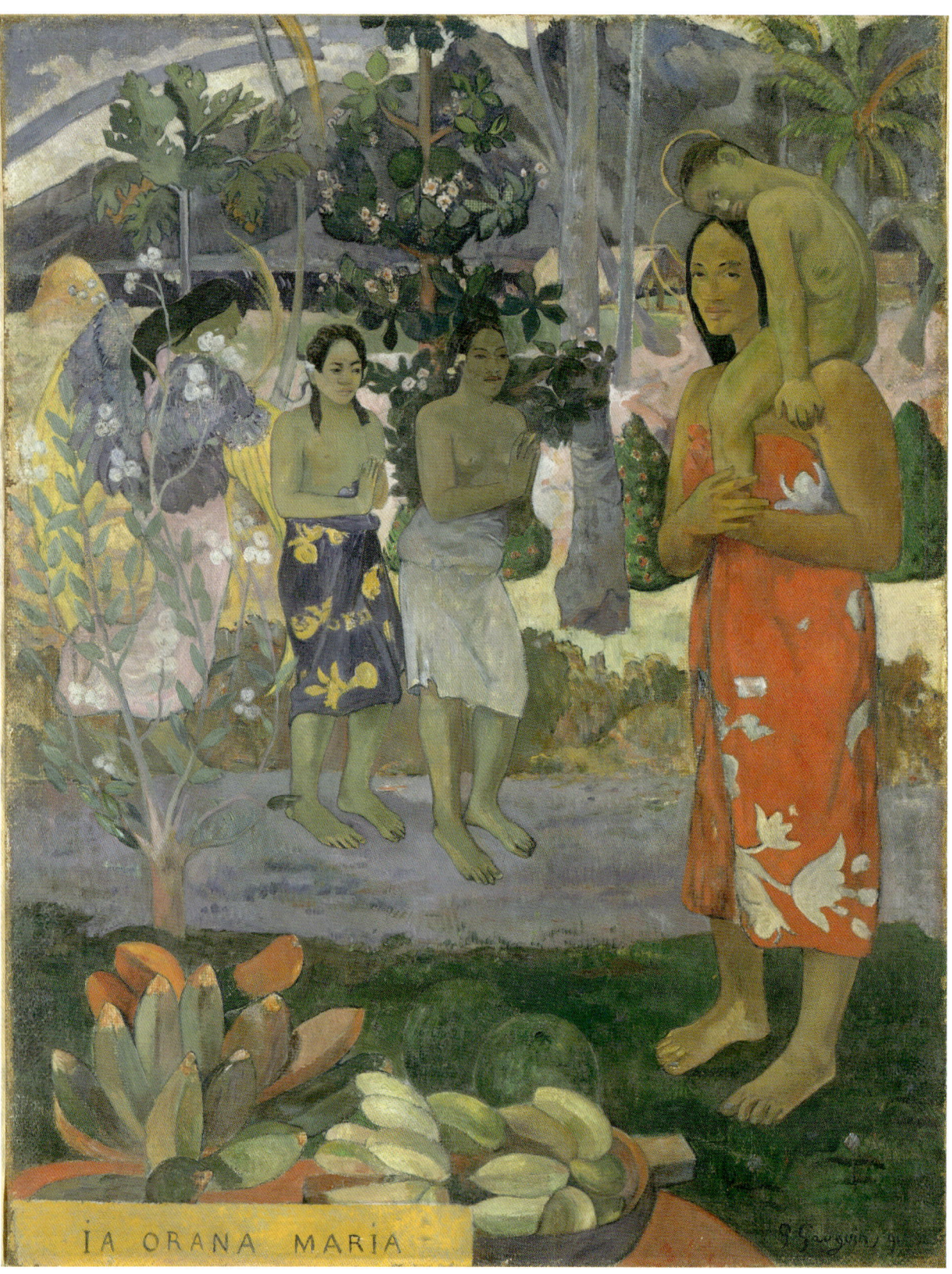

Ia orana Maria (Hail Mary), 1891. *Gauguin decided on a Christian theme for this, his first major Tahitian picture. An angel with yellow wings reveals a Tahitian Mary and Jesus to two Tahitian women dressed in* pareus, *their poses based on a photograph he owned of figures in a carving from Borobudur.*

TAHITIAN WOMEN

Gauguin pondered the new type of beauty he found among the Tahitians, commenting that his neighbour, who appears in *Vahine no te tiare (Woman with a Flower)* was not pretty by European standards but beautiful, her face having 'the melancholy of bitterness mingled with pleasure'. He said that he portrayed the woman as he saw her, while attempting to interpret 'what lay within', yet the Tahitian inscription above her head, which translates as 'woman with a flower', does not name her. The sitter seems to represent an ethnographic 'type' just as much as a specific person. This was the first painting Gauguin sent back to the French capital and he hoped that it would be appreciated for its novelty value. However, he was not the first European to record the appearance of Polynesian women. The French photographer Charles Georges Spitz, who was working in Tahiti at the same time, was also photographing Tahitian women in their best dresses with flowers in their hair, and Gauguin was familiar with his work.

Titi had soon returned to Papeete, but it was not long before Gauguin acquired another companion, Teha'mana, whose name he simplified to Tehura in his writings. Gauguin later gave an account of their meeting in *Noa Noa*, his semi-fictional account of his first stay in Tahiti. He reports that he set off on a voyage around the island, where he came to the district of Fa'aone on the remote eastern coast and was invited to eat with the people who lived there. When he admitted that he was looking for a wife, the woman of the house went and fetched her daughter, whom Gauguin says was 13 years old – significantly, the age of sexual consent in France at the time. He reports that Teha'mana came to live with him as his *vahine*, or wife, and describes a short period

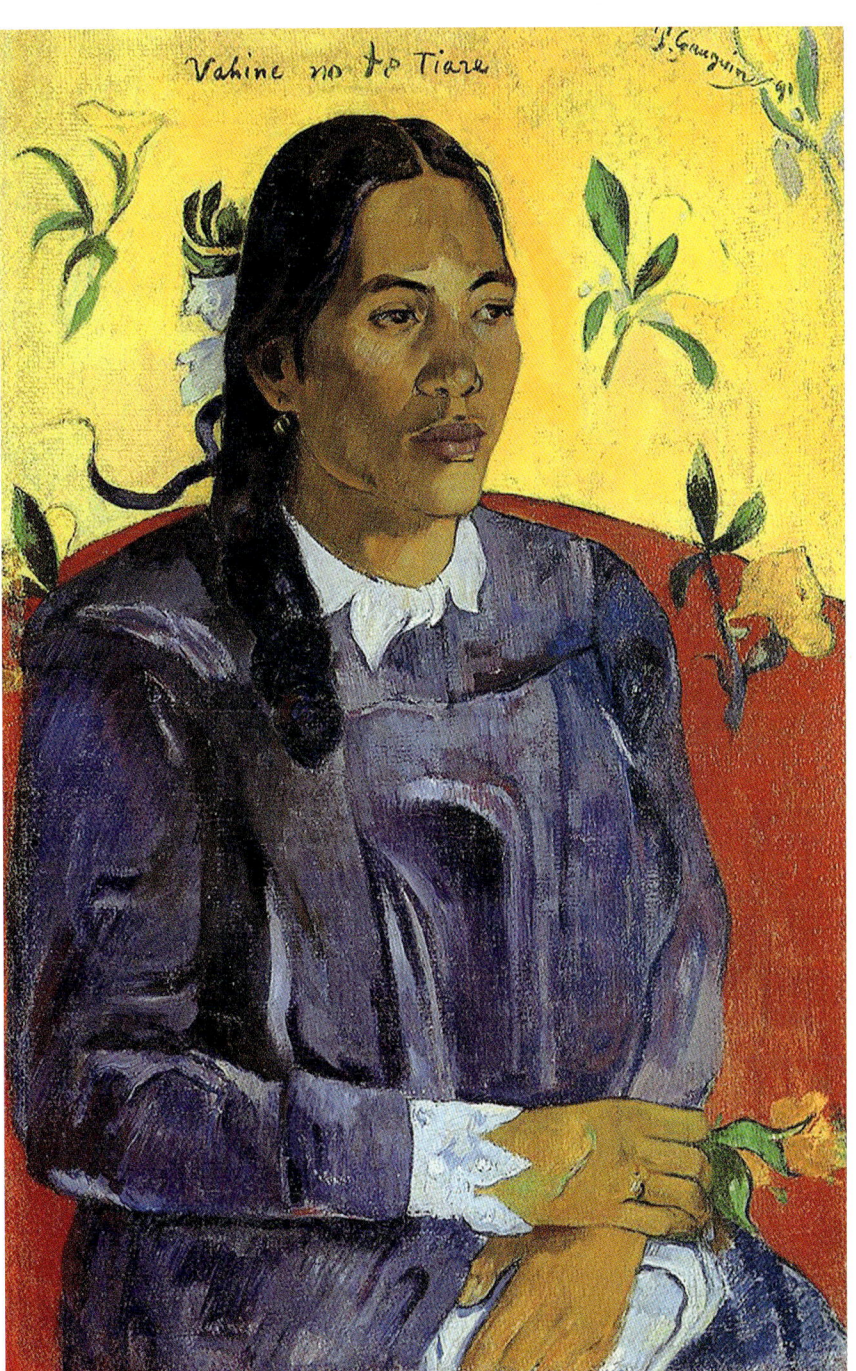

Vahine no te tiare (Woman with a Flower), *1891. This is Gauguin's first portrait of a Tahitian woman. The sitter had insisted on wearing her lace-trimmed smock dress rather than the traditional Tahitian* pareu, *and the blue of her outfit is offset by the brilliant yellow and green of the background, the scattered blossoms echoing the flower in her hair and the one she holds.*

when the two seemed to be studying each other and the domestic idyll that followed: 'A life filled to the full with happiness began. Happiness and work rose up together with the sun … The gold of Tehura's face flooded the interior of our hut and the landscape round about with joy and light.' It seemed that Gauguin had found what he came for: 'Tahitian paradise, *navé navé fénua*, – land of delights.'

At this point, Gauguin was still corresponding with Mette, occasionally expressing the hope that they might be reconciled one day. A letter that he sent her told a rather different story of his domestic arrangements: 'I live more or less alone. That's to say for a model a young girl (vahine – woman) aged 14 – weight about 150[lb] – who is very good at making a fire, doing the washing and smoking cigarettes. (It's pointless asking any more of a Tahitian woman.) She doesn't speak a word of French, and sometimes I chat in Maori, a language I am beginning to speak not too badly.'

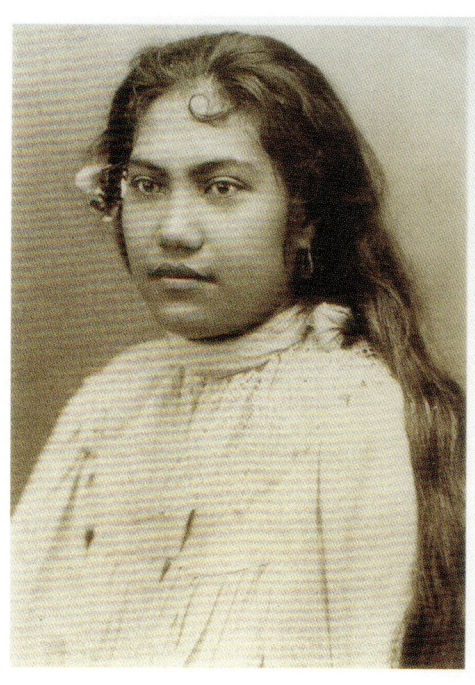

Portrait of a Tahitian Woman, *Charles Spitz, 1888. Charles Spitz's Tahitian subject has a voluminous dress and an impassive expression that resembles Gauguin's* Woman with a Flower. Spitz's *photographs of Tahitian women were created to satisfy European curiosity about Polynesia, and Gauguin was evidently familiar with his work.*

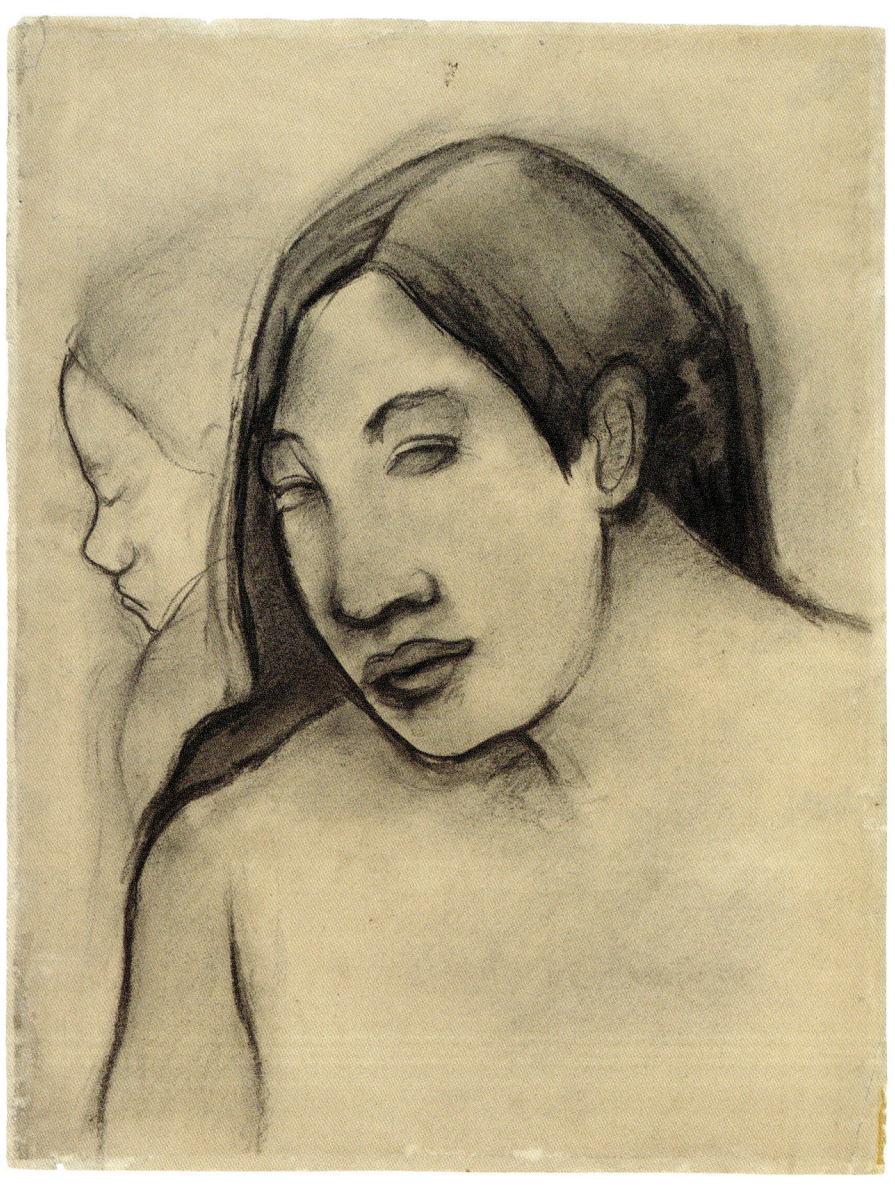

Heads of Tahitian women, frontal and profile views, c. 1891–3. *Gauguin produced several charcoal and black chalk close-up drawings of Tahitians in an attempt to understand their character, studying his subjects from the front and from the side a little like an anthropologist. He regarded such drawings as necessary research in preparation for his paintings.*

FACT OR FICTION?

There is no way of knowing how accurate Gauguin was when he wrote about his relations with women. It should be borne in mind that in *Noa Noa* he was writing for a Western, largely male readership that might have found the exotic sexual encounters titillating. He also co-wrote the text with Charles Morice, a Symbolist poet who may well have embellished it. Indeed, some scholars have even wondered whether Teha'mana was purely a product of Gauguin's fantasy based on his encounters with a number of Tahitian women; a woman of that name even appears in Pierre Loti's novel. However, there is enough evidence to indicate that Teha'mana did exist and that she lived with Gauguin for a while. A letter that Gauguin wrote in 1893 even states that he is about to become a father again, although there is no record of the child. However, since children were commonly adopted in Tahiti it is possible that he or she was raised under another name.

Gauguin's treatment of women in Tahiti has frequently been criticized by commentators, but in part it reflected the colonial behaviour of his time. Since the eighteenth century it had been common practice for Tahitian elders to offer young girls to visiting Western men on the understanding that they would be supported by them. Although Gauguin regarded himself as impoverished, his race and links with France gave him a powerful and prestigious position in Polynesian society that would have made him very attractive even though he was in his forties. Attitudes to sex were more liberal in Tahiti than Europe, and it was not unusual for young women to live with different partners before they married. What Teha'mana probably did not know was that Gauguin was already married, which would have made their liaison unacceptable in her culture. Gauguin described her as 'docile and loving' but we have no record of how she perceived their liaison.

What is also hard to determine is the extent to which she modelled for Gauguin. There is not one photograph that can definitely be said to show her,

and there is only one picture in which Gauguin explicitly mentions her by name: *Merahi metua no Tehamana (Teha'mana Has Many Parents)*. However, it is hard to tell the age of the girl in the picture, who looks older than 13 or 14, and this adds to the uncertainty of her identity. In *Noa Noa* Gauguin says that another of his paintings, *Manao tupapau (The Spirit of the Dead Watching)*, was based on an episode in his daily life with Teha'mana. He recounts how, having returned from a visit to Papeete in the early hours of

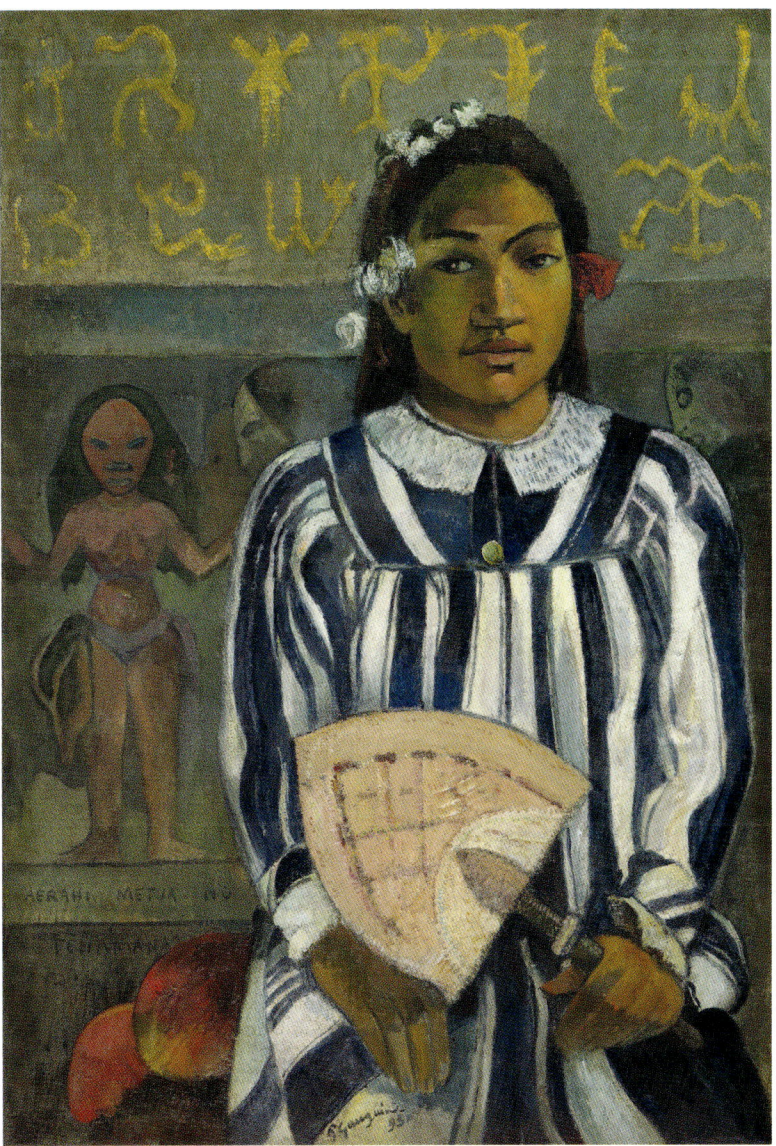

Merahi metua no Tehamana (Teha'mana Has Many Parents), 1893. *The sitter, who may possibly be Gauguin's young companion, is shown in her European-inspired Mother Hubbard dress against a background that features an array of different visual references, from an ancestral goddess to her right to inscriptions from Rapa Nui (Easter Island) and spirits known as* tupapau *behind her.*

the morning, he returned to find the hut in darkness as the lamp had gone out. He lit a match and then he saw his mistress lying immobile and naked on the bed, her eyes filled with fear since she was frightened both of him as he entered the room and of the invisible spirits (*tupapau*) that came out at night. 'Never had I seen her so beautiful, so tremulously beautiful.' Whether or not this is literally true, the painting is an astonishing work that marries both the European artistic tradition of the reclining nude – on the wall of his hut Gauguin had a print of Manet's famous *Olympia*, a portrait of a nude prostitute on a bed – and Tahitian mythology, which was beginning to become familiar to him.

Manao tupapau (Spirit of the Dead Watching), 1892. *Gauguin represents the* tupapau, *or spirit of a dead person, as a hooded black figure seated against a carved post that looks like a ceremonial pillar. On the bed is a flowery* pareu *that the young woman would have worn. As he had done in* The Vision of the Sermon, *Gauguin represents both the human subject and what they are imagining in the same picture.*

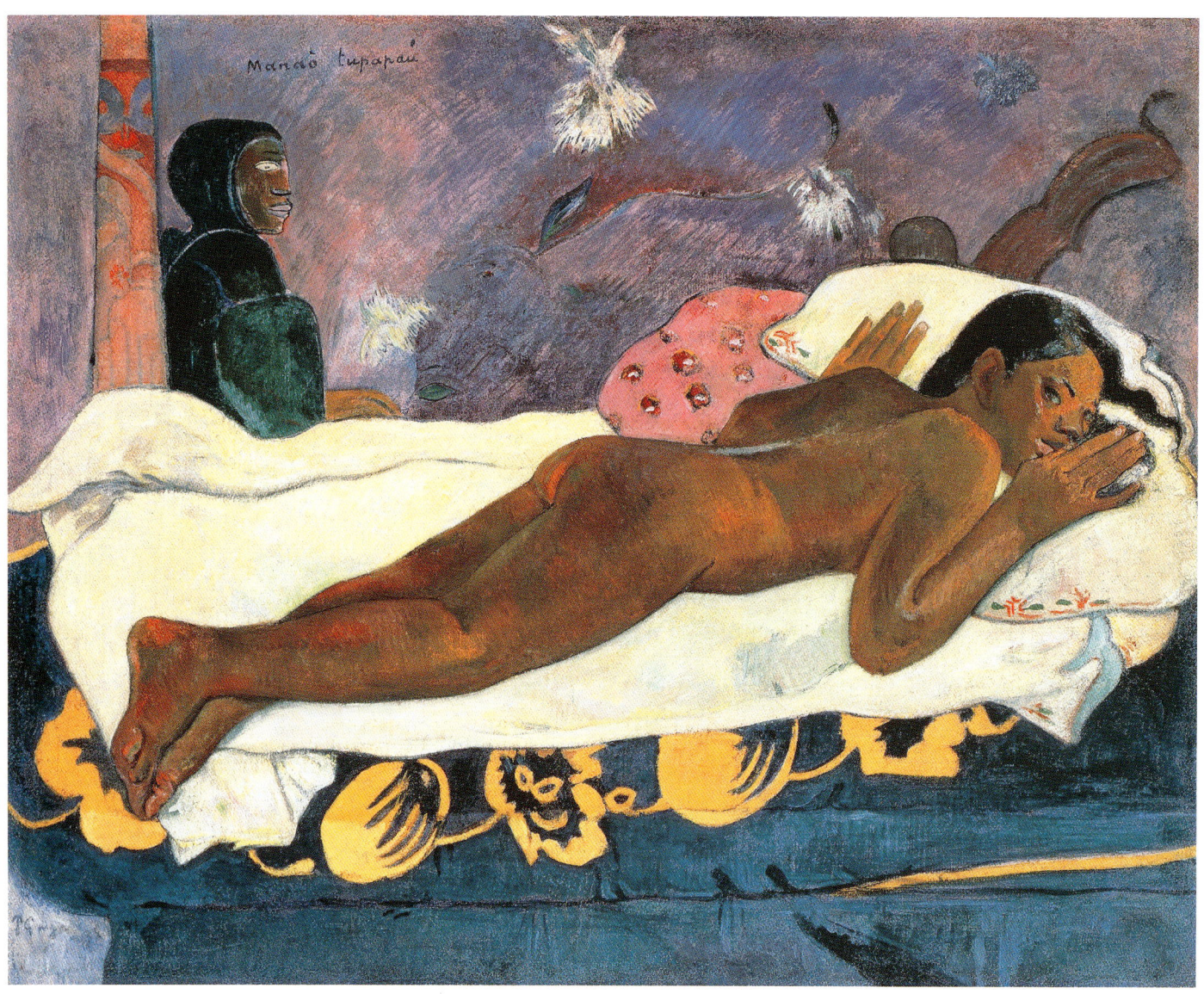

MAORI MYTHS

Gauguin liked to give the impression that he learned about Tahitian beliefs from Teha'mana. He claimed that she 'knows by heart, and that is no small task, the names of all the gods of the Maori Olympus. She knows their history, she teaches me how they have created the world, how they rule it.' But his grasp of her language was shaky at best, and much of what he knew about Oceanic myth was actually taken from a European book that he had been lent by a French colonial resident in Papeete, the two-volume *Voyages aux îles du Grand Océan* by the Belgian author J.-A. Moerenhout. He studied it closely and copied chunks of the text into his own manuscript *Ancien culte mahorie*, where the words are interspersed with watercolour sketches. Gauguin hoped that his interpretation of Maori mythology would intrigue the Parisian public, but Camille Pissarro took a more jaundiced view when he heard about it, writing to his son Lucien: 'He is always poaching on someone's ground; now he is pillaging the savages in Oceania.'

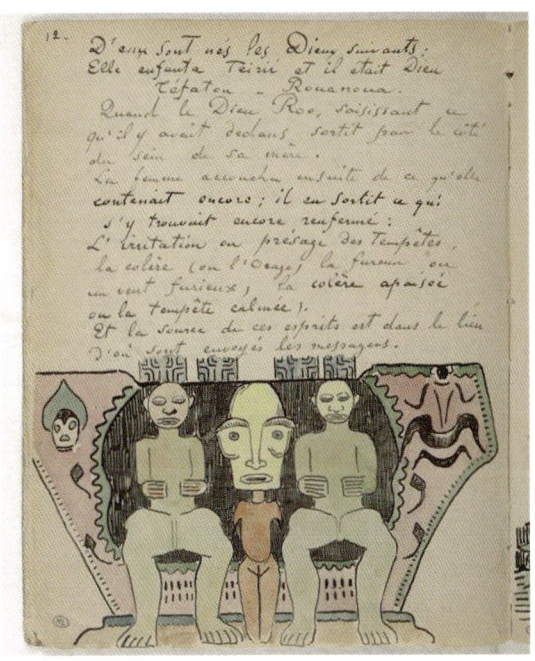

Ancien culte mahorie (Ancient Maori Religion), 1892–3. Gauguin's illustrated record of Polynesian beliefs supplemented with his own interpretations provided him with source material for many of his paintings. He covered his manuscript with native bark cloth to give it a feeling of authenticity.

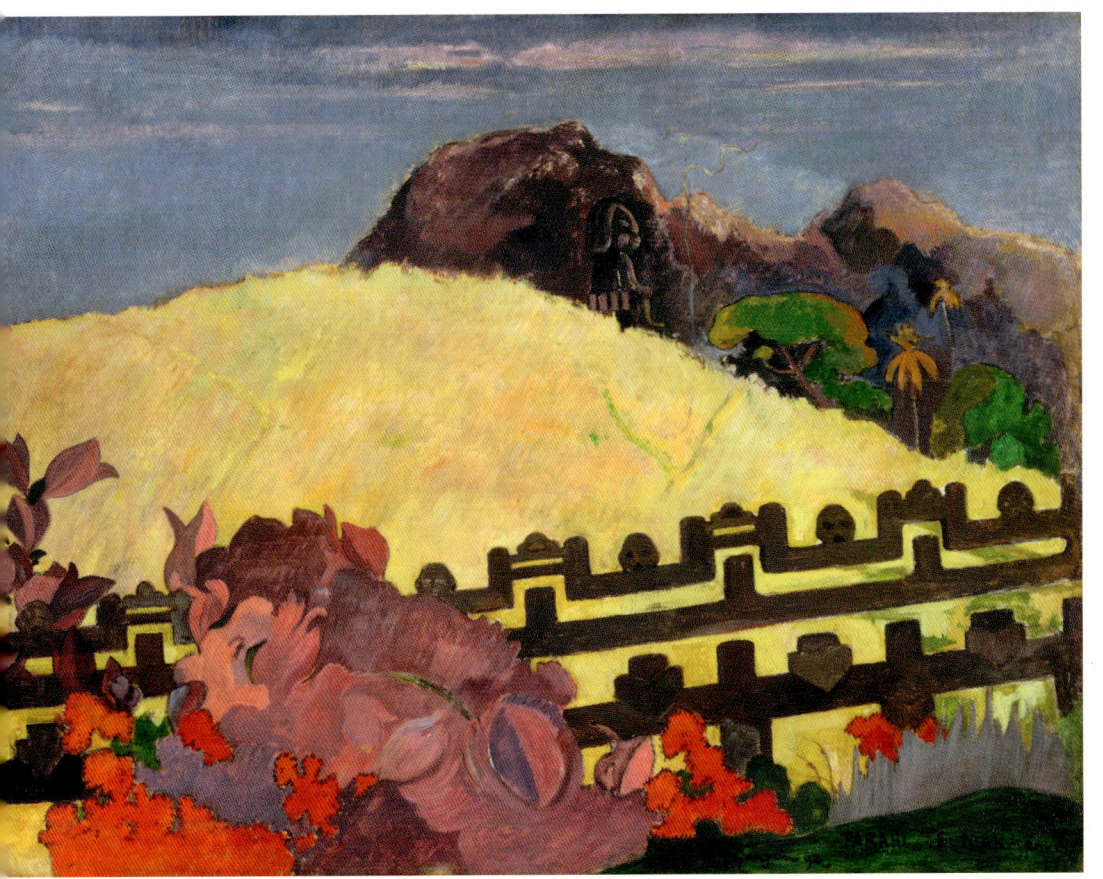

Parahi te marae (The Sacred Mountain, or There is the Temple), 1892. This landscape is a complete invention that purports to show a sacred enclosure where human sacrifices once took place, although this was not part of Tahitian culture. The idol atop the hill is based on Marquesan statues of deified ancestors, while the fence decorations are derived from ear ornaments worn by Marquesan women.

Gauguin's habit of giving his paintings Maori names would have baffled but also tantalized a Western audience. Often the titles invite the viewer to read a narrative into the pictures, so *Aha oe feii?* (*What? Are You Jealous?*) sets up a question that we need to answer, just as *Nafea faa ipoipo?* (*When Will You Marry?*) asks us to interpret the tension between an older woman and the younger one crouching in front of her. But the figures always seem contained in their own world, which is hard to penetrate. Gauguin was intrigued by the Tahitian habit of spending hours sitting in silence, apparently doing nothing: 'Always this silence. I understand why these people can remain seated for hours, days at a time, without saying a word, gazing sadly at the sky. I feel all of this is going to invade my being.' His ample figures are usually static and never shown rushing about or moving quickly, which contributes to their enigmatic, slightly melancholy character.

CARVINGS

Gauguin had gone to Tahiti equipped with his chisels, intending to take up woodcarving again. At first he did not have much access to wood so he modified locally produced objects such as plates and bowls, decorating them with patterns inspired by indigenous decorations and tattoos.

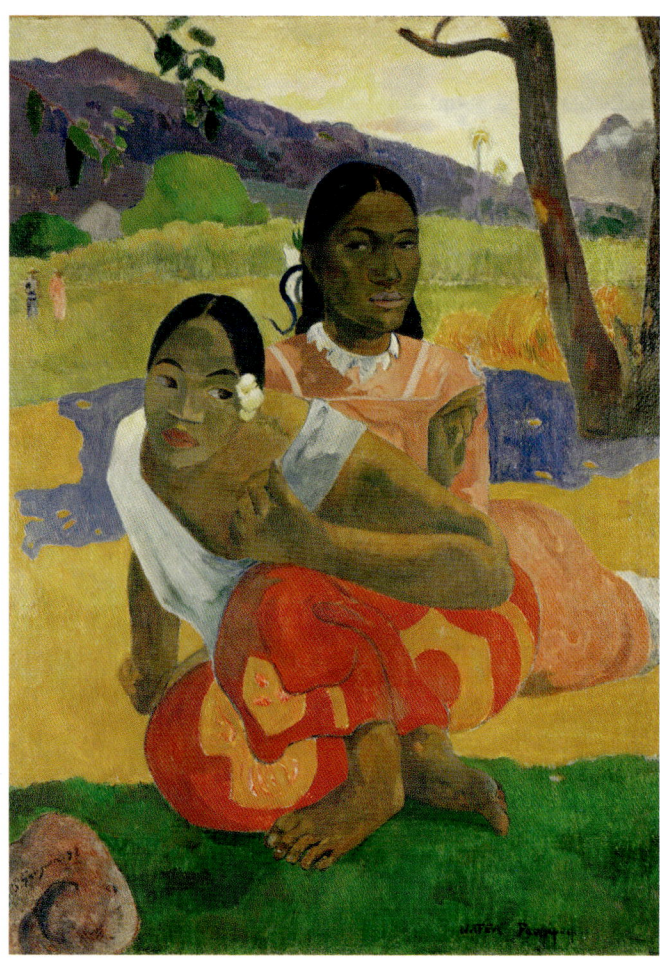

Nafea faa ipoipo? (When Will You Marry?), 1892. An older woman in a colonial dress is sitting in a pose that may be based on Buddhist art, her gesture possibly being one of warning. She is placed behind a younger one wearing the traditional pareu *with a white flower behind her ear, but their exchange is not absolutely explicit.*

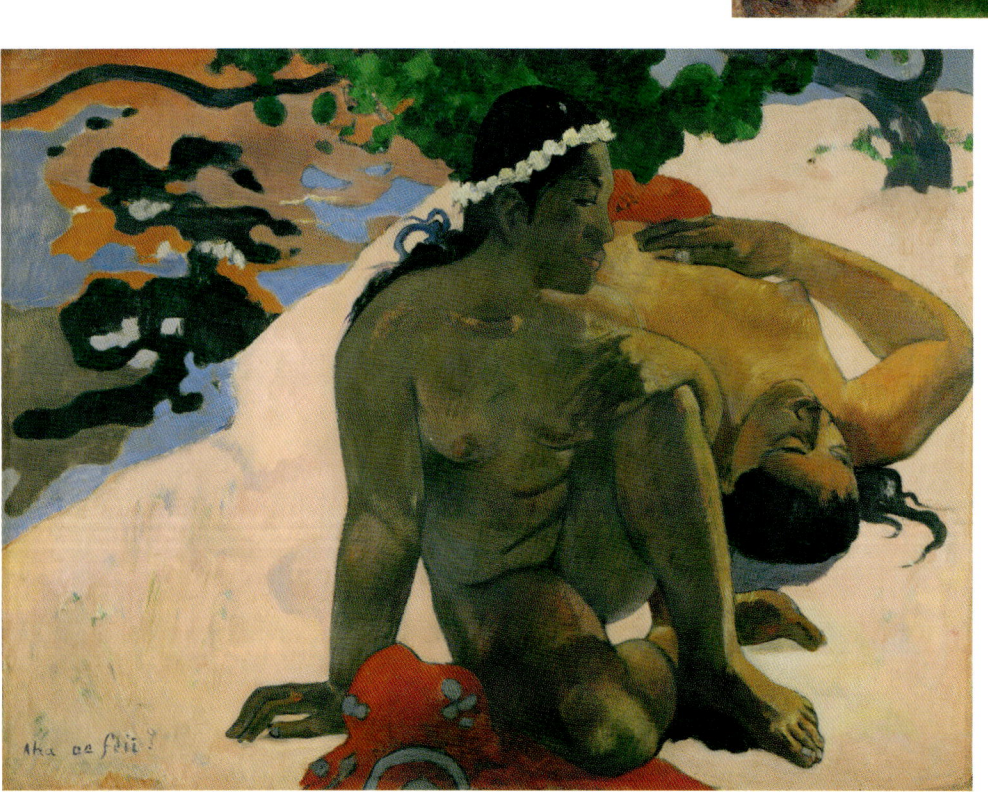

Aha oe feii? (What? Are You Jealous?), 1892. In Noa Noa *Gauguin explained the title of the picture: 'There are two sisters on the shore – they have just had a bathe and are now resting on the sand in casual, voluptuous poses – talking about yesterday's love and the love that will come tomorrow. One remark provokes discord: "What? Are you jealous?"'*

However, he needed to find a fresh supply of wood suitable for carving. In *Noa Noa* he describes how a handsome young Tahitian neighbour took him on an expedition to the mountains in the centre of the island, where they walked naked through the jungle in search of a suitable tree to fell. As very little remained of the ancient sculptures of Tahiti, Gauguin's carvings may have been an attempt to recreate what he thought of as a vanished art and mythology. He had read about the *tii* – wood and stone idols that had once adorned outdoor altars and acted as boundaries of a sacred space – but because they no longer existed he had the freedom to make them according to his own imagination; his three-dimensional sculptures keep the form of the branches from which they were taken. He included them in a number of his paintings. As he wrote to a friend, the artist George-Daniel de Monfreid: 'At the moment I am carving things like savage ornaments on tree trunks.'

FAREWELL TAHITI

Gauguin was enormously productive in Tahiti; during his two-year stay there he produced some 80 paintings and many carvings, but he became increasingly anxious about money as funds from France were drying up and he felt he needed to get back to Paris to promote his art. After just 11 months on the island he was asking the French government to pay for his passage home, but he was not granted free repatriation until June 1893. He landed in Marseilles two months later with four francs in his pocket. 'Farewell, hospitable land, land of delights, home of liberty and beauty!' he wrote in *Noa Noa*. 'I am leaving, older by two years but twenty years younger; more barbarian than when I arrived, and yet much wiser.' In a final poetic flourish he reported that Teha'mana had wept at the quay as he departed, the flower she had put behind her ear wilting on her knee.

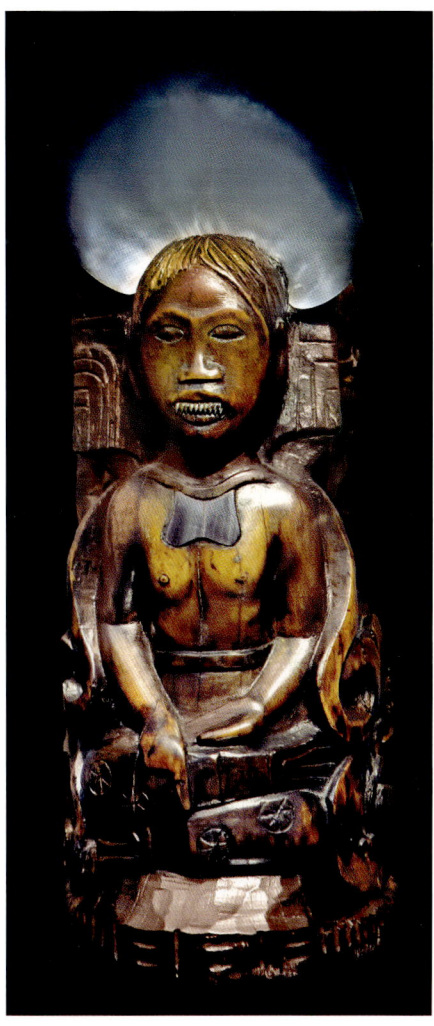

Tii with a Shell, 1892–3. Gauguin's ironwood carving depicts a god sitting in the lotus position reminiscent of the Buddha, with tattooed legs and a mouth full of cannibalistic teeth taken from a parrot fish. Two figures are repeated on the right and left sides of the sculpture.

Cup for Popoi, c. 1891. Gauguin decorated this bowl, which would have been used for serving rice or taro, with carved patterns based on Marquesan designs that he had seen in reproduction.

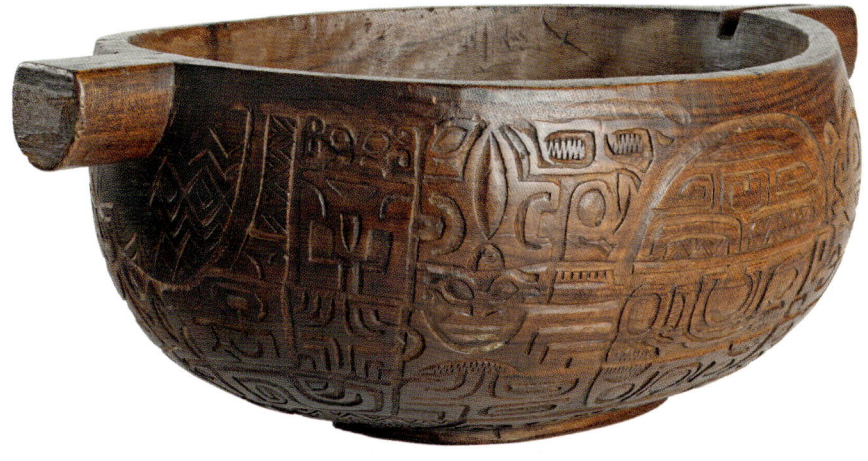

GAUGUIN'S VISUAL SOURCES

Gauguin had eclectic tastes and drew his inspiration from all over the globe, recycling and reassembling designs from many different cultures in his work. He found stimulus in ceramics, tapestries, stained-glass windows, Breton sculpture, popular prints, Peruvian pottery and the artefacts of Oceania. On visits to the Louvre he made sketches of Old Master paintings, Egyptian and Assyrian art. 'Have always before you the Persians, the Cambodians, and a little of the Egyptian,' he advised his friend de Monfreid.

When he went to Tahiti he took with him what he described as 'a whole little world of friends' – a large number of photographs, prints and drawings that would 'speak to me every day'. This imaginary museum provided motifs he could refashion in his own art. The walls of his hut were filled with images, including photographs of dancers from the carvings at Borobudur which he frequently referred to, for example in his painting of a Tahitian Eve who presides over his earthly paradise, *Te nave nave fenua (The Delightful Land)*; sketches he had made of a Peruvian mummy that he had seen in the Musée d'Ethnographie in Paris, which supplied the pose for crouching figures in a number of his paintings; photographs of Egyptian tomb paintings; Greek sculpture from Athens; the Parthenon frieze; Trajan's column in Rome; prints and reproductions of Puvis de Chavannes' painting *Hope* and Manet's *Olympia*. These were complemented by Charles Spitz's photographs of modern-day Tahitians.

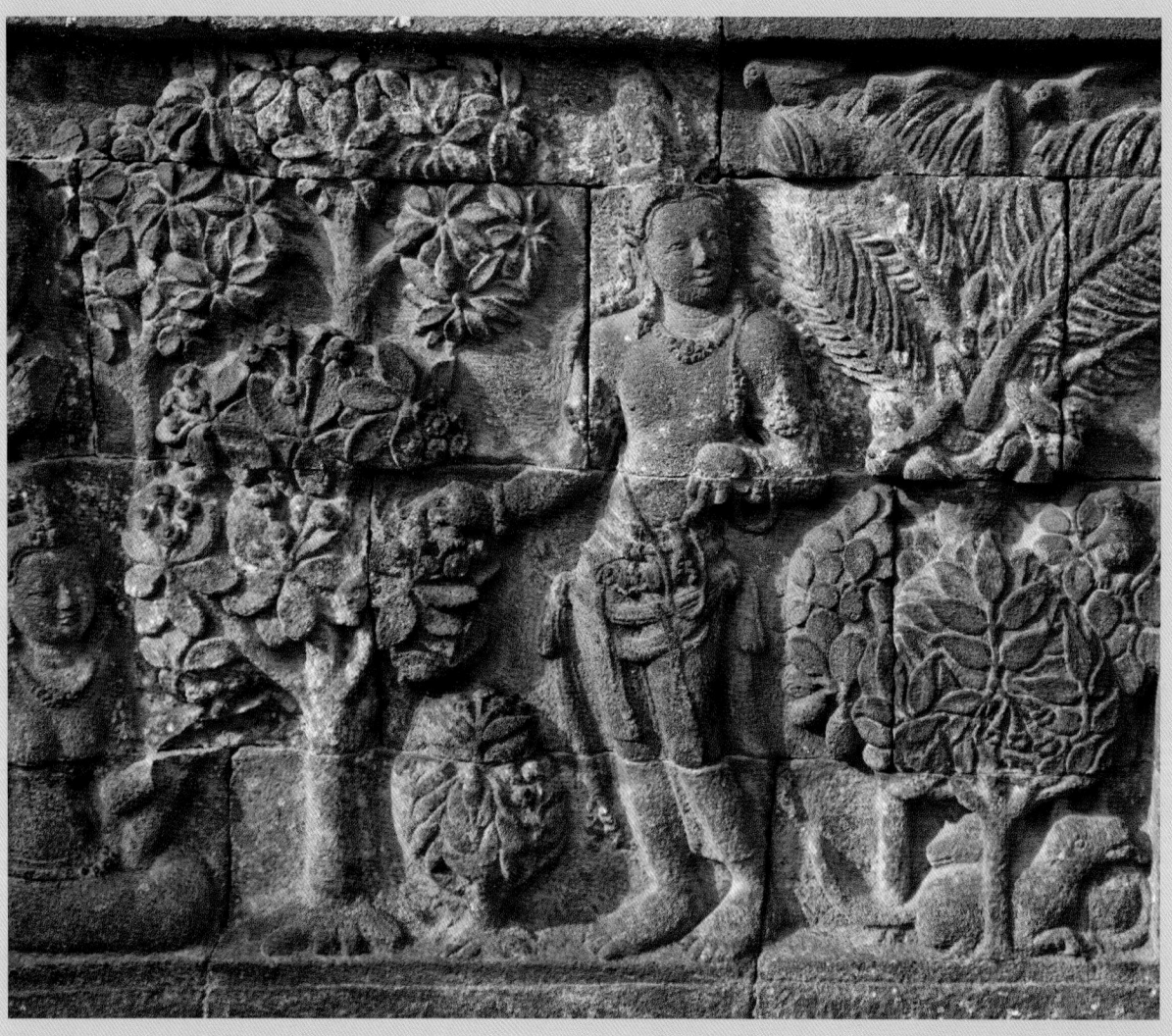

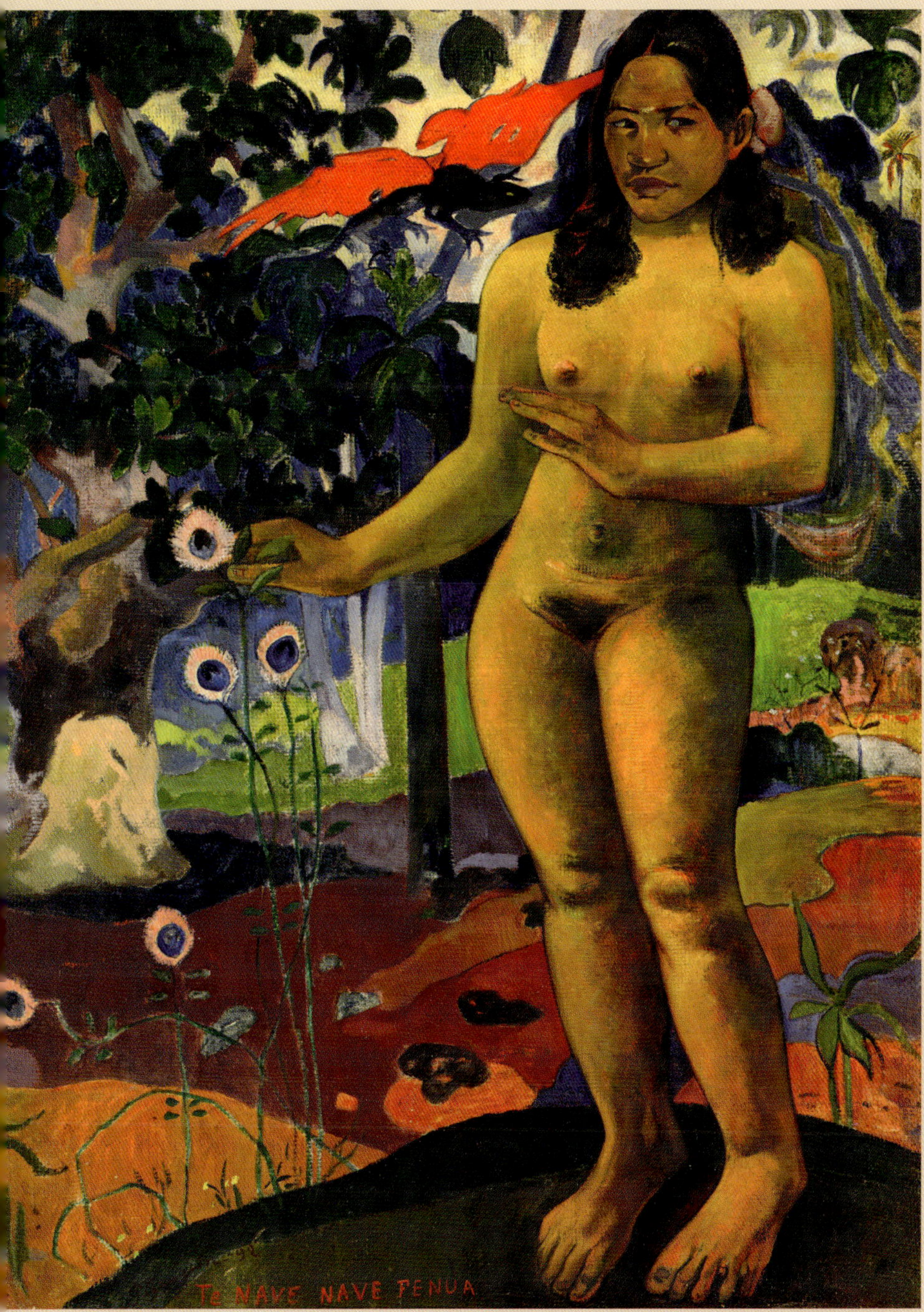

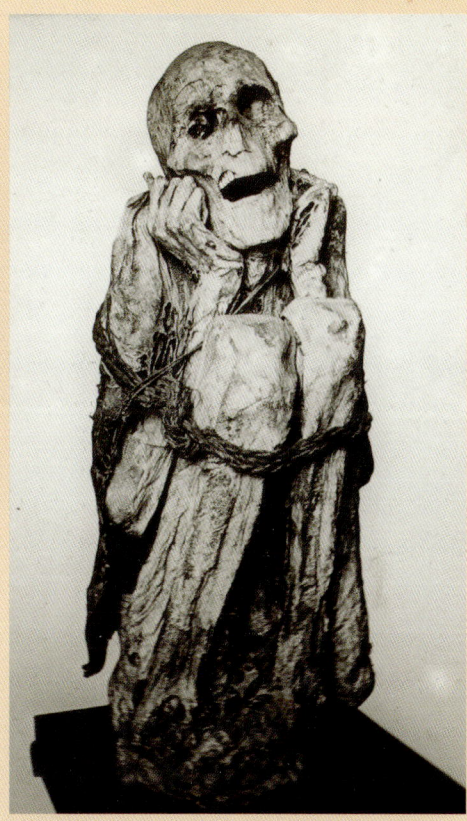

Mummy from the Chachapoya kingdom of Peru, ninth–fifteenth century. This ancient Peruvian mummy went on display in 1882 in the Ethnographic Museum in Paris, where Gauguin saw it. He was no doubt fascinated by its crouching or foetal position, and the way in which this suggested the cycle of life from birth to death.

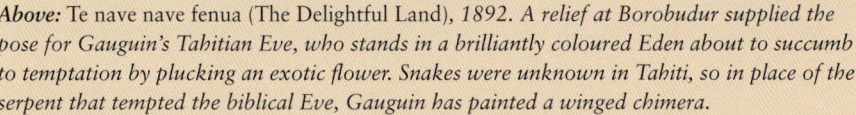

Above: Te nave nave fenua (The Delightful Land), *1892. A relief at Borobudur supplied the pose for Gauguin's Tahitian Eve, who stands in a brilliantly coloured Eden about to succumb to temptation by plucking an exotic flower. Snakes were unknown in Tahiti, so in place of the serpent that tempted the biblical Eve, Gauguin has painted a winged chimera.*

Opposite: Relief on the Borobudur Buddhist temple, Java, Indonesia. Gauguin never saw the ninth-century Buddhist temple in central Java, but he became familiar with it from photographic reproductions. He took photographs of the carved relief panels and statues to Tahiti and made liberal use of the figures in his own art.*

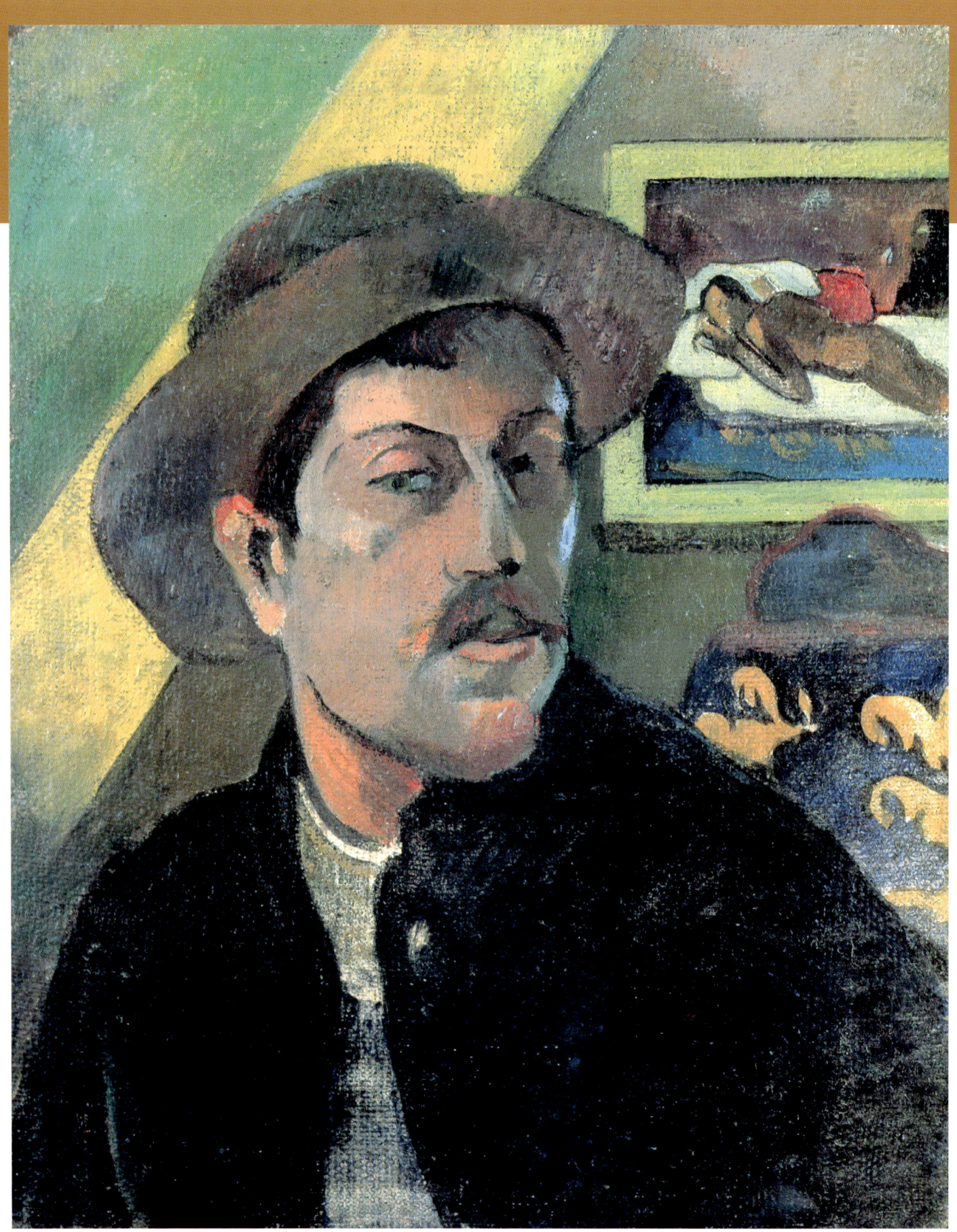

CHAPTER 4
French Interlude

On his return to Paris in the autumn of 1893, Gauguin threw himself into a flurry of activity aimed at re-establishing his position in the art world. Much had changed while he had been away. His friends Theo and Vincent Van Gogh and Meyer de Haan were now dead, as was the writer Albert Aurier, who had championed his work in the press, but Gauguin still had some of his old supporters and he discovered new ones. Degas was helpful; he arranged for the art dealer Paul Durand-Ruel to hold an exhibition of Gauguin's paintings in his gallery, consisting of 41 Tahitian canvases framed in white, yellow or blue frames, three paintings from Brittany and one sculpture. The much-anticipated show opened on 10 November. The catalogue preface, written by a new friend, the poet, playwright and literary critic Charles Morice, urged viewers not to expect a documentary record of life in Tahiti and argued that Gauguin had instead penetrated to the 'primitive' heart of the island. The exhibition generated considerable interest and debate because of its novelty, with the critic Félix Fénéon noting that the canvases were 'barbarous, opulent and taciturn in character'. Despite some favourable reviews, only 11 of the canvases sold, although for high prices. Some were bought by Degas.

A STUDIO IN MONTPARNASSE

Early the following year Gauguin moved into a new apartment in rue Vercingétorix, on the edge of an artists' district in Montparnasse. He painted the walls a brilliant chrome yellow and olive green and decorated the studio with reproductions of works by artists he admired, souvenirs, minerals and shells from his trip and ethnographic artefacts such as tomahawks, pikes and spears. It was an exotic setting, rather like the home of an explorer, in which he could show his work and entertain friends on Thursday evenings with songs and Polynesian dances. He also frequented the Tuesday evening soirées held by the poet Stéphane Mallarmé, where he was a distinctive presence. The poet Henri de Régnier recalled: 'He'd let his bulky body sink ponderously into a chair. The sailor's jersey he'd be wearing, his rugged face, swarthy complexion and huge hands gave an impression of strength and coarseness that was a foil to Mallarmé's exquisite civility and extremely distinguished presence.' Gauguin's appearance was calculatedly outlandish. On the streets of Paris he cut a bizarre figure, decked out in a large blue overcoat with buckles and an astrakhan hat, leaning with a gloved hand on a cane he had carved himself. He would have seemed even more exotic when seen with his new companion, 'Annah the Javanese', an artists' model of Indian and Malay origin, who kept a pet monkey.

Self-Portrait, 1893–4. *Gauguin's self-portrait in his brilliant yellow and green Parisian studio affirms his identity as a painter of the tropics. On the wall behind him is his* Spirit of the Dead Watching *(seen in reverse because he made the picture while looking in a mirror) hanging above a Tahitian* pareu.

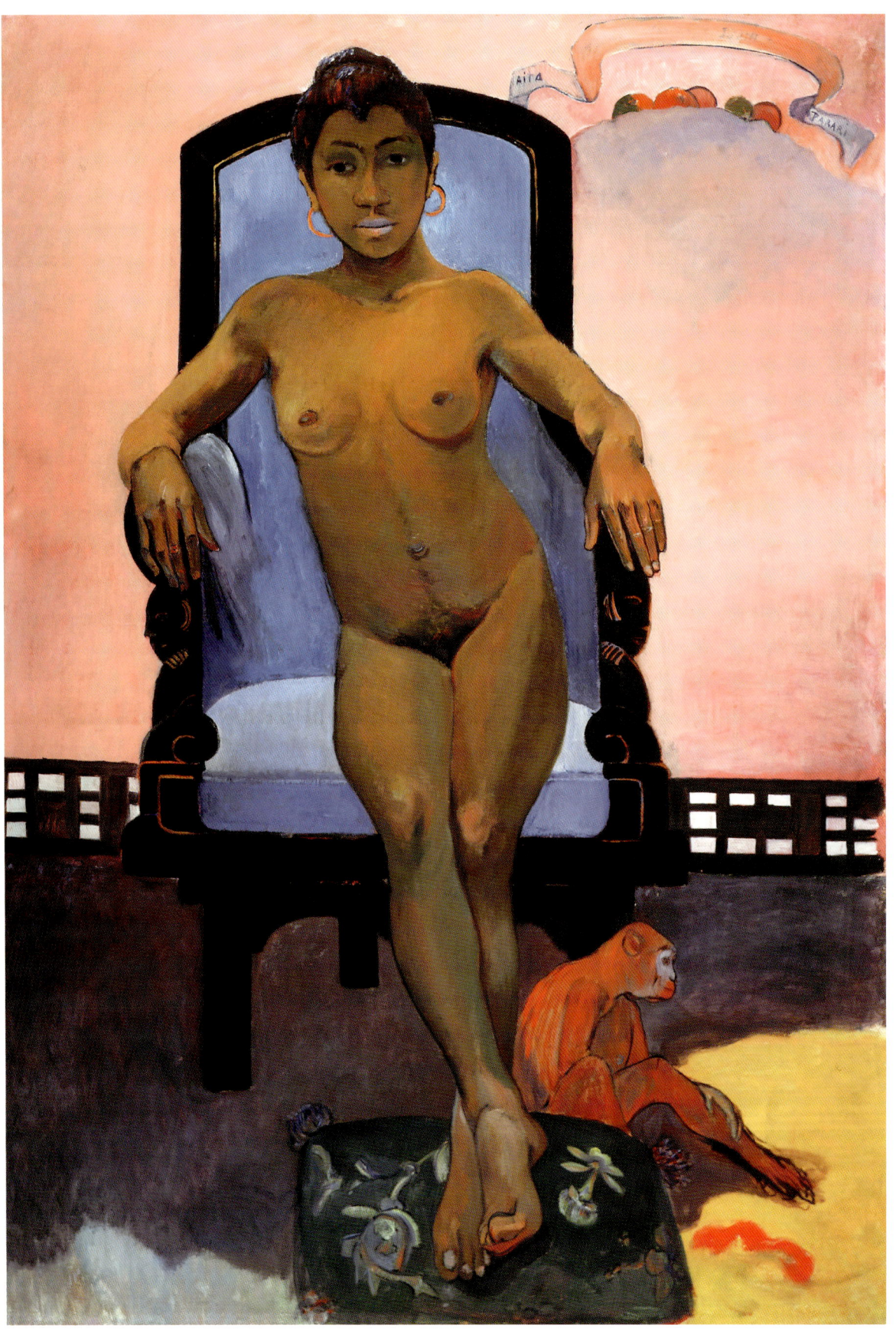

Opposite: Annah the Javanese, 1893. *The art dealer Ambroise Vollard introduced the teenaged Annah, an artists' model, to Gauguin. Her youthfulness and dark complexion would have provided a perfect complement to his stories about his Tahitian adventures. The painting carries a puzzling inscription in Tahitian referring to the virginity of Judith, a 13-year-old neighbour who also posed for him in the nude.*

Below: Gauguin's studio in rue Vercingétorix, 1894. *The Montparnasse studio was the setting for many musical evenings. Standing from left to right are Paul Sérusier, Annah the Javanese and the artist Georges Lacombe. In the foreground are Gauguin in a Buffalo Bill hat, the cellist Fritz Schnedklud and the musician G. Larrivel.*

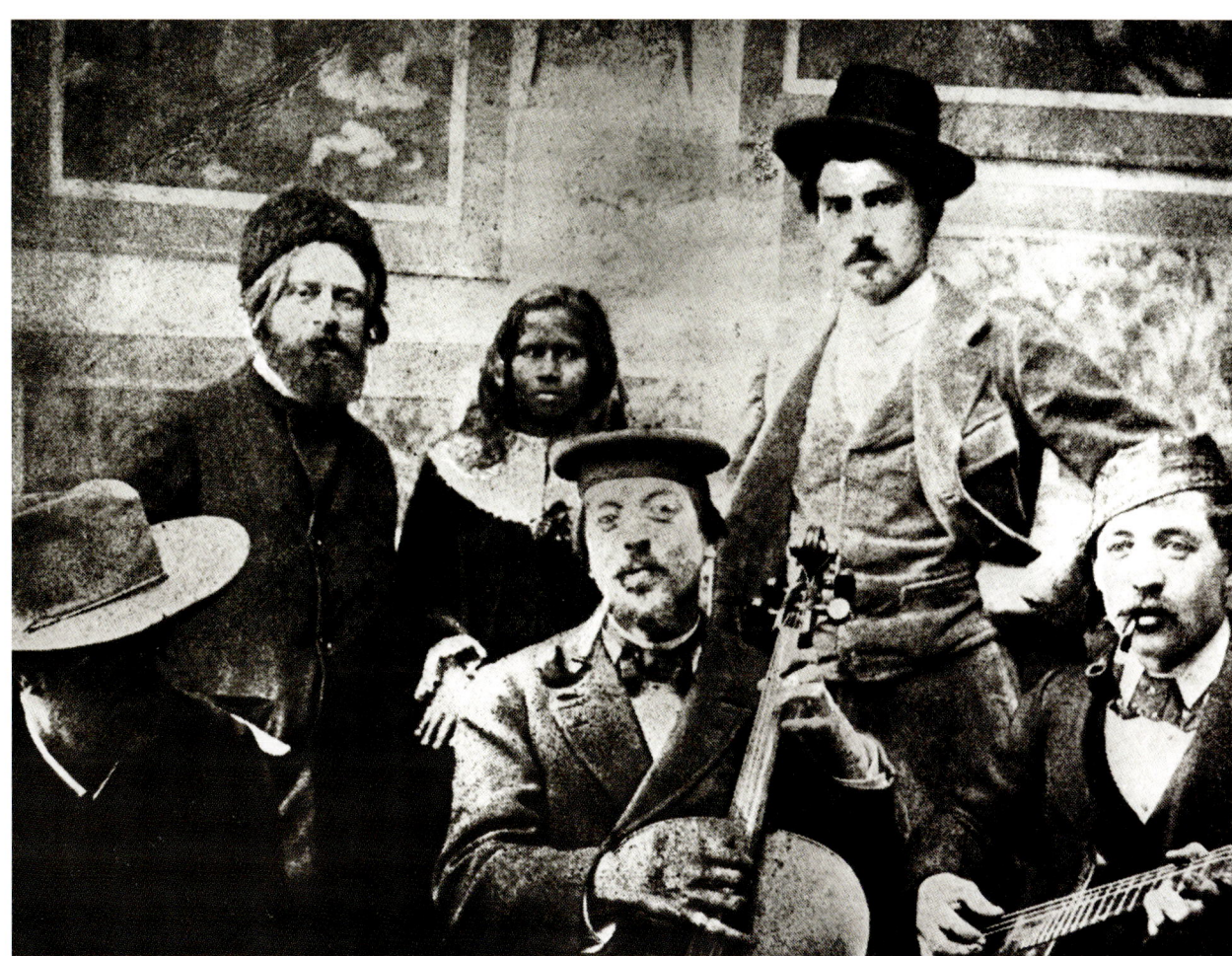

BACK TO BRITTANY

Gauguin made a few trips in Europe, visiting museums in Belgium and exhibiting in Brussels, but stayed away from his family in Copenhagen. By this time it was evident that he was never going to be reconciled with Mette. Furious at his refusal to share a legacy he had received from his uncle Isidore, she broke off contact with him. From now on, Gauguin no longer even attempted to play the part of a respectable married man and that summer he returned to Pont-Aven, taking Annah and her monkey with him. He hoped to retrieve the paintings he had left with Marie Henry in Le Pouldu, but she did not want to part with them, insisting that they were payment for the unpaid hospitality he had enjoyed. Gauguin drank, bragged and got into fights, and a brawl with some sailors in Concarneau resulted in a broken ankle. He would never fully recover from the injury, and during his sustained period of convalescence he was unable to paint. While he was immobile in Brittany he had time to work on his book *Noa Noa*. He also began to compile a scrapbook of press cuttings and philosophical musings that became *Cahier pour Aline (Notebook for Aline)*, which he intended to give to his daughter, writing a dedication to her on the first page: 'She too is a savage, she will understand me.' When Gauguin returned to Paris that November he found that Annah had ransacked his apartment, though fortunately not the paintings.

NOA NOA

Gauguin felt a pressing need to explain his work to a public that found it baffling, and he hoped his written account in *Noa Noa*, which translates as 'very fragrant', would help people understand the paintings. The book is a series of recollections of his life in Tahiti, based on his real experience there but undoubtedly embroidered with fantastical elements, interspersed with Tahitian legends that were derived from Moerenhout's *Voyages aux îles du Grand Océan*. He decided to collaborate with the Symbolist poet Charles Morice, the idea being that the text would have two voices, his own being that of the 'naïve and brutal savage' in contrast to the 'civilized' voice of Morice, which would

reflect the meeting between Europe and Polynesia discussed in the text. Morice and Gauguin worked on the text together until 1895, when Gauguin left for his second and final trip to Tahiti. Morice published a version in 1901, and Gauguin kept hold of his own copy, which he augmented and illustrated. His manuscript is now in the Louvre.

Gauguin had already made a compilation of Maori myth and legend in his illustrated manuscript *Ancien culte mahorie (Ancient Maori Religion)*, which told tales of the Polynesian deities as he understood them, and he used some of this material in his new project. To go with the book he produced a series of ten woodcuts, which he showed

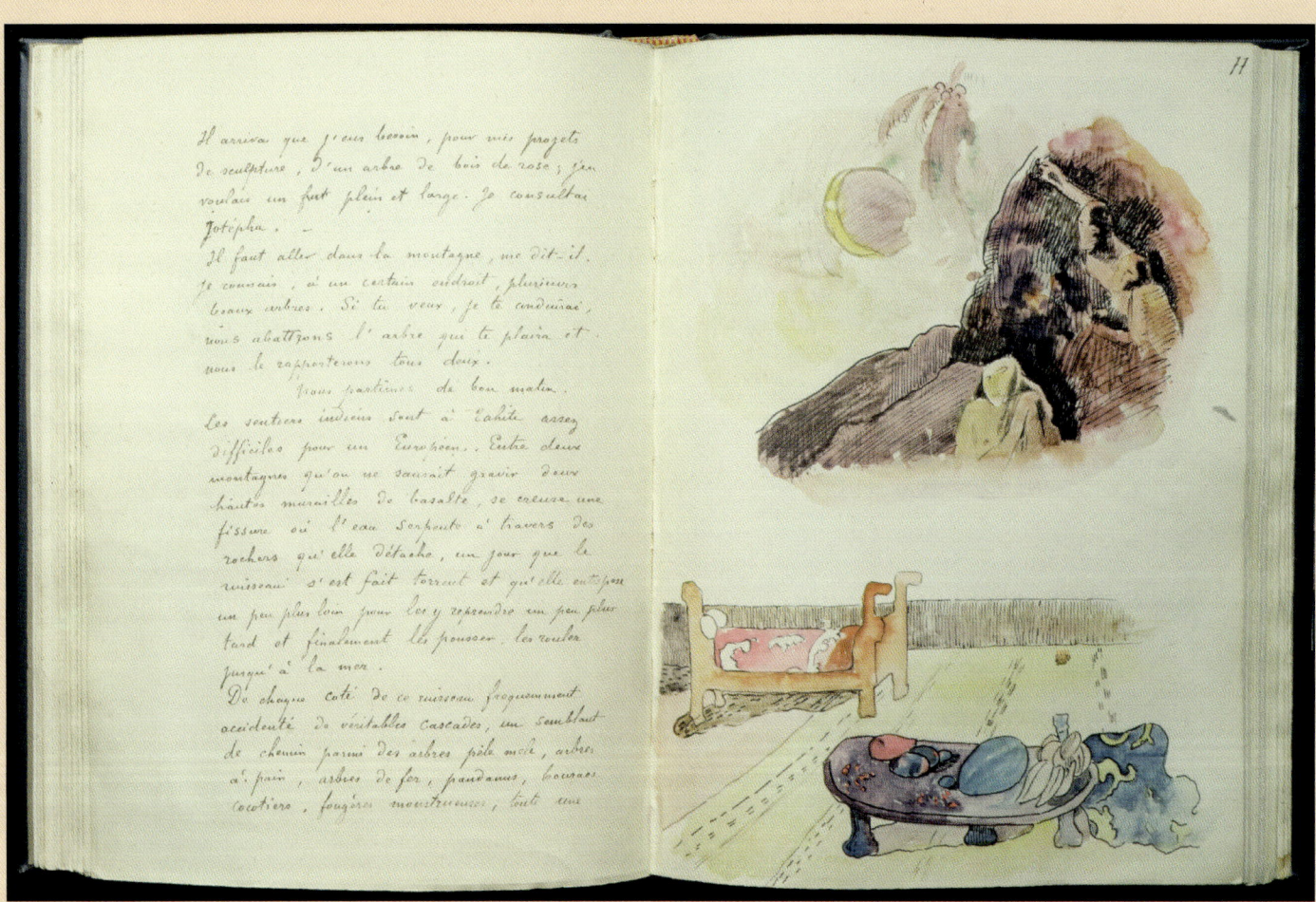

Pages from Noa Noa, *1893–4. Some of the watercolour illustrations in the* Noa Noa *manuscript complement the descriptions that Gauguin gives of his daily life in Tahiti, providing glimpses of where he lived, what he ate and the landscape he observed.*

in his Paris studio when he got back from his ill-fated trip to Brittany in 1894. The woodcut as a print medium had fallen out of fashion and was considered rather archaic, but it was the perfect medium for the consciously 'primitive' style that Gauguin was striving for. The subjects reflect the Tahitian themes explored in the text, telling the story of the origins of life, humanity under the eye of the gods and the influence of the devil. Gauguin pasted these woodcuts into the pages of his manuscript alongside the text, watercolours, drawings and photographs.

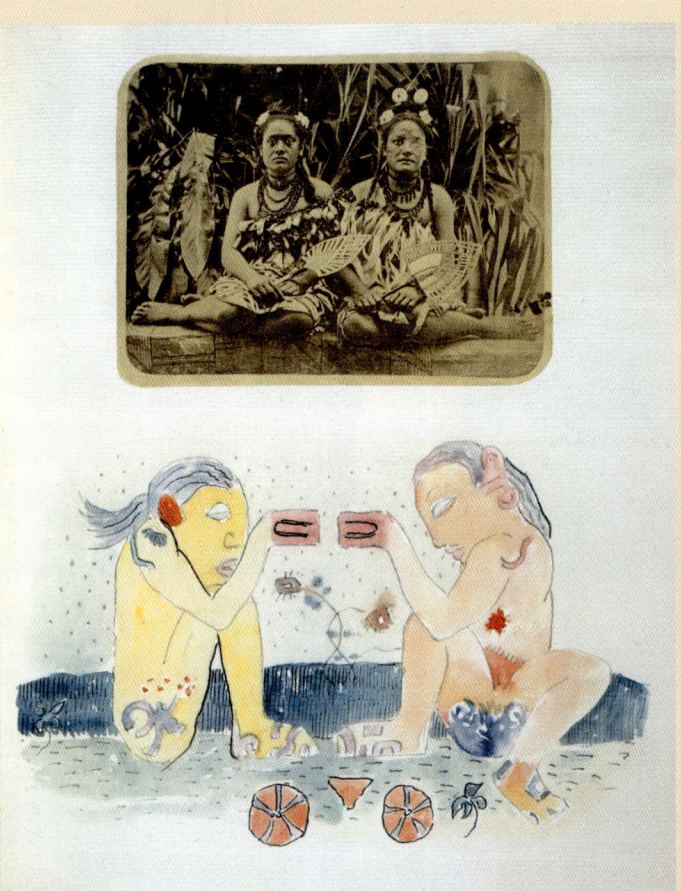

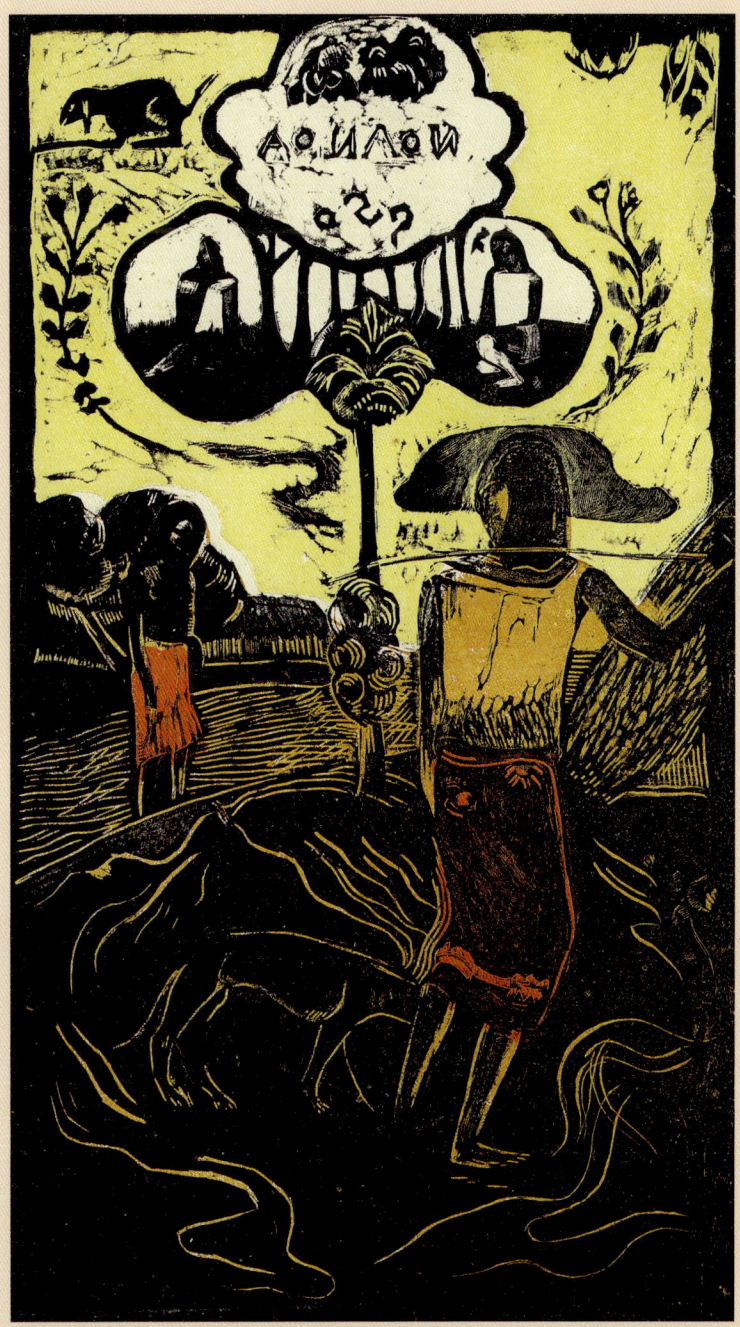

Page from Noa Noa, *1893–4. Gauguin's blend of different media in* Noa Noa *gives a multi-layered appearance and meaning to the manuscript. This page combines a schematic image of two figures, the legendary ancestors of the Tahitians first seen in* Ancien culte mahorie, *with a photograph of contemporary Tahitian women.*

Noa Noa (Fragrant) *from the* Noa Noa *suite, 1893–4. The woman in the foreground carrying fruit on a pole is a recurrent motif in Gauguin's art, conveying an idea of the harmonious relationship between people and their environment in Tahiti. Gauguin printed this woodblock in colour.*

POLYNESIA IN FRANCE

Some of the works that Gauguin produced during his two-year stay in France make a specific link between European and Polynesian culture. *Young Christian Girl*, for example, shows an unidentified red-headed sitter, perhaps a Breton woman or Annette Belfils, the partner of his friend George-Daniel de Monfreid, or even the daughter of William Molard, his neighbour in Paris. While it appears to be an image of Christian devotion (the girl wears a cross round her neck and joins her hands in prayer), she is clothed in the type of missionary dress worn by Tahitian women. Perhaps Gauguin was hoping to combine two 'primitive' expressions of piety from distant parts of the world.

He continued to explore overtly Tahitian subjects in his paintings, reusing and modifying figures that had by now become a familiar part of his visual lexicon. One of these was a woman leaning over a rock to drink from a spring, which he adapted in different ways in an oil painting, a print and a carving, all entitled *Pape moe*

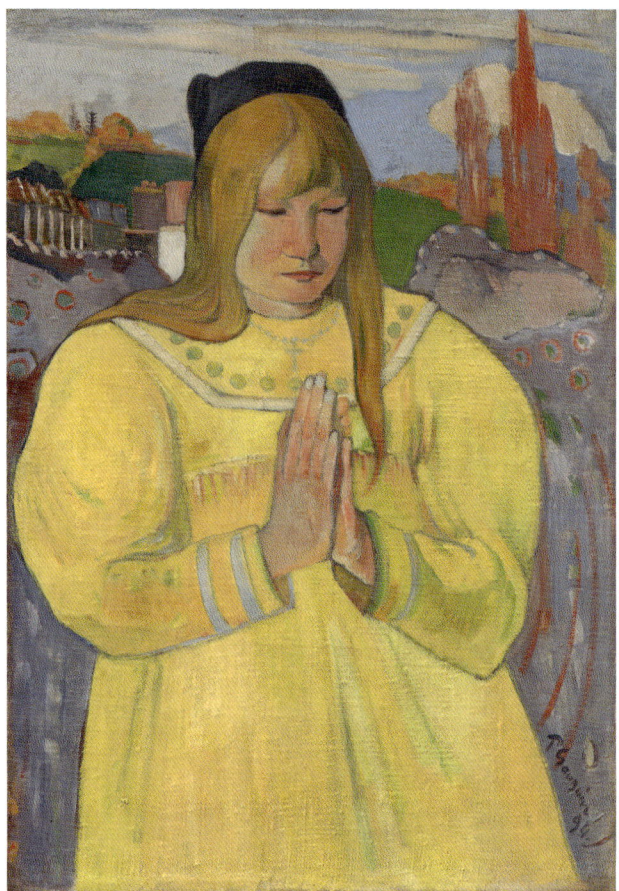

Young Christian Girl, 1894. This portrait blends elements from Gauguin's experiences in France and Polynesia. The girl is praying, and lilac shapes fan out from her shoulders like wings. The trees and hills suggest the landscape of Brittany, but instead of traditional Breton clothing the girl is clad in a yellow Mother Hubbard dress of a type worn by Tahitian women.

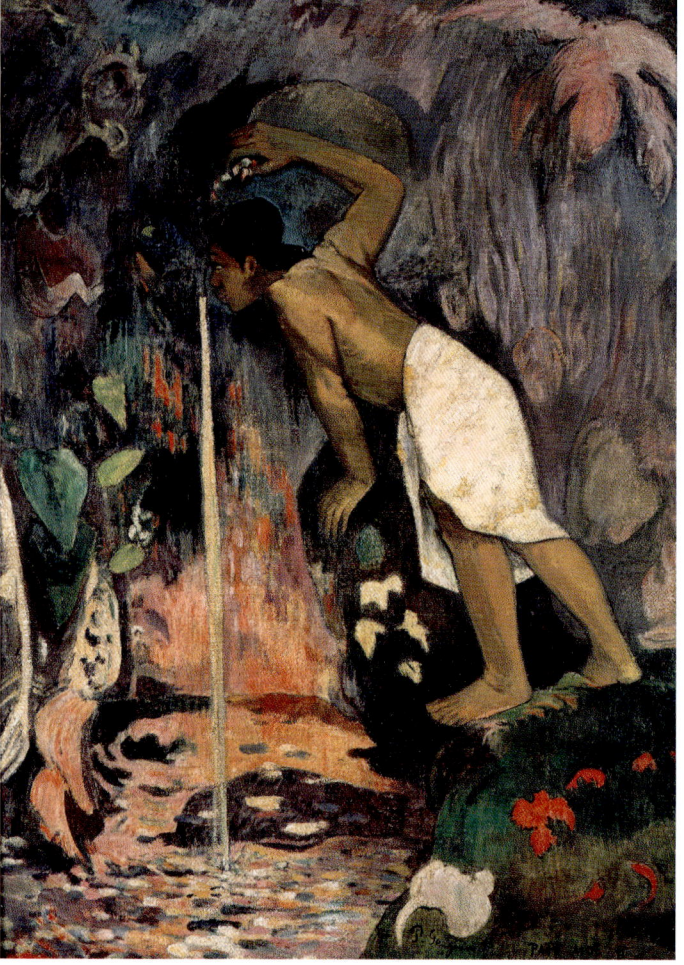

Pape moe (Mysterious Water), 1893–4. *In Noa Noa Gauguin recalls making a trip into the jungle and spotting a naked girl drinking from a spring, who was startled by his presence and fled. Whether or not such an episode did spark the idea for the painting, the sturdy and androgynous figure shown here, based on a photograph, hardly looks frightened.*

(*Mysterious Water*). Gauguin describes having seen such a scene in real life in *Noa Noa*, but the composition was actually based on a photograph of a girl drinking from a pipe taken by Charles Spitz. Whatever the source, Gauguin transformed the simple image into a composition infused with mythical power.

He also painted two large canvases with enigmatic subjects that are hard to interpet. *Mahana no atua (Day of the God)* is an imaginary scene of women on a beach, which is dominated by a statue of the Tahitian goddess Hina. The women on the right are performing a traditional Tahitian dance, the *upapa*, which Christian missionaries had tried to suppress. Pink sand is combined with brilliantly rendered colourful waves that verge on abstraction. The same style with large areas of flat colour contained within curving contours can be seen in *Nave nave moe (Sacred Spring, Sweet Dreams)*. This is a strange mixture of Christian and Tahitian imagery, which includes a young girl with a halo round her head, a lily – long associated with purity in Christian art – and a second woman about to take a bite out of a piece of fruit, perhaps like Eve in the garden of Eden. In the background figures dance in front of a statue of a Maori deity.

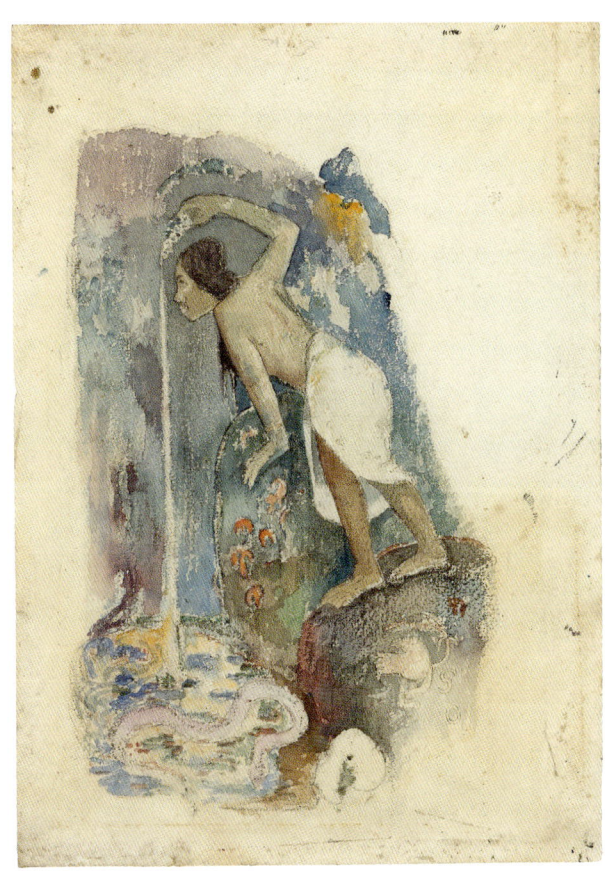

Above: Pape moe (Mysterious Water), *1893–4. Gauguin often reused his motifs in different media. The drinking figure seen in an oil painting, carving and print also appears in this watercolour, although the background details are slightly different in each medium.*

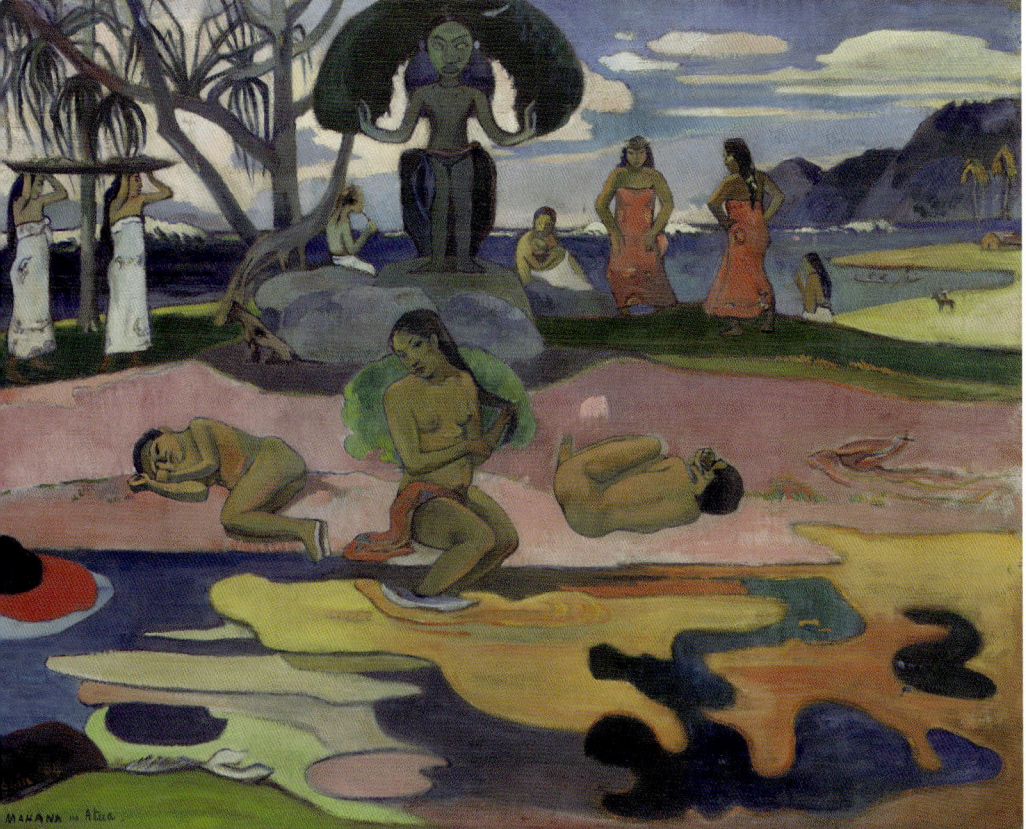

Left: Mahana no atua (Day of the God), *1894. In this fantastic reimagining of Tahitian religious ritual, devotees dance or make offerings to a statue of the Tahitian goddess Hina. The poses of the three figures on the pink sand suggests different stages of life from birth to death, the curled-up figure on the right being reminiscent of the Peruvian mummy Gauguin had seen in Paris. Bold, almost abstract swirls of colour represent sand and sea.*

Nave nave moe (Sacred Spring, Sweet Dreams), 1894. This painting combines elements drawn from Catholic and Tahitian traditions. The figure in the left foreground has a halo, and her companion is about to bite into a piece of fruit, evoking the biblical Eve. The lilies are a flower associated with the Annunciation to the Virgin Mary in Christian art, so purity meets the idea of sin. In the distance a statue of a Maori deity is surrounded by dancers.

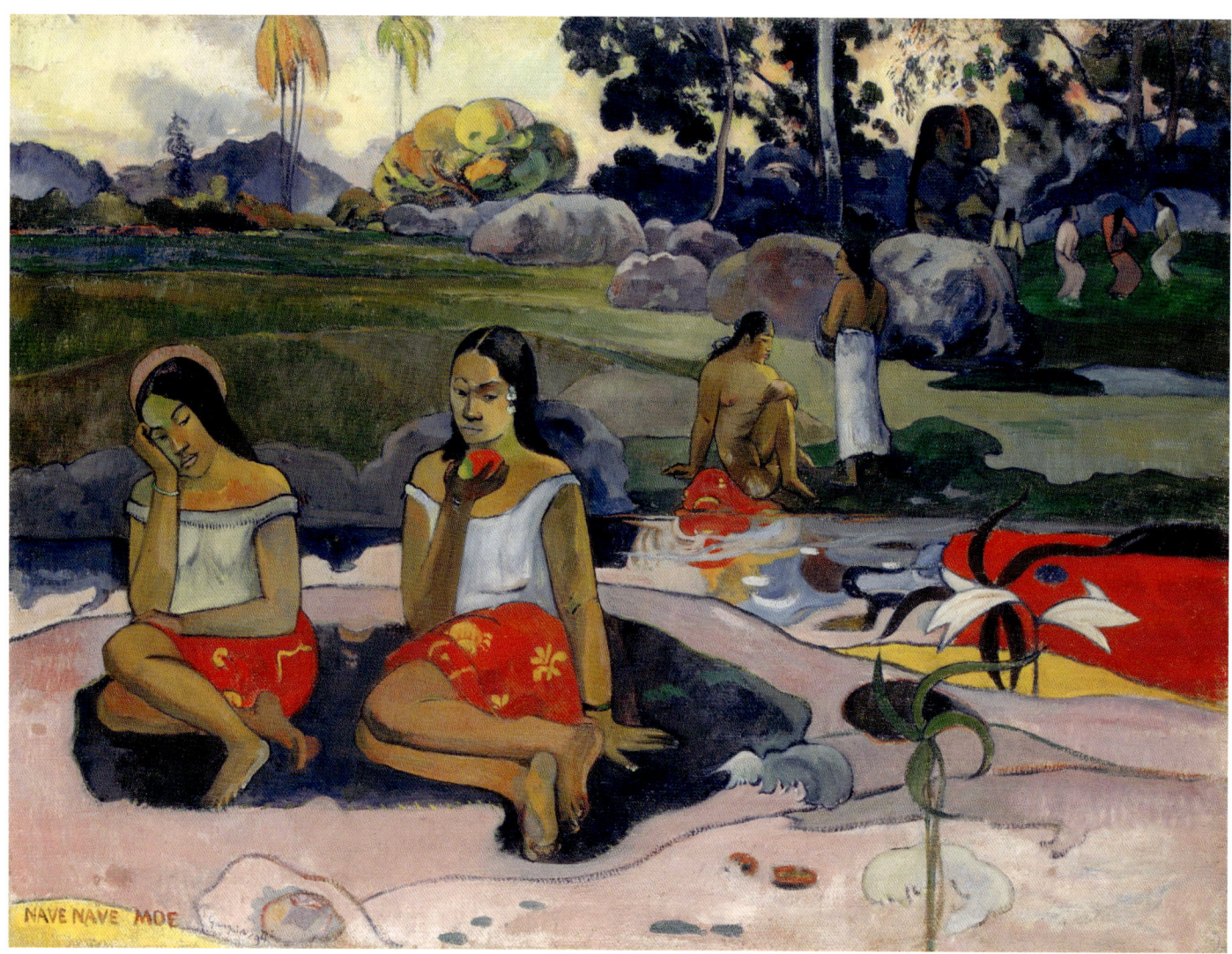

THE IMAGE MULTIPLIED

Not only did Gauguin constantly reuse motifs in his work, he also developed new ways of producing multiple images on paper. Alongside woodcuts, which he sometimes coloured by hand, he also started to experiment with monotypes. He would place a piece of dampened paper on top of an existing drawing or watercolour and press it down in order to transfer the image to another piece of paper, which would then be printed with a mirror image of the original. This process could also be used with an original painted on glass. Each print produced by these methods looked slightly different. One figure that appeared in multiple forms – drawings, monotypes, woodcuts and three-dimensional work – was the distorted and disturbing image of Oviri. In the winter of 1894 Gauguin returned to the studio of Ernest Chaplet, where he produced a number of ceramics, of which *Oviri* was the largest. It represents a woman who has killed a she-wolf; it lies at her feet while she clutches the cub to her hip. It is a curious piece that rejects European ideals of beauty, emphasizing the violent, the ugly and the savage. Gauguin was very proud of it, considering it 'an exceptional piece such as no ceramicist has made until now'. The name 'Oviri', inscribed on the base, can be translated as 'wild' or 'savage', and relates to the Tahitian goddess who ruled over death or mourning. Perhaps at this low point in his life, when he felt the odds were stacked against him, Gauguin identified with this destructive goddess. He may have regarded this strange statue as his alter ego, as he asked de Monfreid to place it on his grave.

By the time he made the sculpture Gauguin had decided to return to Tahiti for good. He told de Monfreid, 'My suffering has cost me all my courage, especially at night, when I do not get a wink of sleep … I've made up my mind to go away to the South Seas and never come back.' He held an auction of his works in February 1895 to raise funds for this new voyage. Only nine of the 47 works sold, some bought by Degas. Disillusioned with the Paris art scene, attacks on him in the press by Émile Bernard who questioned his integrity, and the fact that there was no prospect of reconciliation with his family, Gauguin must have felt he had little to lose by leaving France.

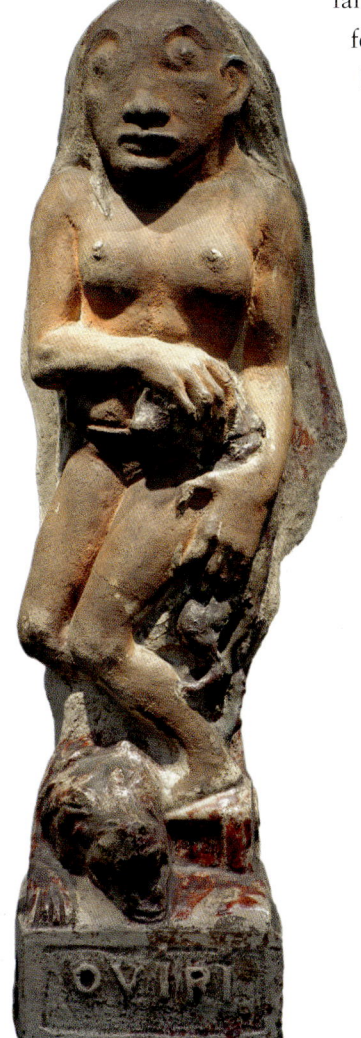

Oviri, *1895–1903. Gauguin dedicated a woodcut of* Oviri *to the poet Stéphane Mallarmé, describing the subject as 'this strange and cruel enigma'. The figure seems to emerge from the shadows, amplifying the sense of menace.*

Oviri, *1894. The statue merges ideas of life, in the young wolf cub the goddess clutches, and death, in the wolf that lies dead at her feet. The pose of the woman relates to figures in the carvings of Borobudur. Gauguin referred to the statue as 'the Murderess' in a letter to Ambroise Vollard, and splashes of reddish glaze indicate the pool of blood at her feet.*

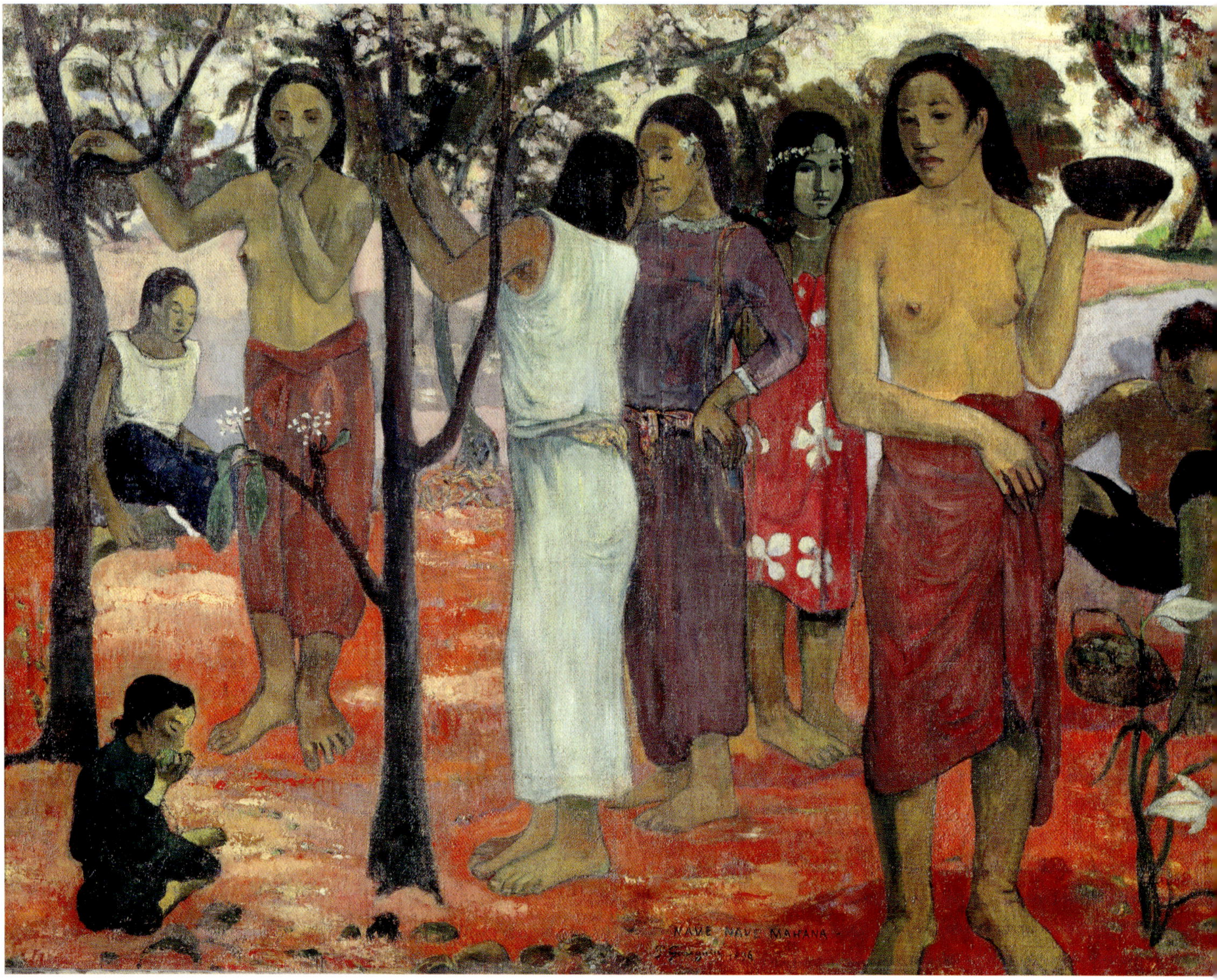

Nave nave mahana (Delicious Days), 1896. A group of women gather fruit, evoking
the idea that they are inhabitants of a primitive Eden, but it is a paradise with a
melancholy atmosphere, conveyed by their sombre expressions and downcast eyes.
The flat, frieze-like arrangement recalls a procession from the Parthenon, of which
Gauguin had a photograph.

CHAPTER 5
Final Years in the Tropics

Gauguin left Paris on 28 June 1895, landing at Papeete two months later. He would never see Europe again. During the voyage the ship had stopped for ten days at Auckland in New Zealand, where he visited the Ethnological Museum and made sketches of the sculptures and carvings that decorated the Maori huts on display.

Papeete had become even more westernized since he had left: there was now electricity in this 'capital of Eden' and a merry-go-round had been installed on the lawn in front of the king's garden. Although Gauguin immediately started talking about moving to the Marquesas Islands 'where I shan't find any Europeans', he was not able to leave until six years later. In the meantime he settled in Punaauia, east of Papeete, where he had a house built complete with a studio. He was certainly not cut off from society: a horse and trap enabled him to travel to the capital to participate in the social life of the colony, and he mixed with prominent French colonial families such as that of the lawyer Auguste Goupil, who invited him to paint a portrait of his daughter. The *Mercure de France*, France's foremost critical journal, and the monthly mail boat kept him in touch with what was going on in France. For a while life seemed to go well. 'How I pity you for not being here,' Gauguin wrote to William Molard in Paris. 'I am sitting quietly in my hut. In front of me is the sea … No such thing as suffering from heat or cold.'

Teha'mana had married someone else while he was away, so he acquired a new young *vahine*, Pahura. She would give birth to two of his children, one of whom died shortly after birth. He was aware of how his abandonment of his European family would look to friends in Europe, but he felt that they would just have to do without him. Refusing to believe that Mette was in straitened circumstances, he wrote to de Monfreid, 'I firmly intend to live my life out here in my hut, altogether peacefully. Oh yes, I'm a great criminal. What does it matter? So was Michelangelo – and I'm not Michelangelo.'

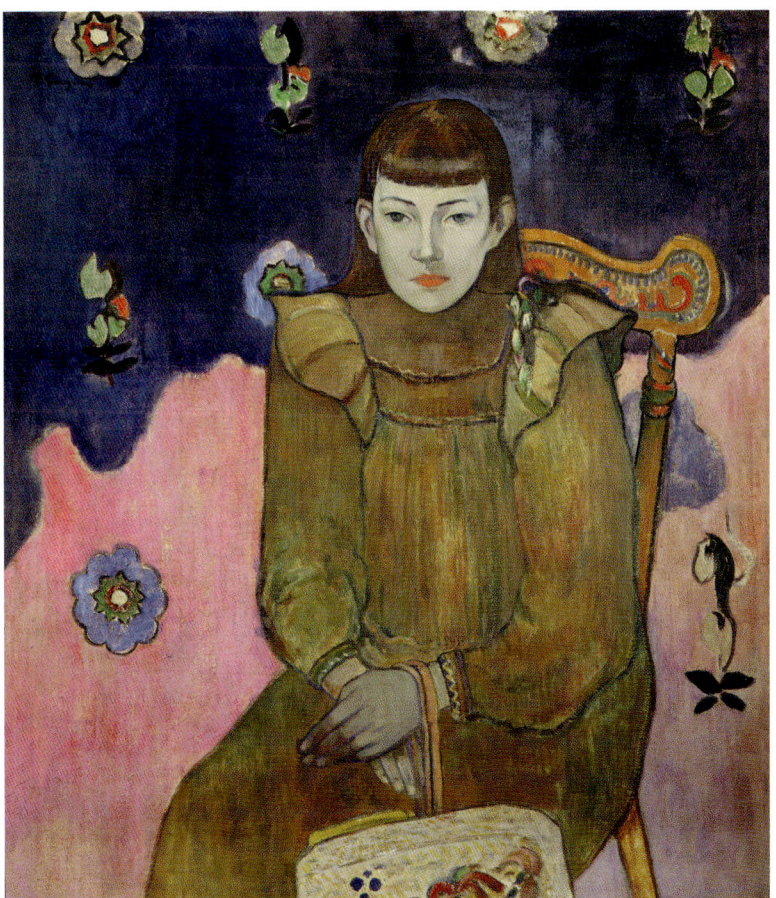

Portrait of a Young Woman. Vaïte (Jeanne) Goupil, *1896.*
Gauguin's portrait of the nine-year-old daughter of Auguste Goupil is conventional in pose, but unusual in other ways. Jeanne has a blank stare and pale, almost mask-like face, and she is seated against an abstract but highly decorative pink and blue background.

AT WORK IN THE NEW STUDIO

For the first year Gauguin concentrated on sculpture, making one of a female nude that he placed outside his house, to the annoyance of the local priest. When he began to paint again he returned to the themes he had tackled on his previous stay in Tahiti, including reclining female nudes such as *Te arii vahine (The King's Wife)*. He was very pleased with this picture, writing to de Monfreid: 'I don't think I have ever done anything with such deep, resonant colours.' His aim had been to suggest 'a luxuriant and untamed type of nature', and dense tropical vegetation is also a notable feature of the other canvases he painted at the time.

Some pictures were set indoors, such as *Nevermore*, another magnificent Tahitian nude that echoes *Manao tupapau*, painted five years earlier. As in that painting, the woman seems subject to some menace. Two figures whisper in the background, but a bird perched on the windowsill might be taken to refer to Edgar Allan Poe's poem *The Raven*, in which the bird flies into the narrator's chamber and repeats 'Nevermore', though Gauguin maintained that it was the Devil's bird that was keeping watch.

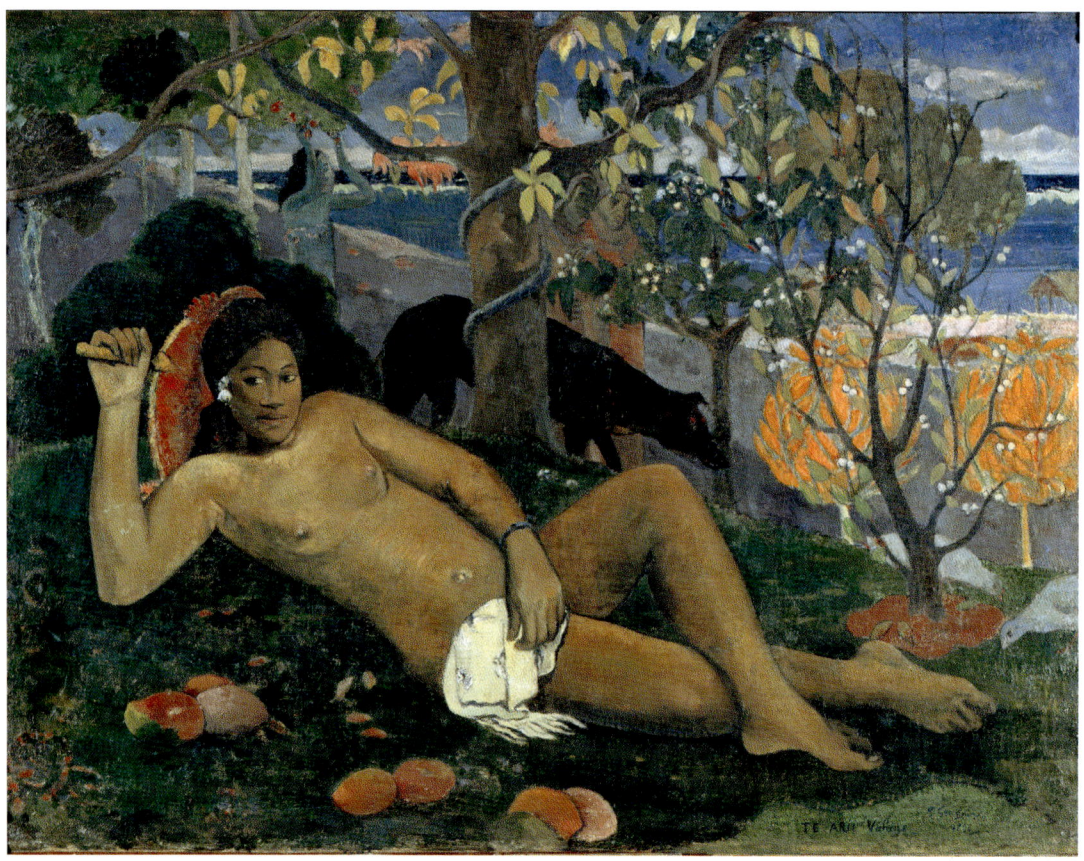

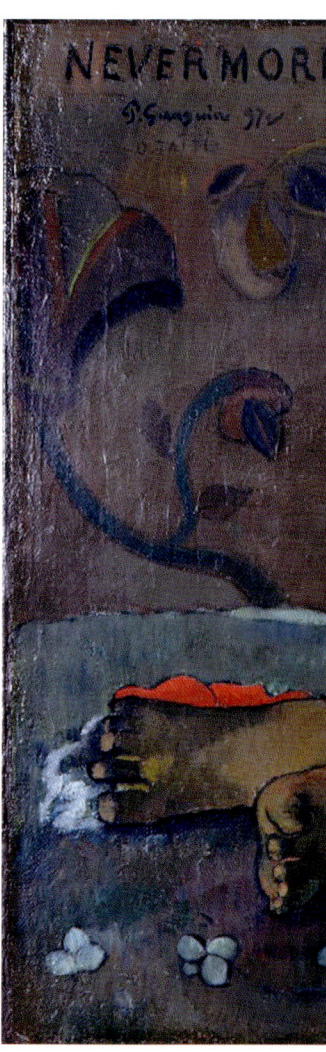

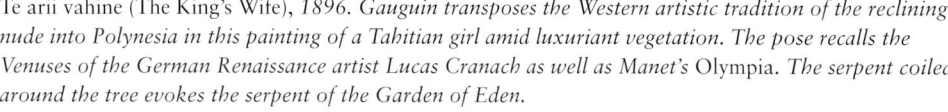

Te arii vahine (The King's Wife), 1896. Gauguin transposes the Western artistic tradition of the reclining nude into Polynesia in this painting of a Tahitian girl amid luxuriant vegetation. The pose recalls the Venuses of the German Renaissance artist Lucas Cranach as well as Manet's Olympia. *The serpent coiled around the tree evokes the serpent of the Garden of Eden.*

Right: Still Life with Teapot and Fruit, *1896. Gauguin's Tahitian canvases contain multiple references to European paintings he admired. In this case, the parallels with a Cézanne still life that was one of his prized possessions is obvious, although there are mangoes in place of Cézanne's apples, a Tahitian cloth in the background and a mysterious figure in a doorway.*

Below: Nevermore, *1897. 'With a simple nude I intended to suggest a certain savage luxuriousness of a bygone age,' explained Gauguin. 'The whole painting is deliberately bathed in colours that are sombre and sad.' That feeling of sadness is also conveyed by the woman's expression, a sense of threat added by the raven perched behind her and the whispering figures in the background.*

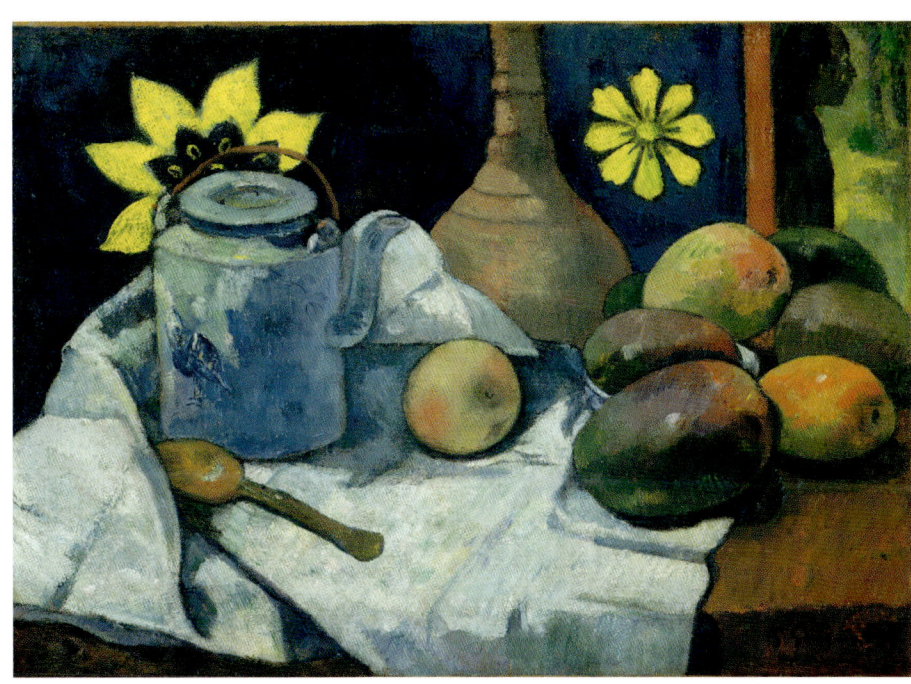

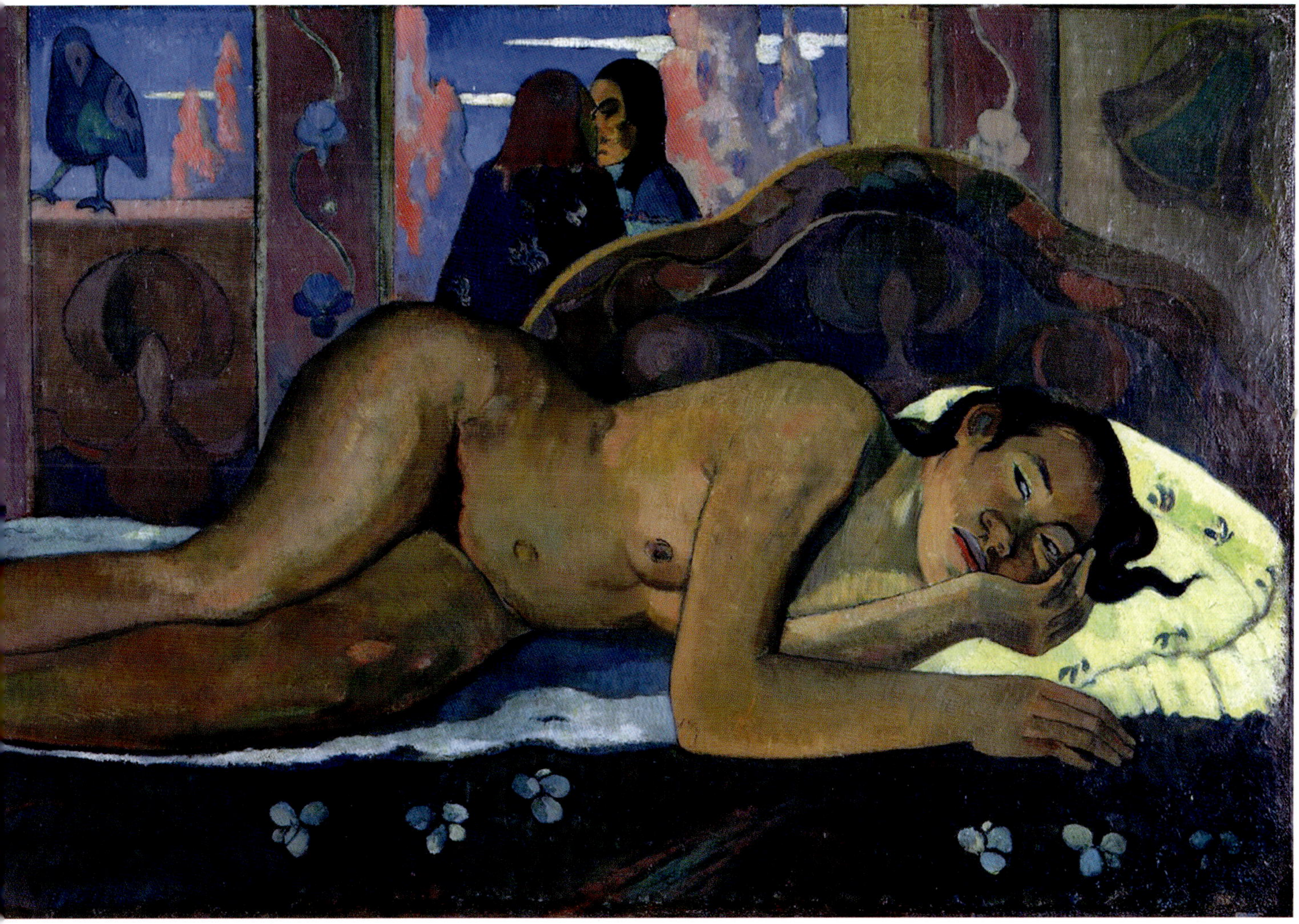

An extraordinary picture, *Te tamari no atua (The Child of God)*, recasts the traditional Christian nativity in Polynesian guise. Gauguin did not have much sympathy for the Catholic and Protestant church establishments that were vying for influence in French Polynesia, but he was interested in spirituality and religions from around the world and blended elements of Christianity, Buddhism, Hinduism and Maori mythology in his art. He would have been aware that mystical themes were increasingly fashionable in French avant-garde Symbolist circles where he might hope to find buyers. *Te rerioa (The Dream)*, which may be set in Gauguin's home, also includes a reference to motherhood: two figures sit silently in an interior, beside a baby in a cradle. 'Everything is dreamlike in this canvas,' he wrote, 'is it the child, is it the mother, is it the horseman on the path? Or is it the painter's dream!'

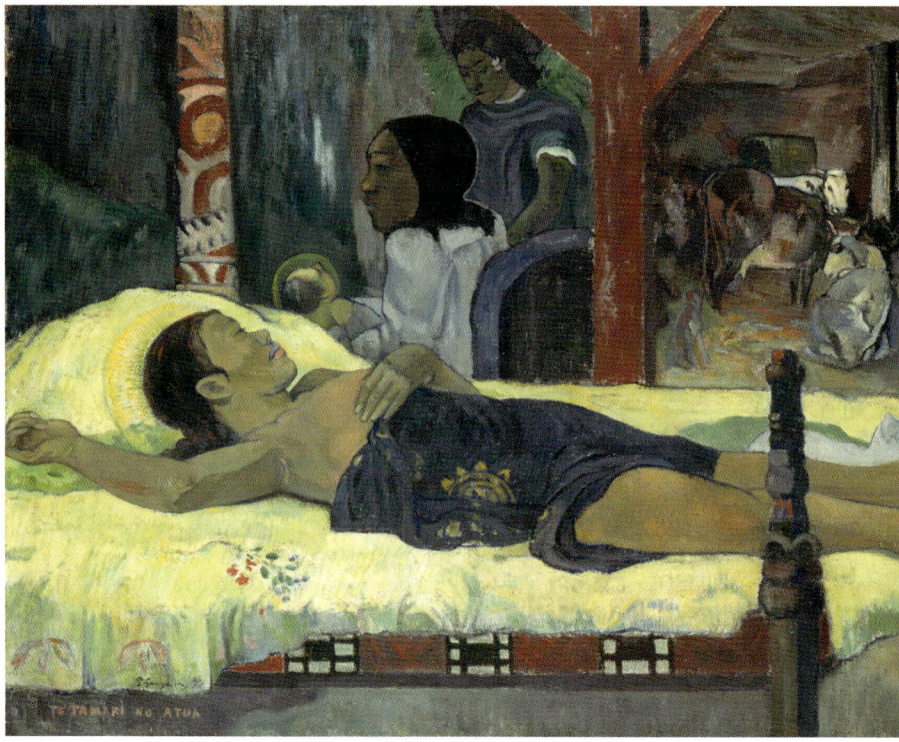

Te tamari no atua (The Child of God), 1896. *A haloed Mary, Christ Child, nurse and attendant are Polynesian figures but the setting is the stable of the Christian narrative. The black-hooded nurse, who resembles a tupapau, a sinister Tahitian ghost, may be about to spirit the baby away. This could possibly reflect the fact that in December 1896 Pahura gave birth to a child that died soon after birth.*

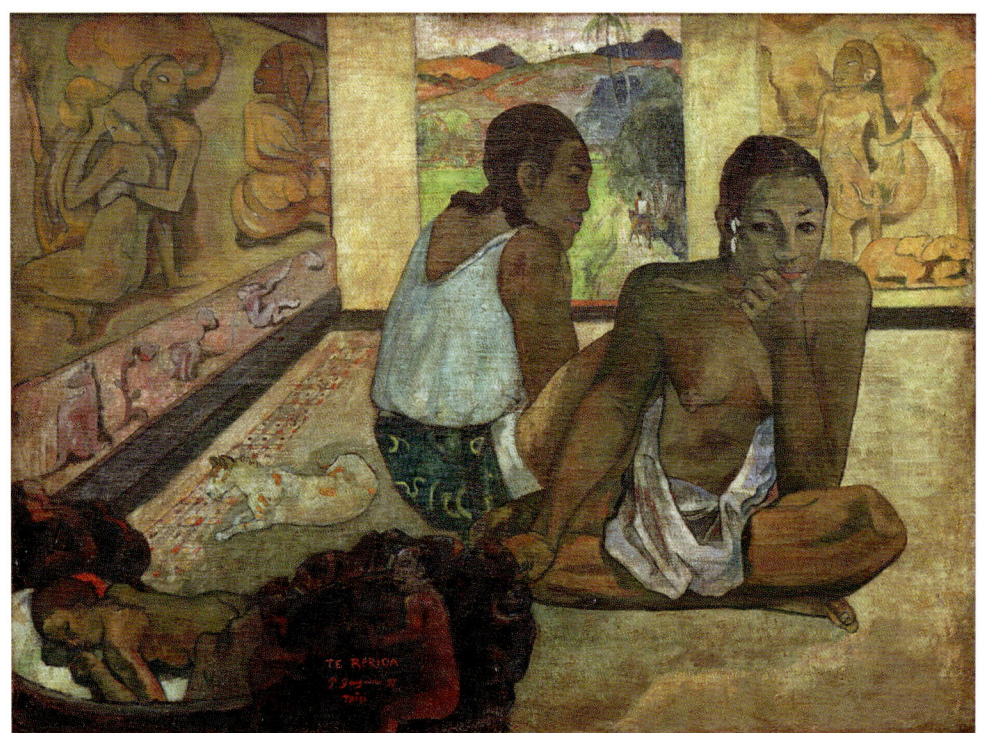

Te rerioa (The Dream), 1897. *Gauguin paid detailed attention to the decoration of his homes in Polynesia, adorning them with carvings. The reliefs on the wall in this picture, which are of his own invention, depict floral and animal motifs, an embracing couple and the goddess Hina. The wooden cradle is based on a carved wooden bowl that he had seen in the Auckland Museum.*

AN AMBITIOUS MASTERPIECE

Gauguin was not absolutely impoverished, but after an initial phase of lavish spending his financial reserves ran low and it was not long before he was sending begging letters to his friends in Paris. He was depressed and in poor health. Complications from the ankle injury he had sustained in Brittany, exacerbated by the worsening symptoms of syphilis and heart trouble, meant several lengthy hospital stays in Papeete. To make matters worse, in April 1897 he received news that his daughter Aline had died from pneumonia. But in the midst of his troubles he produced the largest picture he had ever attempted, a monumental canvas almost 4 m (13 ft) wide – *Where Do We Come From? What Are We? Where Are We Going?* The portentous title hints at the great existential questions faced by humanity, as well as, perhaps, the origins of the Pacific islanders. The figures are all based on sketches or paintings he had made previously, and the groups do not seem to cohere as a single narrative, or appear anchored in a continuous space, but the whole has an undeniable force and sense of mystery. Gauguin saw his painting as a philosophical work on a theme comparable to a Gospel, and it draws heavily on European visual traditions. The two upper corners painted chrome yellow were intended to evoke a fresco applied to a golden wall whose corners had been spoiled with age. The central figure, based on a copy Gauguin had made in the Louvre of a drawing then thought to be by Rembrandt, picks a fruit from a tree in a gesture that recalls Eve's act of plucking an apple from the Tree of Knowledge in the Garden of Eden. Several of the figures appear in other paintings by Gauguin, including the old woman on the far left, originally inspired by the Peruvian mummy he had seen in the Louvre.

Gauguin would have been well aware that large-scale mural painting was undergoing a renaissance in France, with artists such as Puvis de Chavannes, whom he admired, receiving important commissions for decorative schemes. He probably intended the picture to show that he could stand comparison with such artistic contemporaries as well as the great fresco painters of the Italian Renaissance. He may also have seen the picture as his last will and testament, because he was contemplating suicide. He worked day and night to complete it in just one month and was pleased with the result. 'People will say it is slapdash, unfinished,' he wrote to de Monfreid. 'It is true that it is hard to judge one's own work, but in spite of that I believe that this painting is not only the best thing I have ever done, but that I'll never do anything better nor anything to approach it.' Once he had completed the picture Gauguin went to hide in the mountains and took an overdose of arsenic, but it did not kill him.

The large canvas, together with several other works including *Faa iheihe (Tahitian Pastoral)* and *Vairumati*, were exhibited in the winter of 1898 at Ambroise Vollard's gallery in Paris. While critics found some things to admire in the use of colour and form, they were less convinced by the allegorical content of *Where Do We Come From?* and the paintings were sold for a disappointingly small sum.

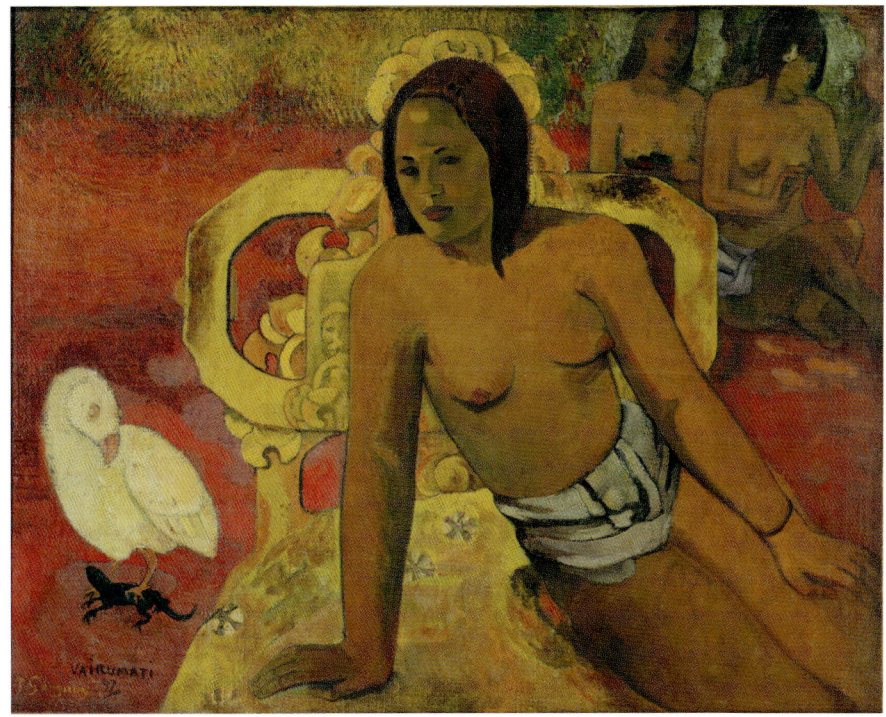

Vairumati, 1897. *Vairumati, a goddess from the Tahitian creation myth, appears in a number of Gauguin's works, including* Where Do We Come From? *Here she is depicted on a bed or altar of gold. When the picture was shown in Paris, the critic Thadée Natanson wrote that it displayed 'a grace to which we were no longer accustomed from the painter'.*

Where Do We Come From? What Are We? Where Are We Going?, *1897. In a letter Gauguin states that the painting begins with the sleeping infant on the right (where do we come from?), moving on through the various figures who ponder the questions of human existence (what are we?); past the blue idol who represents the world beyond and ending up with the woman at the far left, who is close to death and resigned to her fate (where are we going?). The white bird with a lizard in its claws represents the futility of words.*

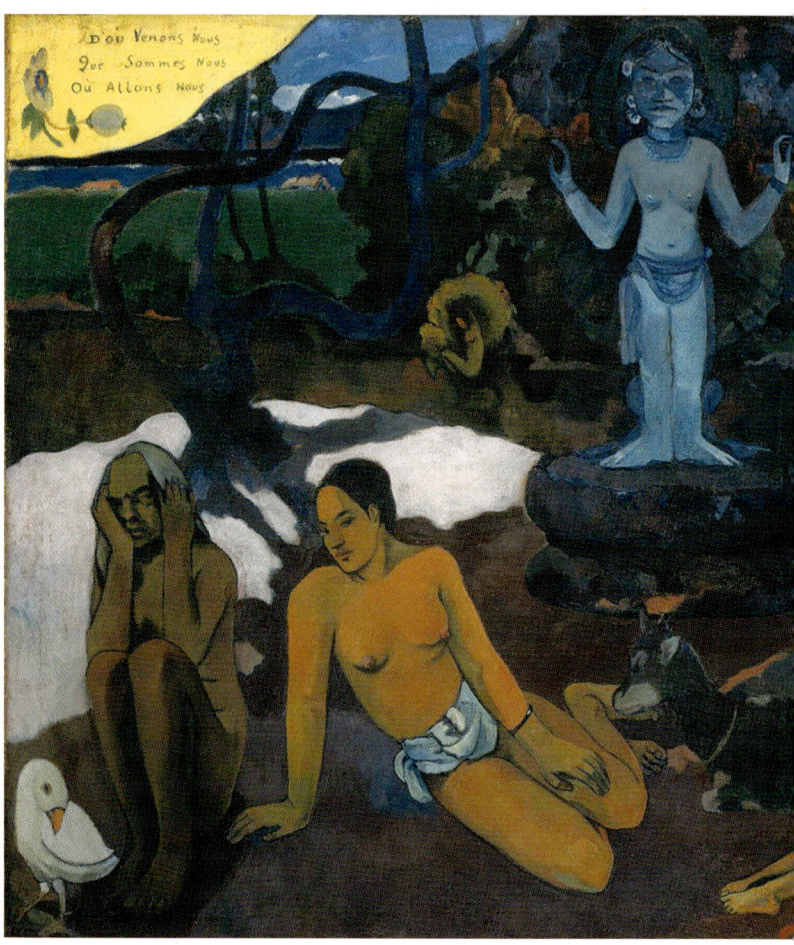

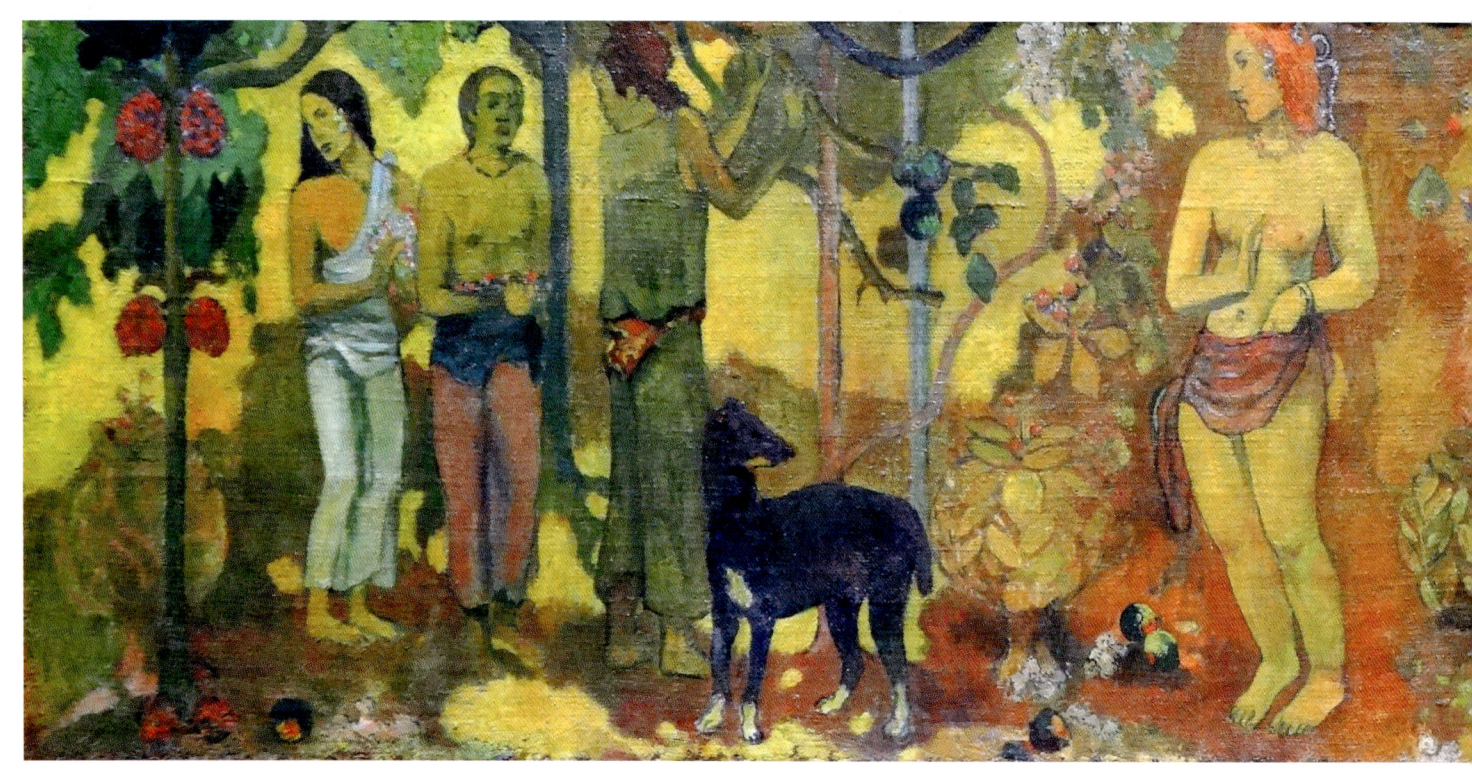

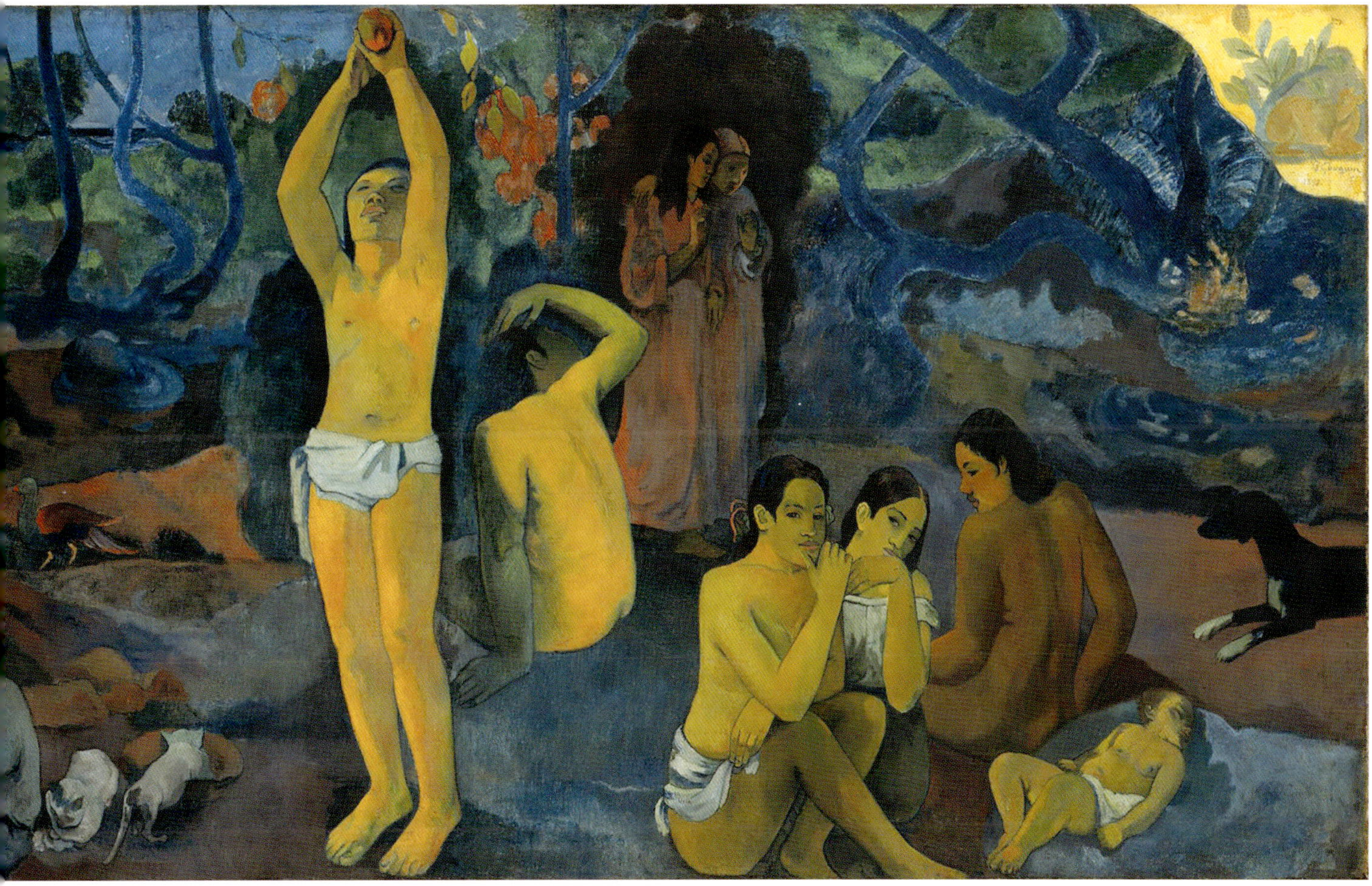

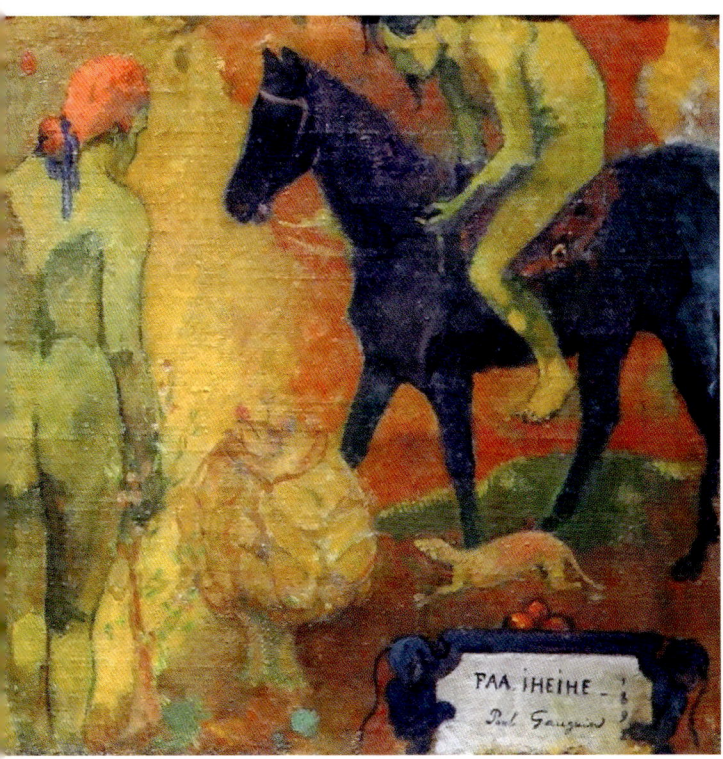

Faa iheihe (Tahitian Pastoral), 1898. *Like the other paintings Gauguin was producing at the time, this work resembles a frieze, inspired by the processional scenes of the Parthenon. The pinecone shapes are derived from the reliefs of Borobudur. The red-haired woman is depicted from front and back, giving her a three-dimensional quality that recalls Gauguin's work as a sculptor.*

GAUGUIN THE JOURNALIST

Gauguin's health and money worries worsened, although
he continued to receive consignments of paint, canvas and
brushes from the faithful de Monfreid. In 1898 he took a
job copying building designs in the Office of Public Works
and Surveys in Papeete, which paid him six francs a day.
In savage mood, he turned to journalism as an outlet.
He became editor, writer and illustrator of a satirical
journal, *Le Sourire (The Smile)* and contributed to another
publication, *Les Guêpes (The Wasps)*. In a series of articles,
Gauguin stood up for the interests of the Catholic white
settlers against the Protestant missionaries and criticized
the increasing influence of Chinese businessmen, the
incompetence of the colonial authorities and French foreign
policy. The viciousness of his attacks in print made him
several enemies.

In the spring of 1900 a new arrangement with Ambroise
Vollard offered Gauguin a steady income, and he quit his
job. He was to send the dealer a regular supply of paintings
as well as drawings and prints in return for a monthly
stipend of 300 francs and materials for his art. He could now
fulfil his ambition of moving to the Marquesas Islands, but
repeated hospitalizations in Papeete delayed his departure
until September 1901. The move was welcome. Gauguin was
worried that the French public was becoming too familiar
with his Tahitian subjects, and he hoped that the Marquesas
would provide 'new and primitive sources of inspiration'.

LIFE IN THE MARQUESAS ISLANDS

Gauguin's new home was a French colony 1,400 km (870
miles) away from Tahiti but linked to it by a regular steamer
service. Authors such as Pierre Loti and Jules Garnier in
his *Océanie* (1871) had described the Marquesas Islands
as an exotic Eden peopled by beautiful inhabitants given
over to pleasures, but the French authorities saw those
who lived there as lawless and resistant to authority. It
was said that they practised cannibalism (though this was
probably an outmoded practice with which they liked to
tease the Europeans) and indulged in drunken orgies. Before
1800 the islands had been thriving communities, but when
Gauguin arrived their population had shrunk to about 4,000
through colonial depredations and the ravages of disease.
Nevertheless, they still had vivid legends and folk tales and a

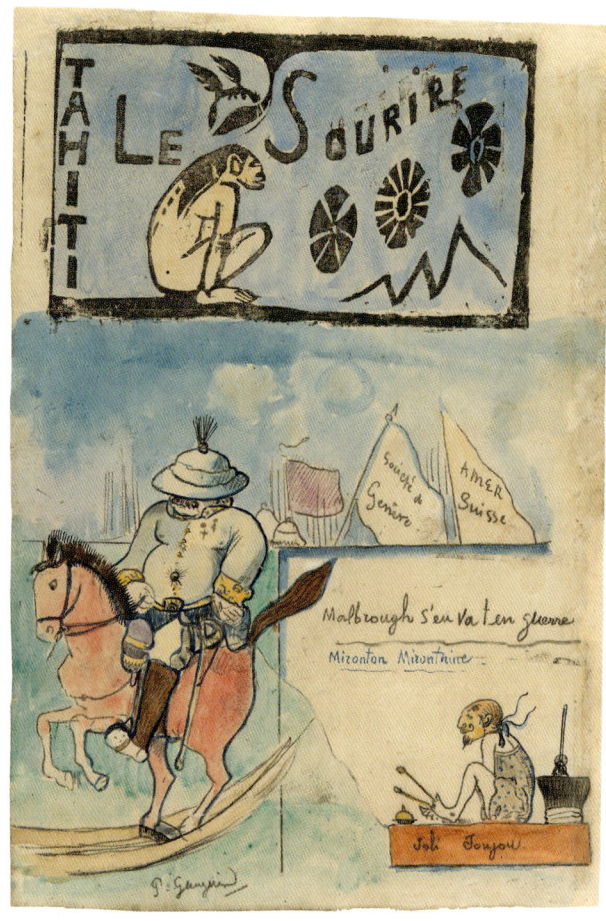

*Le Sourire, 1900. A caricature of a rotund Governor Gallet, Governor
of French Polynesia on a rocking horse is set next to an image of
Gauguin dressed as a savage and beneath a headpiece for* Le Sourire.
*Gauguin wrote the satirical articles, illustrated the pages with woodcut
mastheads and cartoons, and produced no more than 30 crudely printed
copies of each issue.*

rich decorative tradition, which found expression in the art
of tattooing and carving. The Marquesans' sexual freedom
may have appalled the missionaries but naturally appealed
to Gauguin. Filled with enthusiasm about the prospect of
settling in the 'still almost cannibalistic island of Fatu-iva',
he sensed that although his days were numbered the new
location would 'revive in me, before I die, a last spark of
enthusiasm which will rekindle my imagination and bring my
talent to its conclusion'. Gauguin settled in Atuona on the
island of Hiva Oa, a place of dramatic cliffs, volcanic peaks
and dense jungle. He was welcomed into the community
of traders and plantation owners and bought a plot of
land on which to build a house. There was no hospital but
rudimentary healthcare was provided by a Vietnamese exile

named Nguyen Van Cam and the Protestant pastor Paul Vernier, both of whom became friends. Gauguin also had pleasant neighbours, including the American owner of the principal store where he could buy imported French wines and absinthe, and Tioka, an influential Marquesan man who offered Gauguin his nephews as servants. Almost from the start, Gauguin was at odds with officialdom. He initiated a series of challenges to the authorities on issues large and small, including the imposition of previously unheard-of taxes on the islanders, the banning of alcohol and the policy of forcing local children to go to Catholic schools, which was designed to save them from debauchery. Gauguin's discovery that attendance at a school was only compulsory if the child lived within a catchment area of 4 km (2½ miles) led to a number of teenage girls being removed from convents. One of them was Marie-Rose Vaeoho, who became Gauguin's *vahine*. She left him a year later to give birth to a child at her own home. A visiting colonial inspector revealed that Gauguin defended 'all the native vices', and eventually he so incensed officials that he

was placed under constant surveillance, legal actions were started, fines imposed, a prison sentence threatened and plans were made to expel him.

However, Gauguin's hope that the move would prove productive for his art was not in vain. During the final two years of his life, despite debilitating pain in his legs that he dulled with morphine, laudanum and alcohol, and deteriorating eyesight, he painted some extraordinarily beautiful works. 'Here poetry wells up of itself,' he remarked, 'and one has only to drift into dreaming as one paints in order to suggest it.' Some of the pictures were directly inspired by the island's landscape, such as *The Ford*, which shows figures on horseback negotiating a dense forest, and *Riders on the Beach*. He also painted two distinctive Marquesan figures who were unlike the people he had depicted in Tahiti. A beautiful red-haired woman, Tohotaua, sat for a photograph in his studio, which he used as the basis for a spectacular late portrait. Haapuani, a dancer and magician who may have been her husband, posed for a painting of a sorcerer in a red cloak.

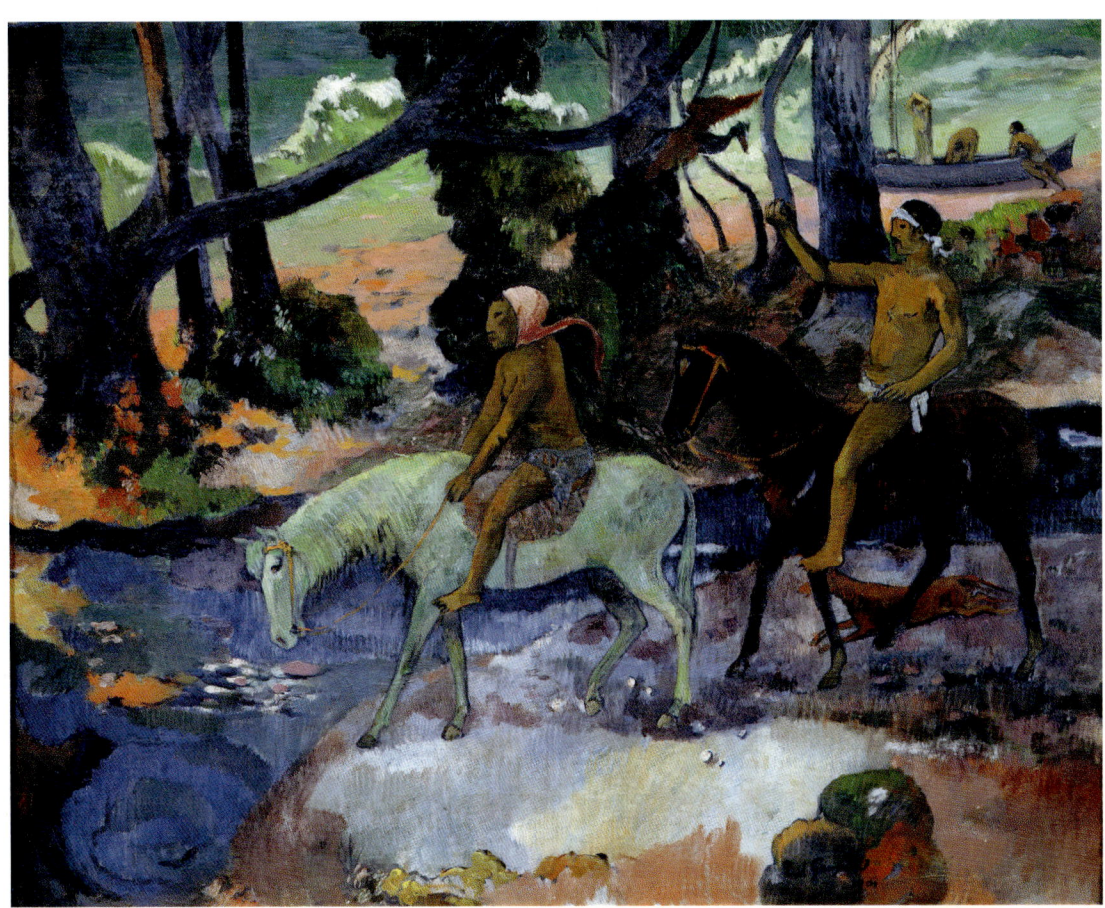

The Ford (The Flight), 1901. *Some of Gauguin's late Marquesan works feature horsemen and travellers. The hooded figure on the white horse here resembles a* tupapau, *the Tahitian ghost that appears in so many of his paintings. He also bears some resemblance to the rider in Dürer's engraving* Knight, Death and the Devil, *of which Gauguin had a reproduction.*

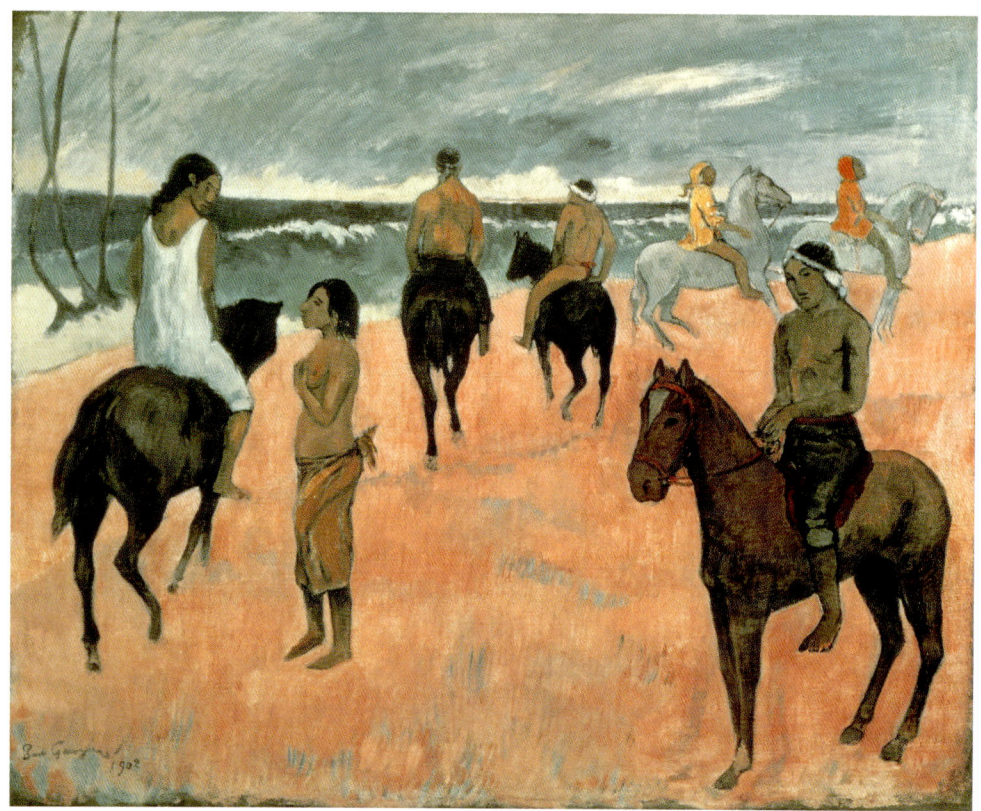

Riders on the Beach, *1902. Riders congregated on the beach at Atuona to exchange ideas and spread news. The elegant poses of the horses here recall Degas' paintings of the racehorses and jockeys at Longchamps, which Gauguin had long admired, but in the background are two decidedly un-European hooded tupapaus, or spirits of the dead.*

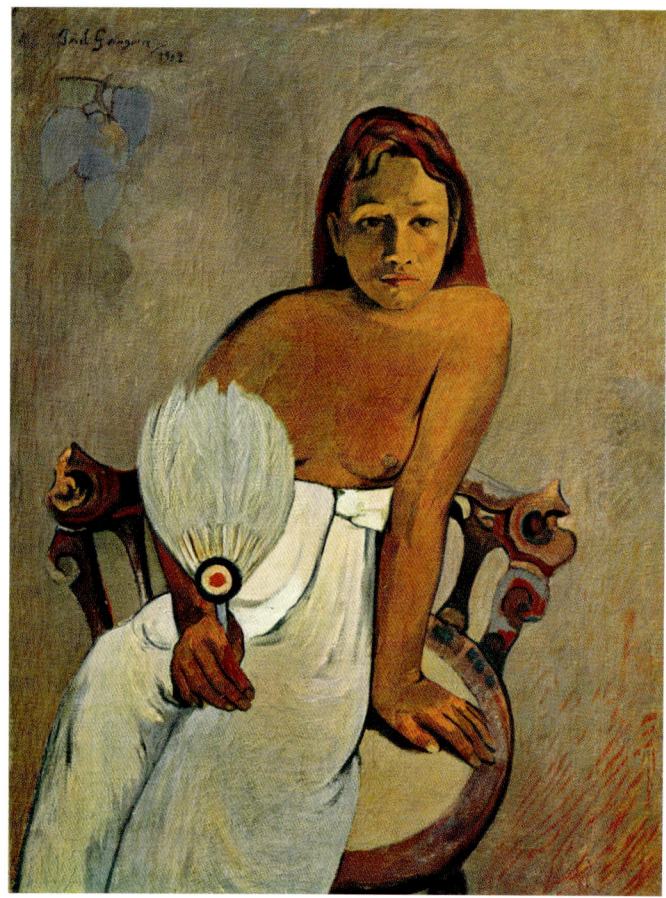

Girl with a Fan, *1902. The photograph on which this is based shows Tohotaua covered up, but Gauguin reveals her breasts. He wrote that, 'A Polynesian woman could never be tawdry or ridiculous, for there is within her that sense of decorative beauty that I have come to admire in Marquesan art.' The red, white and blue ornament at the base of the feather fan recalls the tricolour flag of France – perhaps an oblique reference to liberty.*

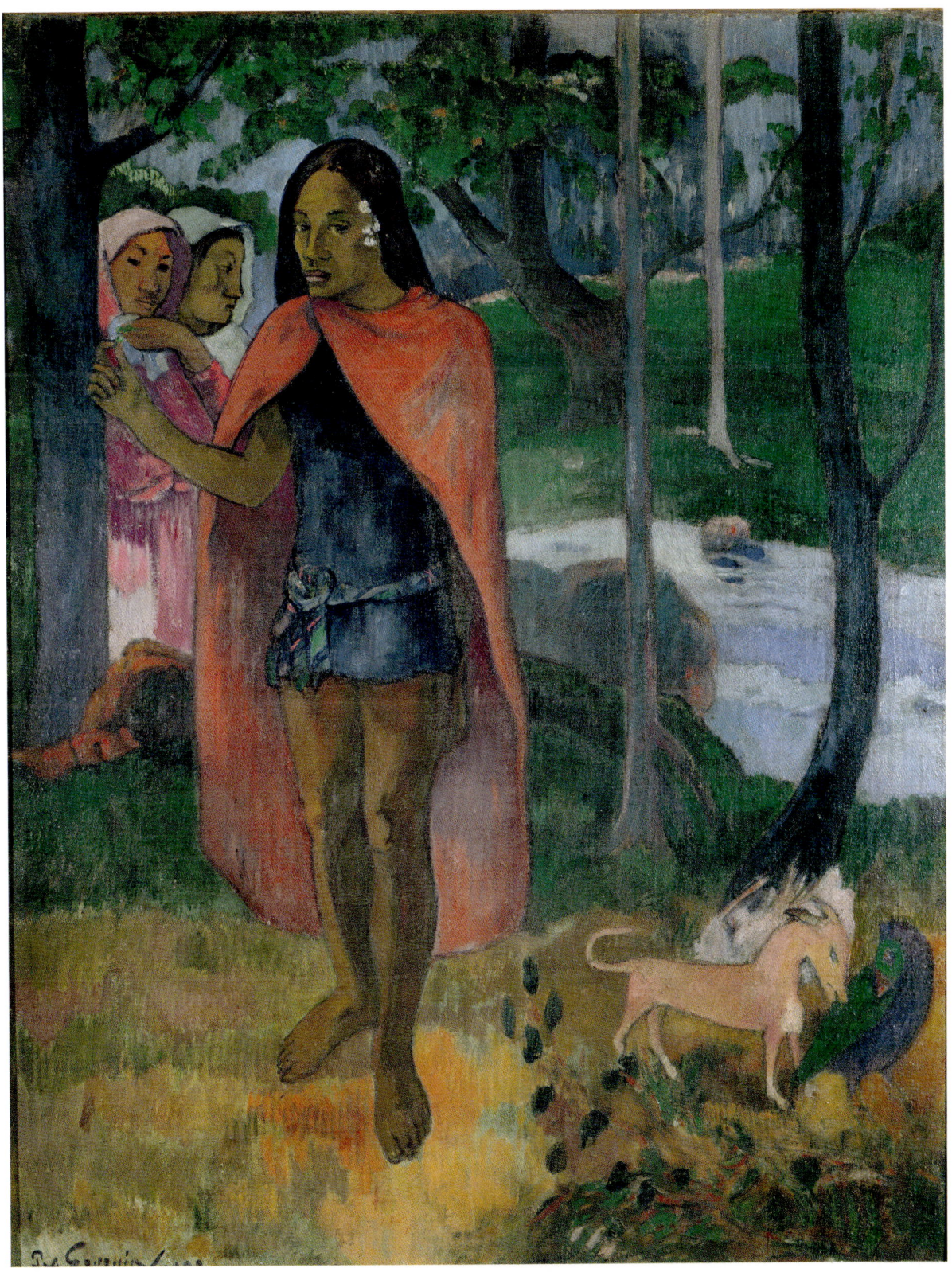

The Sorcerer of Hiva Oa, 1902. Portrayed in his ceremonial cape, this man was
an indigenous healer and musician who conducted religious rituals on Hiva Oa. A
Polynesian man would normally have covered his legs with a pareu, but Gauguin gives
him erotic appeal by exposing his legs and tucking a sprig of flowers behind his ear.

THE HOUSE OF PLEASURE

Gauguin built his new house on land sold to him by the local Catholic bishop, Joseph Martin, who would soon condemn him for depravity. A two-storey building made of wood, bamboo and plaited leaves, it was modelled on Maori meeting houses and raised storage huts. The ground floor, open on two sides, was used for living, dining and drinking with his male friends. The upper storey, where Gauguin had his bedroom and a light-filled studio, was reached by a ladder. At the foot of the ladder stood two of Gauguin's wooden sculptures, *Father Lechery*, which depicted Joseph Martin as a horned devil with a pious Western face, and *Thérèse*, which portrayed the bishop's housekeeper. These were intended to mock the hypocrisy of their secret affair. The wooden door frame consisted of carved panels showing massive nude figures, flowers and animals depicted in a deliberately crude 'primitive' style. Three horizontal panels bore the inscriptions 'Maison du Jouir' (House of Pleasure), 'Soyez mystérieuses' (Be mysterious) and 'Soyez amoureuses et vous serez heureuses' (Be in love and you will be happy'), advertising Gauguin's intentions.

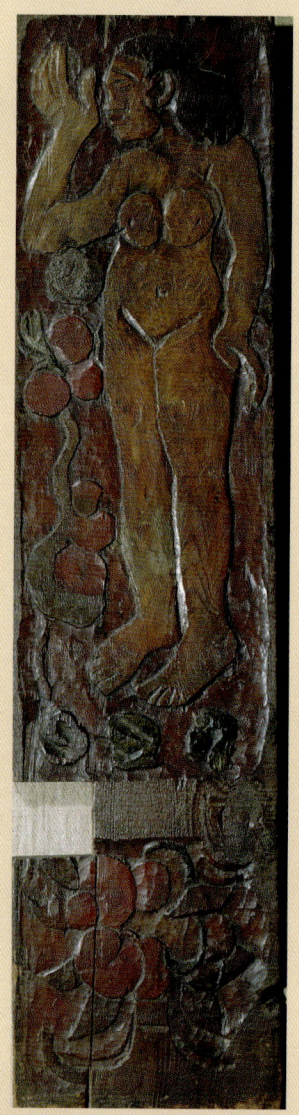

Carvings from the Maison du Jouir, *1901–2. The crudely carved painted panels of sequoia wood that Gauguin made to decorate his 'House of Pleasure' led to his bedroom at the top of the stairs. Several of the motifs that he had used in previous works reappear in them. The two horizontal base panels, for example, echo carvings he had made in Brittany years earlier.*

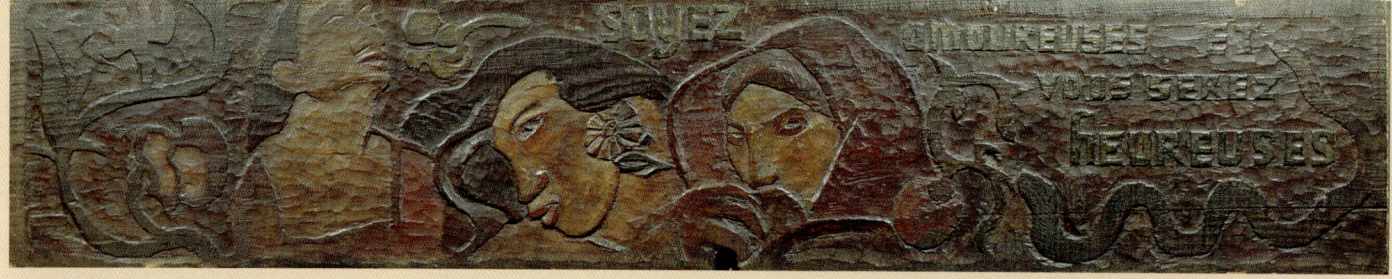

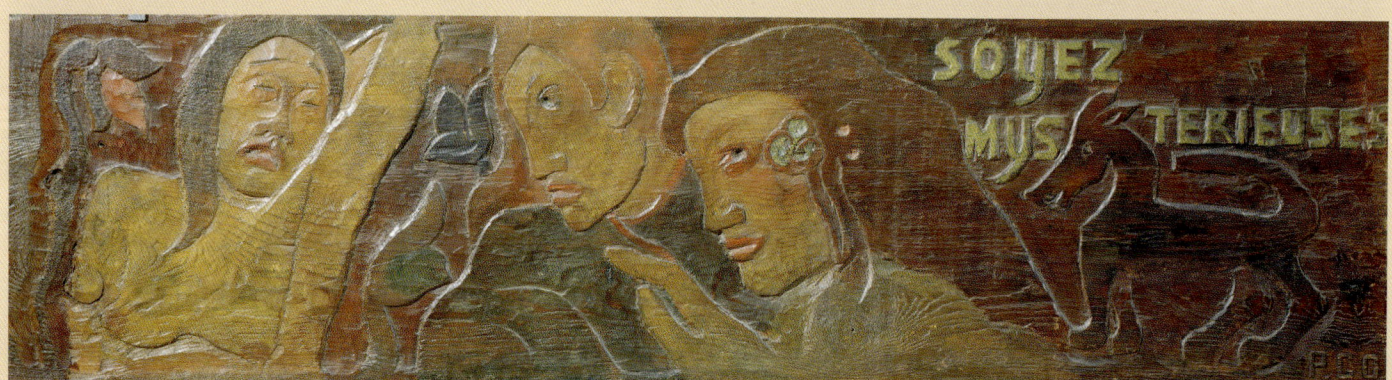

Gauguin acquired two houseboys, a cook, a dog and a cat. He furnished his home with a harmonium, a harp and some ill-matched furniture as well as a guitar, a rifle, some sacred sculptures, novels and newspapers. On the walls he hung photographs of paintings by his favourite artists, erotic images and Japanese prints. 'I have everything a modest artist could wish for,' he wrote to de Monfreid. 'A large studio with a small sleeping area; everything to hand arranged on shelves; the whole thing raised two metres above the ground where we eat, do carpentry and cooking. A hammock for siestas sheltered from the sun and cooled by breezes from the sea 300 metres away blowing through coconut palms.'

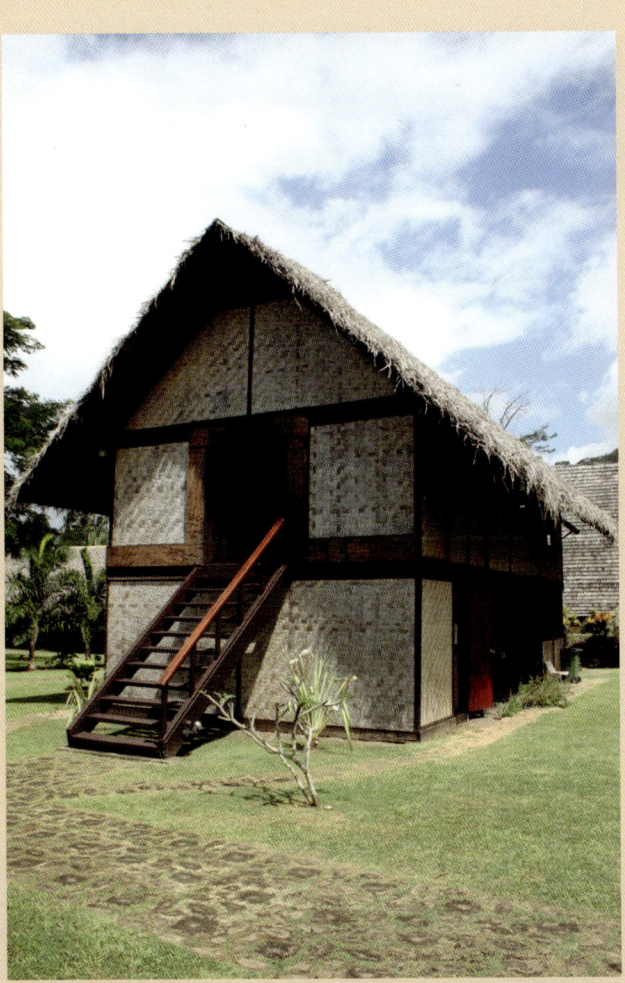

Reconstruction of Gauguin's Maison du Jouir.

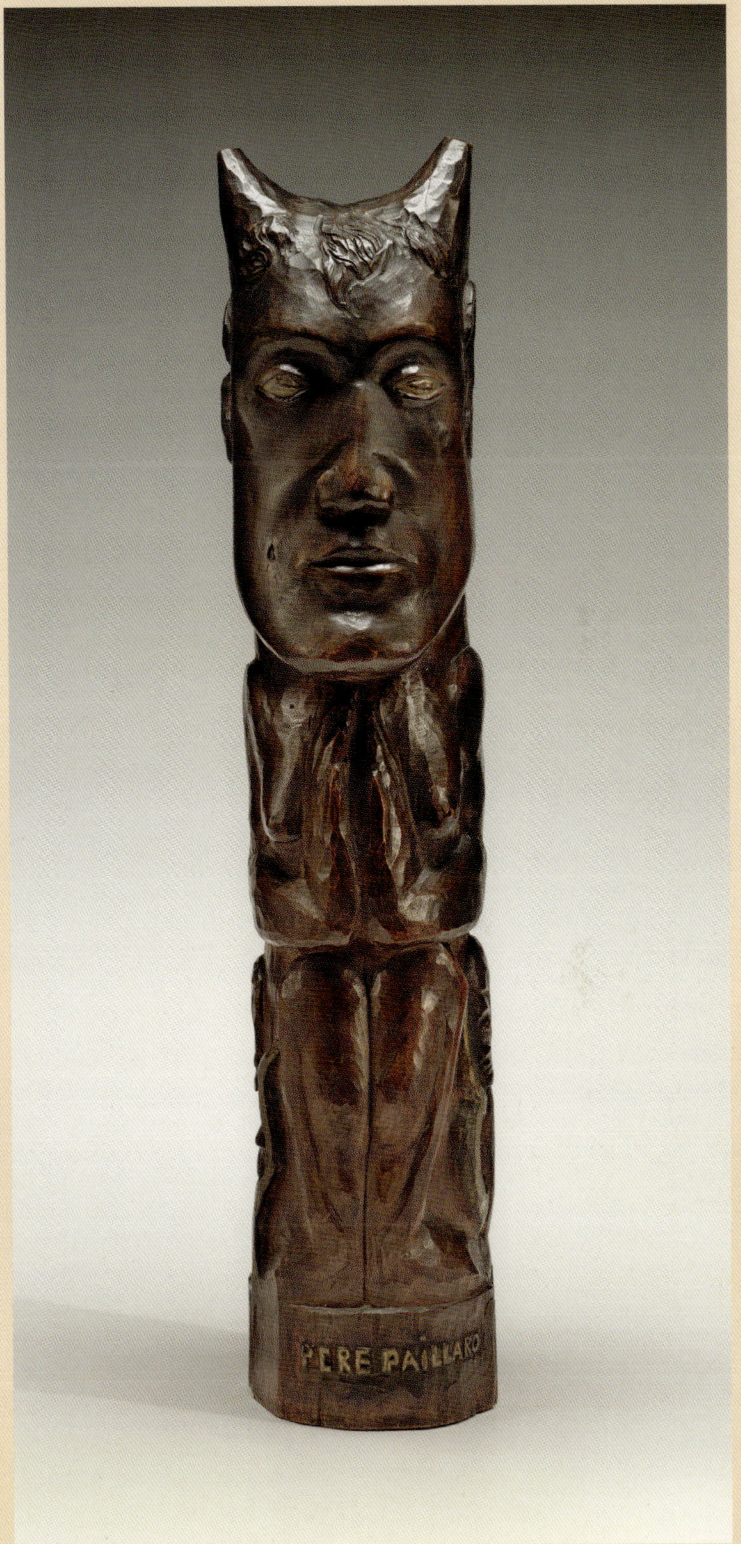

Père Paillard (Father Lechery), *1902. Gauguin intended this sculpture to mock the hypocrisy of the local bishop who castigated him for his immoral behaviour while he himself had a secret affair with his housekeeper despite his vows of celibacy. Two nude women carved at the base of the sculpture allude to the bishop's various liaisons.*

GHOSTS OF FORMER FRIENDS

Even though his surroundings were idyllic, Gauguin missed discussions with his European friends. Starved of their conversation, he wrote long letters and penned a rambling memoir and series of reflections on life and art that he entitled *Avant et Après (Before and After)*. Former friends are referred to in a few still lifes, which almost function as surrogate portraits. De Monfreid had sent sunflower seeds, and when they bloomed in his garden, Gauguin painted still lifes of them that evoked memories of Van Gogh and the Yellow House. Another still life of flowers included a mask-like face in the background that is a caricatural version of his old friend and pupil from Brittany, Meijer de Haan, who had died seven years previously. De Haan also appears in *Barbarian Tales* as a devil-like creature with clawed feet and hands and glowing green eyes, his features grotesquely exaggerated.

Not long before his death, in poor health, at odds with the Marquesan authorities and pursed by creditors, Gauguin was contemplating a return to Europe. He was reflecting on the lonely path he had pursued as an artist, while also congratulating himself on his ability to withstand its rigours. 'Solitude should not be recommended to everyone', he wrote to Charles Morice, 'for you have to be strong in order to bear it and act on your

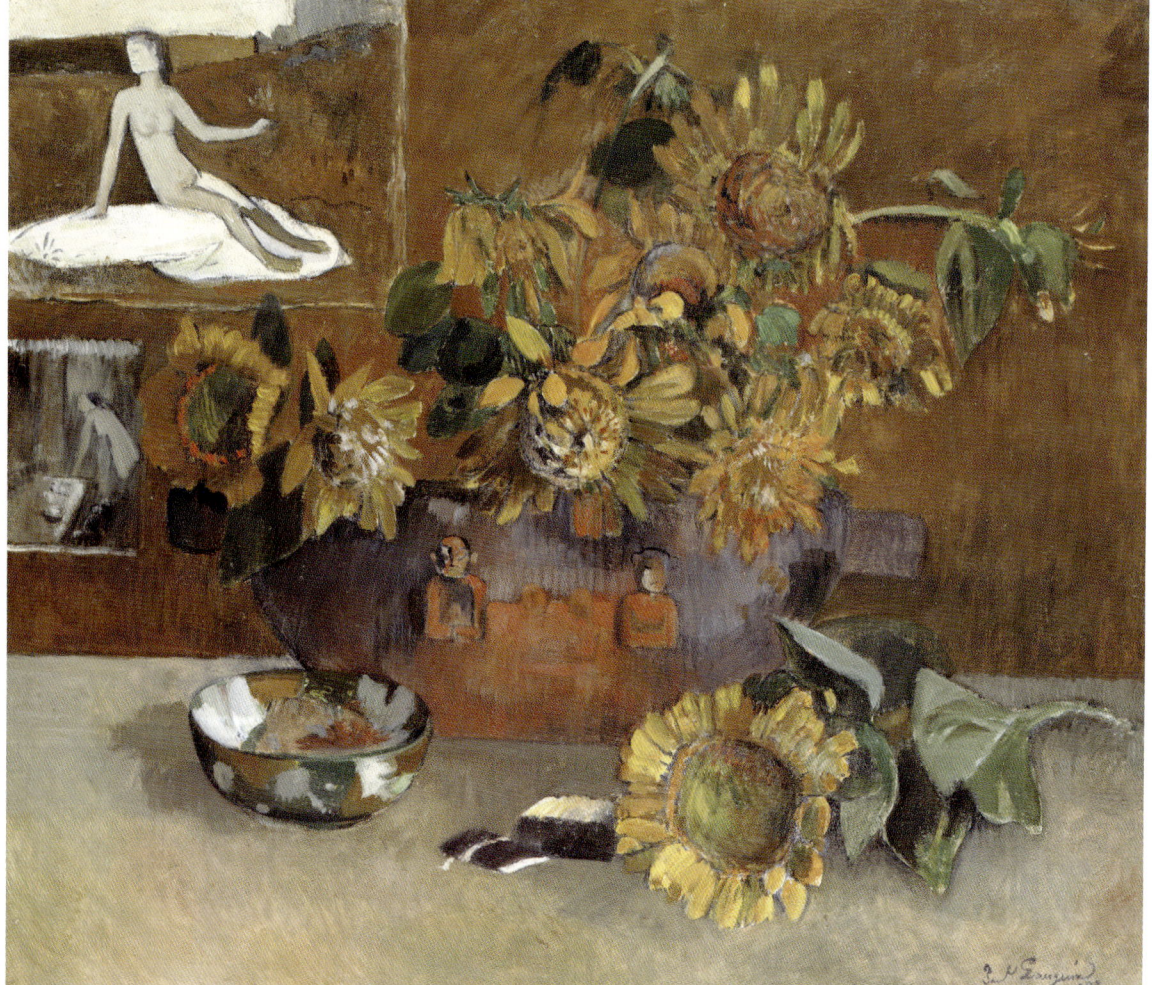

Still Life with 'Hope', 1901. This still life is an assembly of tributes to artists and decorative traditions that Gauguin admired. The sunflowers – an obvious homage to Van Gogh – are displayed in a Meso-American pot beside a Japanese bowl. On the wall behind is a reproduction of Puvis de Chavannes' painting Hope *and a print by Degas.*

own.' De Monfreid advised him against returning: 'Now you are that legendary artist, who, from out of the depths of Polynesia, sends forth his disconcerting and inimitable work ...Your enemies (and you have many, as have all who trouble the mediocre) are now silent ...You must not return. You are now as the great dead. You have passed into the history of art.'

De Monfreid's words were prophetic. On 8 May 1903 Gauguin's neighbour Tioka found him lying lifeless in bed, having had a heart attack. The funeral was hurried and he was buried the next day in the Catholic cemetery in Atuona. Today, the grave is guarded by a bronze cast of *Oviri*.

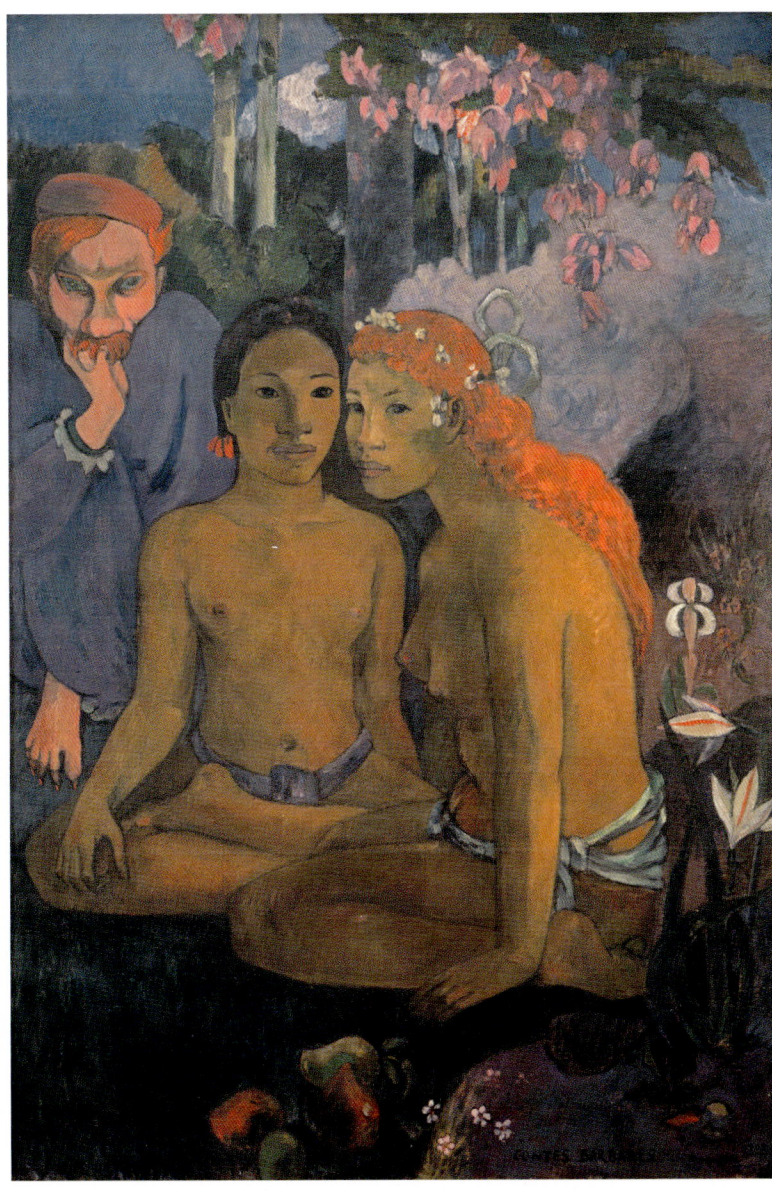

Barbarian Tales, 1902. *Meijer de Haan, the Jewish intellectual, is shown wearing a Christian missionary dress. He may represent the Judeo-Christian tradition and the 'civilized' world that Gauguin despised. The central figure is seated in a Buddhist pose while the Polynesian woman on the right, the red-headed Tohotaua, may stand for Maori beliefs.*

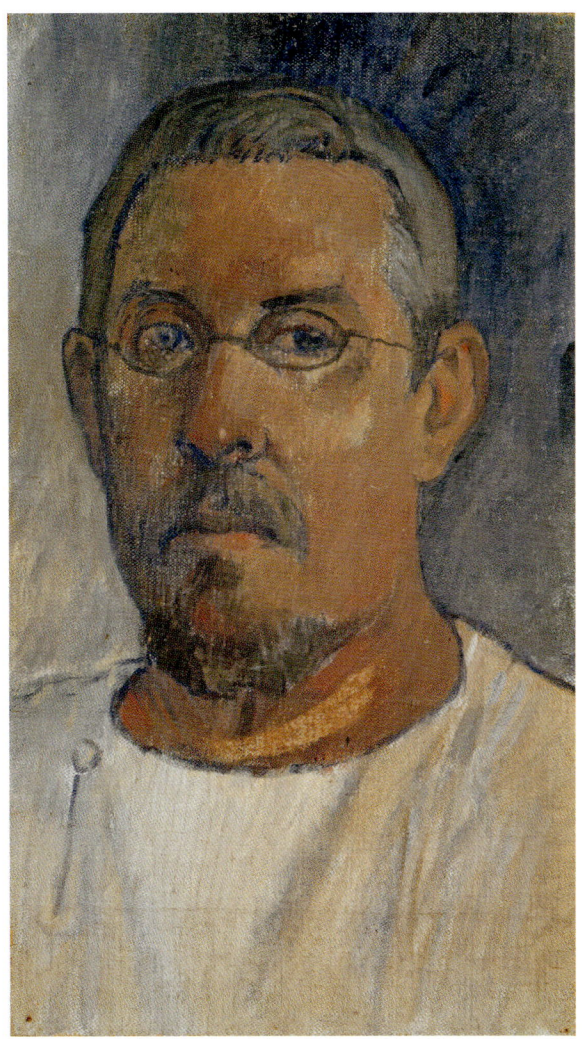

Self-Portrait, 1903. *Gauguin's final self-portrait is strikingly honest in its simple presentation: no longer adopting a pose or different persona, Gauguin shows the bespectacled man in the mirror unembellished, plainly dressed and with his hair cut short.*

EPILOGUE: GAUGUIN'S LEGACY

At the time of his death Gauguin had been absent from the Paris art scene for eight years, but he had not been forgotten. Six months later Ambroise Vollard held an exhibition of his works that was attended by the greatest artists of his time, such as Degas. Younger artists also came, including André Derain, Raoul Dufy and Henri Matisse (who was inspired to make his own trip to Tahiti in 1930). For them, Gauguin's bold use of brilliant and unnaturalistic colour, the daring simplicity of his compositions and their decorative quality was a revelation. In his fascination with non-Western art, Gauguin also anticipated the concerns of the next generation of artists who embraced the notion of 'primitivism', finding in non-Western art and artefacts a revolutionary directness that would rejuvenate their work. Prime among them was Pablo Picasso, who owned a copy of *Noa Noa* and saw the Gauguin retrospective at the 1906 Salon d'automne in Paris. He was particularly struck by *Oviri*, which stimulated his interest in sculpture and ceramics and encouraged him to explore 'primitive' forms in his groundbreaking *Demoiselles d'Avignon* (1907).

In Britain considerable interest was aroused when Gauguin's work went on show in the *Manet and the Post-Impressionists* exhibition that Roger Fry organized at the Grafton Galleries in 1910, where responses ranged from laughter to admiration. The show of Cézanne's and Gauguin's work at the Stafford Gallery in Mayfair the following year evoked a more considered appraisal. Frederick Spencer Gore's painting of the show includes the artists Augustus John and Philip Wilson Steer, revealing a growing appreciation of Gauguin's work in the British artistic establishment.

Gauguin's colourful life left a literary legacy, too. Somerset Maugham visited Tahiti in 1914 on the trail of Gauguin, and his novel *The Moon and Sixpence* (1919), loosely based on Gauguin's life, did a great deal to stir up interest in the life and work of this most singular artist on both sides of the Atlantic. In the years following the devastation of the First World War Gauguin's rejection of European civilization and his flight to Polynesia must have felt very attractive, and the appeal of his colourful canvases, with their visions of an imaginary paradise, has not faded since then.

Les Demoiselles d'Avignon, *Pablo Picasso, 1907. Picasso admired Gauguin's use of motifs and ideas drawn from non-Western cultures and art that was considered 'primitive'. The two female figures on the right of this painting of a brothel have features inspired by African masks, while the other figures show the influence of ancient Iberian sculptures from Picasso's native Spain. The fragmented and faceted forms and abandonment of conventional perspective heralded the birth of Cubism.*

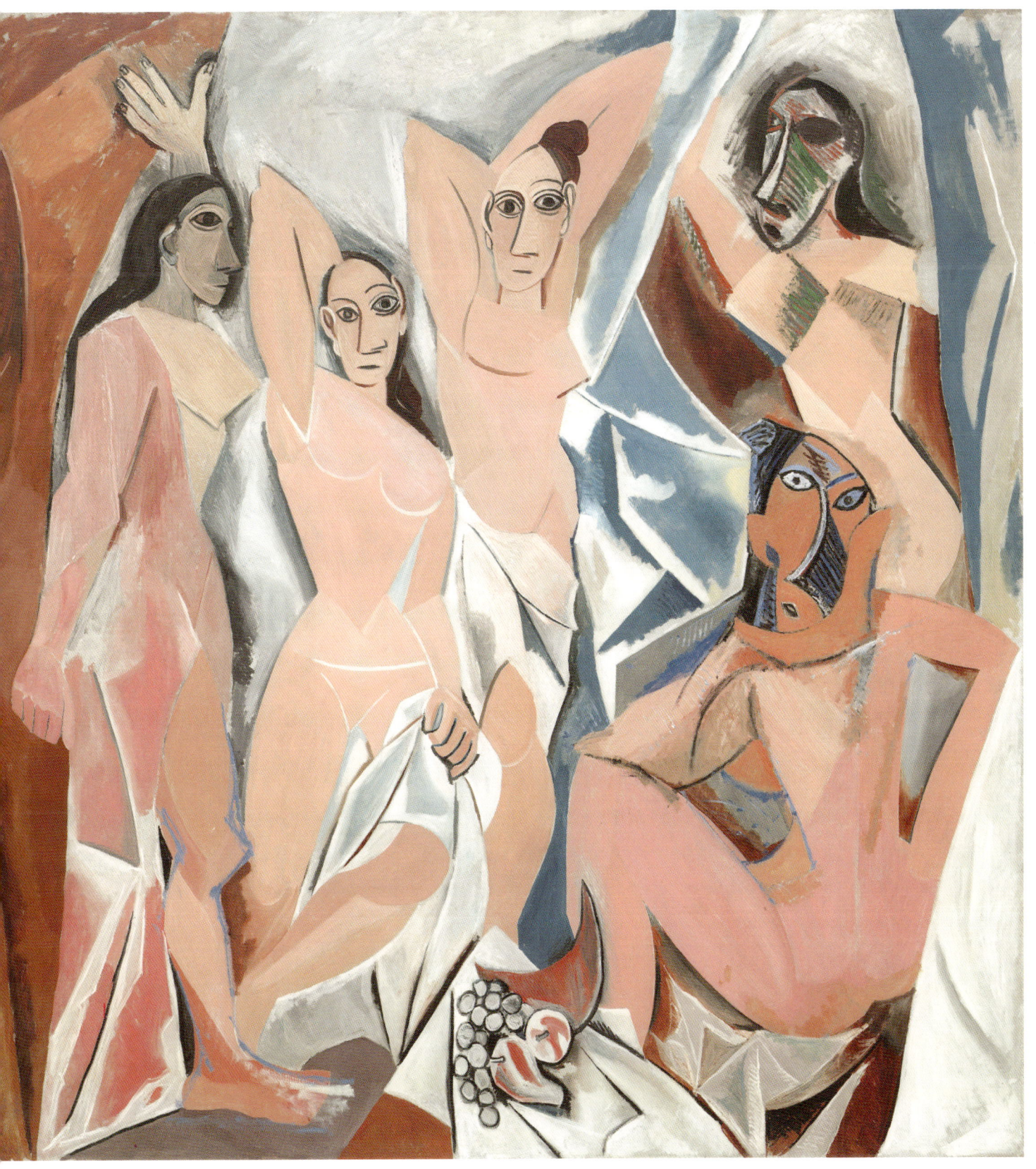

TIMELINE

1840s

'48 Eugène Henri Paul Gauguin is born in Paris on 7 June, the second child of Clovis Gauguin, a journalist, and his wife Aline Chazal.

'49 The Gauguin family leaves France for Peru. Clovis dies on the voyage, but Aline and her two children continue to Lima, where they stay with relatives for five years.

1850s

'54 The family returns to France and settles in Orléans.

'59 Gauguin enrols at the Junior Seminary of the Saint Mesmin Chapel in Orléans, where he remains for three years.

1860s 1870s

1865–71 After enlisting in the merchant marines and then the French Navy, Gauguin spends much of his time at sea.

'72 With help from Gustave Arosa, who was appointed his guardian after his mother's death, Gauguin gets a job as a stockbroker in Paris.

'73 On 22 November Gauguin marries a Danish woman, Mette Gad. By this date he is painting in his spare time.

1870s continued

'74 Gauguin and Mette's first son, Emil, is born on 31 August. Four more children follow: Aline (b.1877); Clovis (b.1879); Jean René (b.1881) and Paul (b.1883).

'76 The Paris Salon accepts a forest landscape by Gauguin.

'78 Gauguin starts to buy works by his contemporaries, including Pissarro, who becomes his artistic mentor and introduces him to Impressionist circles.

'79 Gauguin is invited to participate in the Impressionist group exhibition. From 1880 to 1886 he shows work in the final four Impressionist exhibitions.

1880s

'83 Following the stock market crash, Gauguin leaves his job in finance and decides to paint full time.

'84 The family moves to Rouen in January, but when it proves impossible for Gauguin to make enough money from his art, Mette and some of the children move to Copenhagen. Gauguin joins them there in November and works briefly as a tarpaulin salesman.

'85 Gauguin returns to Paris in June and takes odd jobs to make ends meet while he continues to paint.

'86 In July, Gauguin goes to Pont-Aven in Brittany for the first time. There he attracts a number of admiring younger artists, including Charles Laval. In the autumn he makes ceramics in the Paris studio of Ernest Chaplet.

'87 With Laval, Gauguin travels to Panama and Martinique. Back in Paris in November he meets Vincent Van Gogh and his brother Theo, who becomes his dealer.

'88 After a prolonged visit to Pont-Aven, where he works alongside Émile Bernard, in October Gauguin joins Vincent Van Gogh in the Yellow House in Arles. He travels back to Paris in December after Van Gogh mutilates his ear.

'89 The Universal Exhibition in Paris reawakens Gauguin's desire to go to the tropics. He exhibits his works at the Café des Arts inside the exhibition grounds.

In the summer he returns to Brittany and, finding Pont-Aven too busy, he retreats to the remote hamlet of Le Pouldu.

1890s

'90 While spending the summer in Le Pouldu, Gauguin receives the news of Van Gogh's suicide. In Paris that winter he becomes a regular at gatherings of Symbolist artists and writers.

'91 Gauguin visits his family in Copenhagen for the last time in March, then travels to Tahiti, landing on 9 June. Papeete is too westernized for his taste, so in September he moves to the remoter Mataeia, living there with his *vahine* Teha'mana.

'93 Gauguin leaves Tahiti on 4 June. His exhibition in Durand-Ruel's Paris gallery is a critical success.

'94 In his new Paris studio in rue Vercingétorix, Gauguin hosts weekly gatherings of musicians, artists and writers. During a visit to Brittany he receives an ankle injury in a brawl from which he never fully recovers.

'95 Gauguin leaves for Tahiti on 28 June, stopping at Auckland on the way, where he studies Maori art in the Ethnological Museum. He settles in Punaauia, where he lives with his *vahine* Pahura.

1900s

1898–1901 In increasing ill health and short of funds, Gauguin takes a job as a clerk in Papeete. Critical of the colonial administration, he starts a satirical journal, *Le Sourire*. In 1900 an arrangement with the dealer Ambroise Vollard provides him with a regular income.

'01 In September Gauguin leaves Tahiti and settles on the Marquesan island of Hiva Oa, where he builds his 'House of Pleasure'.

'03 Gauguin dies on 8 May. Later that year eight of his paintings are shown in the Paris Salon d'Automne and a small retrospective exhibition is arranged by Ambroise Vollard.

FURTHER INFORMATION

Gauguin, Belinda Thomson, Thames & Hudson, new edition 2019.
Gauguin: Artist as Alchemist, Gloria Groom (Editor), Art Institute of Chicago, 2017.
Gauguin and Impressionism, Richard R. Brettell and Anne-Birgitte Fonsmark, Yale University Press, 2005.
Gauguin: Maker of Myth, Belinda Thomson (Editor), Tate Publishing, 2010.
Gauguin Portraits, Cornelia Homburg and Christopher Riopelle (Editors), National Gallery of Canada, 2019.
Gauguin's Skirt, Stephen F. Eisenman, Thames & Hudson, 1997.
Paul Gauguin: An Erotic Life, Nancy Mowl Mathews, Yale University Press, 2001.
Savage Tales: The Writings of Paul Gauguin, Linda Goddard, Yale University Press, 2019.

Paul-Gauguin.net provides images of Gauguin's complete works, but no commentary.

LIST OF ILLUSTRATIONS

Title page (2)
Vahine no te tiare (Woman with a Flower), 1891, oil on canvas, 70.5 × 46.5 cm (27¾ × 18⅓ in), Ny Carlsberg Glyptothek, Copenhagen, Denmark. akg-images/Pictures from History.

Page 6
Gauguin at his Easel, 1885, oil on canvas, 65.2 × 54.3 cm (25⅔ × 21⅓ in), Kimbell Art Museum, Fort Worth, USA. akg-images/Erich Lessing.

Page 8
Portrait of Aline Gauguin, c. 1893, oil on canvas, 41 × 33 cm (16⅛ × 13 in), Staatsgalerie, Stuttgart, Germany. akg-images.

Page 10
Still Life with Oysters, 1876, oil on canvas 53.34 × 93.35 cm (21 × 36¾ in), Virginia Museum of Fine Arts, Richmond, Virginia, USA. Art Heritage/Alamy Stock Photo.

Page 11
The Little Dreamer, 1881, oil on canvas 60 × 74 cm (23⅔ × 29⅛ in), Ordrupgaard Museum, Charlottenlund, Denmark. akg-images.

Page 12
Drawing of Baby Jean René Gauguin, 1881, black fabricated chalk, red chalk, brush and brown wash, with pen and brown ink, on cream wove paper, with later additions in graphite, 11.9 × 12.2 cm (4⅔ × 4⅞ in), Art Institute of Chicago, USA. H. Karl and Nancy won Maltitz Endowment.

Page 13
Landscape, 1873, oil on canvas, 50.5 × 81.6 cm (19⅞ × 32⅛ in), Fitzwilliam Museum, Cambridge, UK. akg-images/De Agostini Picture Library.

Page 14
Study of a Nude (Suzanne Sewing), 1880, oil on canvas, 114.5 × 79.5 cm (45 × 31¼ in), Ny Carlsberg Glyptotek, Copenhagen, Denmark. Heritage Images/Fine Art Images/ akg-images.

Page 15
The Seine at Pont d'Iena, 1875, oil on canvas, 65.4 × 92.4 cm (25¾ × 36⅜ in), Musée d'Orsay, Paris, France. akg-images.

Page 16
Diego Martelli, Edgar Degas, 1879, oil on canvas, 110.4 × 99.8 cm (43⅝ × 39¼ in), National Gallery of Scotland, Edinburgh, UK. Bridgeman Images.

Page 17
Interior of the Artist's Home, rue Carcel, 1881, oil on canvas, 130.5 × 162.5 cm (51⅜ × 64 in), Nasjonalmuseet, Oslo, Norway. akg-images/Erich Lessing.

Page 18
Double portrait drawing of Gauguin and Pissarro, Camille Pissarro and Paul Gauguin, 1883, charcoal with coloured pencils on paper, 31.5 × 48.5 cm (12⅜ × 19 in), Department of Prints and Drawings, Musée de Louvre, Paris, France. akg-images/Erich Lessing.

Page 19
Edge of the Woods near L'Hermitage, Pontoise, Camille Pissarro, 1879, oil on fabric, 125 × 163 cm (49⅕ × 64⅙ in), Cleveland Museum of Art, Cleveland, Ohio, USA. Gift of the Hanna Fund.

Snow at Vaugirard II, 1879, oil on canvas, 60.5 × 80.5cm (23⅞ × 31¾ in), Szépmüvészeti Museum, Budapest. akg-images/Album.

Page 20
Portrait of Mette Gauguin, 1877, marble, height 34.5 cm, (13⅝ in) Courtauld Institute Art Gallery, London, UK. Bridgeman Images.

Page 21
Gauguin's Family, rue Carcel, (Garden in Vaugirard), 1881, oil on canvas, 87 × 114 cm (34¼ × 44⅞ in), Ny Carlsberg Glyptotek, Copenhagen, Denmark. akg-images/Erich Lessing.

La Toilette, 1882, pear wood, 34.1 × 55 × 7 cm (13⅜ × 21⅔ × 2 ¾ in) Museum of Modern Art, Strasbourg, France. akg-images.

Page 22
Blue Roofs, Rouen, 1884, oil on canvas, 74 × 60 cm (29⅛ × 26⅔ in), Collection Oskar Reinhart 'Am Romerholz', Winterthur, Switzerland. akg-images/André Held.

Page 24
Still Life with a Mandolin, 1885, oil on canvas, 61.7 x 51.3 cm (24¼ x 20⅛ in), Musée d'Orsay, Paris, France. Photo © Josse/Bridgeman Images.

Page 25
Guests and staff in front of the Pension Gloanec in Pont-Aven, Brittany, France, 1888, photograph. akg-images/De Agostini Picture Library.

Breton Pardon (Pardon Day in Brittany), Pierre-Charles Poussin, 1851, oil on canvas, 146 × 327 cm (57½ × 128¾ in), National Gallery, London, UK. akg-images.

Page 26
Women and children in traditional Breton costumes, Pont-Aven, c. 1900, photo postcard. Collection Dupondt/akg-images.

Breton Women Chatting (Four Breton Women), 1886, oil on canvas, 71.8 × 91.4 cm (28¼ × 36 in), Neue Pinakothek, Munich, Germany. akg-images.

Page 27
Breton Woman and a Young Breton, 1886–7, partially painted unglazed stoneware vase, height 26 cm (10¼ in), private collection. Photo © Christie's Images/ Bridgeman Images.

Portrait Vessel of a Ruler, Moche culture, Peru, 100 BC–AD 500, ceramic and pigment, 35.6 × 24.1 cm (14 × 9½ in). Art Institute of Chicago, Illinois, USA. Kate S. Buckingham Endowment.

Page 28
Still Life with Laval's Profile, 1886, oil on canvas, 46 × 38 cm (18⅛ × 15 in), Indianapolis Museum of Art, Indiana, USA. akg-images.

Page 29
Tropical Vegetation (Martinique Landscape), 1887, oil on canvas, 117 × 89.8 cm (46 × 35⅓ in), National Galleries Scotland, Edinburgh, UK. Heritage Images/ The Print Collector/akg-images.

Page 30
Picking Mangoes, Martinique, 1887, oil on canvas, 86 × 116 cm (33⅞ × 45⅔ in), The Van Gogh Museum, Amsterdam, The Netherlands.

Page 31
The Swineherd, 1888, oil on canvas, 28¾ × 36⅝ in. (73 × 93 cm), Los Angeles County Museum of Art, USA. Gift of Lucille Ellis Simon and family.

Page 32
The Pardon, or *Breton Women in the Meadow*, Émile Bernard, 1888, oil on canvas, 74 × 92 cm

(29¼ × 36¼ in), private collection. Bridgeman Images.

Page 33
The Talisman, Paul Sérusier, 1888, oil on wood, 27 × 21 cm (10⅔ × 8¼ in), Musée d'Orsay, Paris, France.

Pages 34–5
Plum Garden at Kameido, from the series 'One Hundred Famous Views of Edo', Utagawa Hiroshige, 1857, woodblock print, 36 × 24.4 cm (14⅛ × 9⅔ in), Art Institute of Chicago, Illinois, USA. Clarence Buckingham Collection.

The Vision of the Sermon (Jacob Wrestling with the Angel), 1888, oil on canvas, 72.2 × 91 cm (28⅓ × 35⅝ in), National Galleries Scotland, Edinburgh, UK. Heritage Images/Fine Art Images/akg-images.

Page 36
Self Portrait with Portrait of Émile Bernard (Les Misérables), 1888, oil on canvas, 44.5 cm × 50.3 cm (17½ × 19⅞ in), Van Gogh Museum, Amsterdam, The Netherlands. akg-images/Album.

Page 37
Café at Arles, 1888, oil on canvas, 72 × 92 cm (28⅓ × 36⅕ in), Pushkin Museum, Moscow, Russia. akg-images.

Page 38
The Grape Harvest (Human Misery), 1888, oil on jute sackcloth, 73.5 × 92 cm (29 × 36⅕ in), Ordrupgaard Museum, Charlottenlund, Denmark. akg-images.

Page 39
Sunflowers, Vincent Van Gogh, 1887, oil on canvas, 43.2 × 61 cm (17 × 24 in), The Metropolitan Museum of Art, New York, USA. Rogers Fund, 1949.

Gauguin's Chair, Vincent Van Gogh, 1888, oil on canvas, 90.5 × 72.7 cm (35½ × 28½ in), Van Gogh Museum, Amsterdam, The Netherlands. Bridgeman Images.

Vincent's Chair, Vincent Van Gogh, 1888, oil on canvas, 91.8 × 73 cm (36 × 28¾ in), National Gallery, London, UK. Bridgeman Images.

Page 40
Schuffenecker's Studio, 1889, oil on canvas, 72.7 × 92 cm (28⅔ × 36¼ in), Musée d'Orsay, Paris, France. akg-images/Laurent Lecat.

Page 41
Dancers in the Javanese village at the Universal Exhibition, Paris, 1889, engraving. akg-images/Pictures from History.

Page 42
La Belle Angèle (Portrait of Mme Satre), 1889, oil on canvas, 92 × 73.2 cm (36¼ × 28⅞ in), Musée d'Orsay, Paris, France. akg-images/Album.

Page 43
The Kelp Gatherers II, 1889, oil on canvas, 87 × 123.1 cm (34¼ × 48½ in), Museum Folkwang, Essen, Germany. Bridgeman Images.

The Yellow Christ, 1889, oil on canvas, 92 × 73.3 cm (36¼ × 28⅞ in), Albright-Knox Art Gallery, Buffalo, New York, USA. Heritage Images/Fine Art Images/akg-images.

Page 44
In the Waves, 1889, oil on fabric, 92.5 × 72.4 cm (36⅜ × 28 1½ in), Cleveland Museum of Art, Cleveland, Ohio, USA. Gift of Mr and Mrs William Powell Jones.

Page 45
The Loss of Virginity, 1890–1, oil on canvas 89.5 × 130.2 cm (35¼ × 51¼ in), Chrysler Museum of Art, Norfolk, Virginia, USA. akg-images.

Emil, Paul and Aline Gauguin, *c.* 1891, photograph. © SZ Photo/Bridgeman Images.

Page 46
Self-Portrait, 1889, oil on wood, 79.2 × 51.3 cm (31⅛ × 20⅛ in), National Gallery of Art, Washington, USA. Chester Dale Collection.

Page 47
Bonjour Monsieur Gauguin, 1889, oil on canvas, 93 × 74 cm (36⅔ × 29⅛ in), Národní Galerie, Prague, Czech Republic.

Christ in the Garden of Olives, 1889, oil on canvas, 72.4 × 91.4 cm (28½ × 36 in), Norton Museum of Art, Palm Beach, Florida, USA. Bridgeman Images.

Page 48
Portrait of Suzanne Bambridge, 1891, oil on canvas 70 × 50 cm (27½ × 19⅔ in), Royal Museum of Fine Arts of Belgium, Belgium. akg-images/Album/Joseph Martin.

Page 50
Arii matamoe (The Royal End), 1892, oil on coarse fabric, 45.1 × 74.3 cm (17¾ × 29¼ in), The J. Paul Getty Museum, Los Angeles, California, USA.

Page 51
Man with an Axe, 1891–3, thinned gouache with pen and black ink, over pen and brown ink, on cream wove paper (discoloured to tan), laid down on cream Japanese paper, 31.7 × 22.8 cm (12½ × 9 in), Art Institute of Chicago, Illinois, USA. Gift of Edward McCormick Blair.

A Tahitian man carrying bananas, photographed *c.* 1920. Getty images/Paul Popper/Popperfoto.

Pages 52–3
The Meal, 1891, oil on paper glued on canvas, 72.5 × 91.5 cm (28½ × 36 in), Musée d'Orsay, Paris, France. akg-images.

Fatata te miti (By the Sea), 1892, oil on canvas, 67.9 × 91.5 cm (26¾ × 36 in), National Gallery of Art, Washington, USA. Chester Dale Collection.

Page 54
Ia orana Maria (Hail Mary), 1891, oil on canvas, 113.7 × 87.6 cm (44¾ × 34½ in), Metropolitan Museum of Art, New York, USA. Bequest of Sam A. Lewisohn, 1951.

Page 55
Vahine no te tiare (Woman with a Flower), 1891, oil on canvas, 70.5 × 46.5 cm (27¾ × 18⅓ in), Ny Carlsberg Glyptothek, Copenhagen, Denmark. akg-images/Pictures from History.

Page 56
Portrait of a Tahitian Woman, Charles Spitz, 1888, photograph. Zip Lexing/Alamy Stock Photo.

Heads of Tahitian women, frontal and profile views, *c.* 1891–3, charcoal and wetted charcoal, with stumping and erasing, on cream wove paper, selectively fixed, 41.3 × 32. 5 cm (16¼ × 12¾ in), Art

Institute of Chicago, Illinois, USA. Gift of David Adler and his friends.

Page 57
Merahi metua no Tehamana (Teha'mana Has Many Parents), 1893, oil on jute canvas, 75 × 53 (29½ × 20⅞ in), Art Institute of Chicago, Illinois, USA. Gift of Mr and Mrs Charles Deering McCormick.

Page 58
Manao tupapau (Spirit of the Dead Watching), 1892, oil on jute mounted on canvas, 73 × 92.4 cm (28¾ × 36⅜ in), Albright-Knox Art Gallery, Buffalo, New York, USA. akg-images/De Agostini Picture Library.

Page 59
Ancien culte mahorie (Ancient Maori Religion), p 12, folio 6 verso, 1892–3, black ink and watercolour, 21.5 × 17 cm (8½ × 6⅔ in), Collection of the Musée d'Orsay, held in the Department of Prints and Drawings, Musée du Louvre, Paris, France. Photo RMN-Grand Palais (Musée d'Orsay)/Stéphane Maréchalle.

Parahi te marae (The Sacred Mountain or *There is the Temple)*, 1892, oil on canvas, 66 × 88.9 cm (26 × 35 in), Philadelphia Museum of Art, Philadelphia, Pennysylvania, USA. Gift of Mr and Mrs Rodolphe Meyer de Schauensee, 1980/Bridgeman Images.

Page 60
Nafea faa ipoipo? (When Will You Marry?), 1892, oil on canvas, 101.5 × 77.5 cm (40 × 30½ in), private collection. akg-images/Erich Lessing.

Aha oe feii? (What? Are You Jealous?), 1892, oil on canvas 66 × 89 cm (26 × 35 in), Pushkin State Museum of Fine Arts, Moscow, Russia. akg-images/Erich Lessing.

Page 61
Tii with a Shell, 1892–3, ironwood, mother-of-pearl and parrot fish teeth, 34.4 × 14.8 × 18.5 cm (13½ × 5⅞ × 7¼ in), Musée d'Orsay, Paris, France. Peter Horee/Alamy Stock Photo.

Cup for Popoi, *c.* 1891, carved tamanu wood, 14.5 × 44 × 26.5 cm (5⅔ × 17⅓ × 10½ in), Musée

INDEX